Israeli
War Widows

ISRAELI
WAR WIDOWS

Beyond the Glory
of Heroism

LEA SHAMGAR-HANDELMAN

BERGIN & GARVEY PUBLISHERS, INC.
MASSACHUSETTS

First published in 1986 by
Bergin & Garvey Publishers, Inc.
670 Amherst Road
South Hadley, Massachusetts 01075

6 7 8 9 9 8 7 6 5 4 3 2 1

Printed in the United States of America

Library of Congress Cataloging-in-Publication Data

Shamgar-Handelman, Lea.
   Israeli war widows.

   Bibliography: p.
   Includes index.
   1. War widows—Israel—Social conditions. 2. War
widows—Israel—Psychology. 3. War widows—Services
for—Israel. I. Title.
UB405.I75S53   1986   305.4'90654'095694   85-20131
ISBN 0-89789-094-9

310608

To the memory of
AHARON SHAMGAR
(Harry Schwager)
1924–1961

CONTENTS

Acknowledgments

The people I encountered in the course of my research and study on war widows were never indifferent—they were either very much for it, or vehemently against it. It gives me a great deal of pleasure to pay this personal tribute to those who supported my work. It goes without saying that I owe the greatest debt of gratitude to the war widows, a gratitude expressed by the book itself.

I mention first my friend Mrs. Hannah Barag who, from the beginning of the study to the end of the field work, gave me, besides much practical help, constant encouragement to continue, encouragement that came out of her own genuine interest and involvement in the subject of this study.

Professor Rivka Bar-Yosef undertook the task of supervising my doctoral thesis which was based on this study, even against the opinions of other experts who did not see either much purpose or potential in the subject and the material.

The Director of the NCJW Research Institute for Innovation in Education, Profesor Chaim Adler, gave me a professional home and a base from which to continue the study once the support of the Rehabilitation Department of the Ministry of Defense was withdrawn. Since then, he has continued to give me personal support and encouragement. The Institute and its staff were generous with their help whenever it was needed.

At a time of professional crisis, when it seemed that my work was coming to a dead end, it was Professor Michael Inbar, with his sharp critical approach to work in the field of sociology, who gave me renewed courage to pursue my writing.

Unexpected support was offered by organized groups of parents of widows, as well as by individuals among them. Hearing of my study, they contacted me and impressed upon me the importance of the work I was doing.

Not less unexpected was the help I got from people within the Rehabilitation Department of the Ministry of Defense who, even after the official support for my study ended, continued to deliver relevant and important information. Their names, for obvious reasons, cannot be mentioned here.

A Fulbright Scholarship helped me to spend a year in the stimulating, friendly atmosphere of the Center for Family Studies of the University of Minnesota. During that year I was able to reanalyze and rethink the material of the study that would be included in this book.

Mrs. Irma Rosen was instrumental in giving this book its English format, and Mrs. Kay Weinberger generously devoted her editorial talents to shape the final product. Both of them, while doing their job, pampered me with their genuine friendship.

My very special thanks go to my friend and agent, Sheila Even-Tov, who undertook to deal with the tedious process of bringing this book to publication.

And then there is my family. At many points of the study and the writing of this book, my daughter, Ronit, expressed the viewpoint of young people on the subjects dealt with in the book and her insight forced me to reconsider and revise many points discussed in the book. And Don, who went hand-in-hand with me through this long journey, both before and even after he became my husband—without him and his support I could not have come to the end of this ordeal.

Prologue

This book is about war widows. War widows everywhere are among the lesser known casualties of war. Sociological interest has been directed to the fighting soldier, to prisoners of war, to returning soldiers, and even to the families of soldiers. The wives of soldiers who never came back, however, have rarely been the focus of sociological attention. When, at the end of 1969, the Israeli Ministry of Defense commissioned a study concerning war widows, I saw it as an opportunity to remedy this omission, at least in part. The aim of this commissioned study was to find ways to improve and ease the adjustment of war widows to their situation. More specifically, the study was expected to identify the needs of war widows, and accordingly to evaluate the services offered to them by the Rehabilitation Department of the Ministry of Defense.[1] With this practical and applicative purpose in mind, the study was focussed on the group of widows considered to be in most need of help and services—widows of the Six-Day War (the last war at the time) who were also mothers of children who were minors. This study was carried out in the period between 1970 and 1972. In 1972, the final report was submitted to the Israeli Ministry of Defense.

The data collected during the first stage of the study convinced me that the problem of adjustment to war-widowhood in Israeli society had far-reaching implications. So many aspects of adjustment were called into question by the data: what was considered to be good adjustment and by whom; how much and what kind of adjustment was "allowed" by society; who set the limits of adjustment; and how much of the adjustment process was borne by the widow and how much by those around her. It seemed to me that the answers to these kinds of questions went far beyond the definition of need and provision of services, and even beyond the problems of personal adjustment to loss.

They concerned issues which deeply affected the lives of the war widows, of their families and their friends, but yet which lay totally outside the scope of their bureaucratic encounters with the Rehabilitation Department of the Ministry of Defense. Studying the experience of the war widow in different spheres of Israeli society offered, I felt, a new way of looking at that society as a whole. This awareness prompted me to venture into a prolonged study of the situation of war widows in Israeli society.

A second stage of field work was carried out between 1972 and 1975. During this stage, a follow up of the widows studied in the first stage was supplemented by data that concerned war widowhood in general. These data were collected from a wide variety of sources that covered, whenever possible, periods both prior to, and later than, the Six-Day War. In addition, a much wider range of subjects was covered than in the original stage.

Widowhood, as the findings of my study show very clearly, is a "master status," to borrow Becker's term (Becker 1963, 31-35). As such, it expresses itself in every area of the lives of those so entitled. The women who are discussed here were war widows at home and at work, among friends and within their extended families, in their dealings with officials and in their most intimate relationships. As the focus of this book is on the state of widowhood, I could begin by writing on any one of these or of the other subjects of this book, yet the way in which these women were enshrouded by the widowhood would always be in the focus. Although this is a sociological book, it presents the phenomenon of widowhood mainly from the point of view of the widows rather than from that of society.

Five of the chapters in the book are devoted to those subjects that became the most salient in the course of the interviews. In each of these chapters, the findings are analyzed in relation to relevant sociological approaches. At the end of the chapter, an example of all that was said on the subject by one widow in the sample is presented in full. The order of the chapters could be understood as a linear progression from the widest context of the state to the narrowest one of individual status, or as a circular shift from the way the state defines and sees the widow to the way the widow sees herself within society. But no such sophisticated decisions were made in the organization of the book. The ordering of chapters follows, more or less, the sequence of subjects presented spontaneously by most of the widows during the interviews. If there is any implicit meaning to this order, it should be sought in the widows' organization of their perceptions and presentation of their situation. The dividing line between one subject and the next was not very clear in the interviews, and I kept this fuzziness in the book as well. As they spoke of their roles as mothers and homemakers, the widows usually talked about the composition of their households and of their extended families as well. In their descriptions of their struggles for status they also spoke about their work and career opportunities. Wherever possible, I left it this way. The division of lives and of living conditions into neat categories of topic and chapter contains a high degree of the arbitrary. Therefore this book can be read from beginning to end and the other way around.

One of the purposes of writing this book was to fulfill an obligation to the women who shared with me the essence of their tragedy and the struggle of their lives. My role was that of interpreter and discussant, but the story belongs to the widows. They deserve to be heard, and what they have to say is worth listening to. They also want to be heard. During the course of the interviews it was common for a widow to express the wish that her painful experience, her mistakes and successes and the knowledge that she had gained, would not be wasted. "I am telling you my story," said one, "with the hope that others will be able to learn from it." I hope so too, and this desire determined the way the widows themselves are presented in this book. It is written and organized to give them pride of place in their own story.

This story is both that of the widows as a group and the very personal story of each one of them. In order to introduce each widow to the reader, a few lines of general description of each of the seventy-one studied is given at the end of the book. I trust that these personal vignettes will enable the reader to relate the quotations in the text to more intimate images of the women who uttered them.

Israeli
War Widows

I

Theoretical Points
of Departure

Our century has been saturated with war, and wars themselves have attracted the interest of many social scientists. Yet war widowhood as a social phenomenon has never been the subject of serious study. Moreover, in the sociological literature, widows are dealt with mainly in the context of aging, and widowhood is regarded as the last inevitable stage in a woman's life. Thus, in four social science encyclopedias I consulted, the entry "widowhood" is conspicuous by its absence, although these works offer a good deal of information on "marriage," "divorce," and "parenthood," subjects related to personal and familial status (Kna'ani 1962; Gould & Kolb 1964; Seligman 1931; Sills 1968). This subject is also neglected in most introductory works of sociology, even in those of the sociology of the family, where little or no mention is made of widows as a social category. The few works that refer to this subject dismiss it with several sentences of a general nature.[1] For this reason, in studying widowhood and related topics, scholars have had difficulty in finding any conceptual frameworks that are relevant to the subject. For example, Aitken-Swan (1962) found herself compelled to define the term "widow" before she could discuss the population of her survey. This she did in the following simplistic way, perhaps because a more refined definition was not available:

> The Social Services Act, 1947–1959, grants a "widow's pension" to various categories of women temporarily or permanently without their husbands. For this reason, the term "widow" has lost its meaning in Australia and requires to be defined. For the purpose of this survey, a widow is a woman whose husband has died (Aitken-Swan 1962, 6).

Lopata (1973A) found that the only way to learn anything on the subject of widowhood was to research it, or in her words:

1

This study resulted from my realization that I knew nothing about what happens to families, particularly to wives, after the death of the husband, in spite of the fact that I had been studying American urban women for more than twelve years. I soon learned that most literature dealing with family relations does not contain adequate data about widows. (Lopata, x)

The present work is about war widows in Israel. In particular, I have responded to the question, implicit in Lopata's words, of what has happened to the families, and especially to the wives, of soldiers killed in Israel's five major wars and many lesser clashes. Given the virtual lack of information and substantive theory on the subject, I was forced, like others before me, to draw upon existing theories on closely related and relevant subjects. These theories stem from different disciplines and touch, each in its own way, upon some aspects of my subject of interest. As general points of departure, I draw on the considerable body of knowledge accumulated in three areas of research and theory: (I) widowhood, (II) family in crisis, and (III) social catastrophe.

Widowhood

Widowhood is a subject dealt with by several disciplines, among them psychology, psychiatry, social work, and to a much lesser extent, anthropology and sociology. One could expect each discipline to treat the subject in its own distinctive way, yet in fact, the borders between the disciplines tend to blur. As a result, it is hard to distinguish any characteristic differences between the contributions of various disciplines, either in method or in content.

On inspection, much of the work on widowhood turns out to focus on problems of mourning and bereavement. That this should be so is in no small measure due to the initial and definitive works of Freud and Durkheim. In his famous article, "Mourning and Melancholy," Freud dealt with the psychopathological reaction to the loss of a close person, and compared it to a healthy reaction to such an event (Freud [1917] 1959). Durkheim, in discussing the general meaning of ritual, also dealt with rites of mourning and their social meanings (Durkheim [1915] 1961). The majority of scholars who have followed in the wake of Freud and Durkheim acknowledge their debt to either or both; their work derives its impetus and direction from them, and accordingly, for the most part, is concerned with the process of becoming a widow and the reaction to it. This focus has diverted attention from an examination of widows as a unique social category with its own typical patterns of interaction with others. Consequently this aspect of widowhood research has been quite neglected. Psychologists, rather than sociologists, have held sway in this area, and psychologistic interpretations of mourning dominate the literature. Most scholars of the subject have tried to discover the psychological processes a person goes through in adjusting to the loss of someone close. The capacity of a mourner to face loss, the way of doing it, and the resources that aid in the process, are all discussed from a psychological viewpoint (Rees 1971). Thus the process of coping with loss can be "normal" or "pathological" (Bowlby 1961; Lindemann 1944), as can be the effect of this loss on the mourner (Bunch 1972; Stein & Susser 1969).

Scholars (usually psychologists) agree that the adjustment of a mourner to loss is a sequential process, commonly called "grief-work" (Lindemann 1944), but they seldom agree on the substance of this process or on the number of stages it comprises (Eliot 1969; Parkes 1972; Pollock 1961). In describing the process of psychological adjustment of a person to the loss of a "meaningful other," the analogy is sometimes made with that of adjustment to a new physical condition, and sometimes with the adjustment to the loss of a meaningful component in the self-identity and ego definition of the mourner. Others conceive the loss as similar to an amputation, and mourning is seen as equivalent to the process by which the crippled person comes to terms with the condition by creating a new personal context of meaning (Pollock 1961; Waller 1951).

Besides its dependency on the personal characteristics of the mourner, the process of adjustment is also conditional upon a host of other factors which may make it easier or more difficult to cope. These include the extent to which the death was anticipated (Lehrman 1956), the type of relationship between the mourner and the deceased (Waller 1951), the possibility of finding a substitute to fill the roles of the deceased (Averill 1968), the sources of help and support for the mourner (Lindemann 1944; Maddison & Walker 1967), and other such factors.

The length of the period of grief-work cannot be accurately determined, in the opinion of most researchers, but it appears from their conclusions that one year, more or less, may be considered a reasonable period for this process (Glick, Weiss & Parkes 1974). After grief-work has ended successfully, the mourner is expected by most researchers to return to a capacity and an ability to function comparable with that before the mourning period. The works mentioned above deal almost exclusively with the mourner. To the extent that they deal at all with social surroundings, the focus is on the degree to which the environment (including children and family, as well as the sources of help available) aids or hinders the mourner's grief-work (Scott

1967). The results of the loss and the period of mourning which follows are measured by criteria relating to the individual. This psychological approach to coping with death has given rise to a web of theories and practical guidance intended mainly to direct those who work with people in mourning. Their purpose is to ensure the proper expressions of sorrow, anxiety, rejection, and so on, that are considered integral to the situation of loss (Engel 1961).

The absence of external expressions of grief, such as crying or withdrawal, is considered by those working with mourners as a repression of feeling and/or a denial of reality. This, in their opinion, indicates the absence of the process of grief-work. According to these theories, the lack of grief-work would most probably express itself later in psychological or psychosomatic symptoms (Brewster 1950; Deutsch 1937). A large part of the psychiatric literature dealing with widowhood is concerned with this type of reaction (Bowlby 1961; Greengain 1942; Maddison & Walker 1967). In the field of social work, the emphasis has shifted from dealing with concrete problems (economic, organizational, and others), to dealing with mental problems, on the assumption that mourners who successfully pass through the process of grief-work will be able to solve other problems through their own resources (Abrahams 1972; Silverman 1963).

That there is a clear lack of sociological orientation to problems of mourning and bereavement is recognized by many scholars. Eliot, who is considered the pioneer among those dealing with this subject, in his early work on the adjustment of families to loss, drew attention to the dearth of empirical studies dealing with the sociological aspects of this adjustment process (Eliot 1930A, 1930B). In a later article, he introduced sociological perspectives and pointed to the effects of the death of a member of a family on its organization of roles and on its way of functioning (Eliot 1932). Yet, although he drew attention to the lack of empirical work on the sociological aspects of loss, Eliot himself never carried out research of this kind. In his later articles, he touched now and then upon questions related to the social life of the mourner, to the reaction of friends and strangers to the newly widowed, to the change in relationships within the kinship unit and so forth. However, all of these points were supported by theoretical discussion only (Eliot 1955).

More recently, the subject of widowhood was the focus of work by Glick, Weiss and Parkes (1974). In *The First Year of Bereavement,* the authors summarized a study based on some 150 widows and widowers. In their survey of relevant literature, they state, "The exploration of the social aspect of bereavement seems to have a brief history. The emotional aspects of bereavement have, however, received more attention" (Glick, Weiss & Parkes, 6).

Given this neglect of such social aspects, the authors stress their importance and undertake as their aim to correct these lacunae:

> One aim of this book is to provide a response to this need to understand bereavement as a social as well as an emotional event. Indeed, our view is that the social and emotional aspects are so intermeshed that neither can be understood apart from the other. (Glick, Weiss & Parkes, 6)

In spite of this declared aim, the social problems presented by widowhood are treated in this book from a very specific perspective. The authors deal with many social variables, such as economic problems, support systems, and contacts with family members and friends. But the emphasis is always on the question of how these variables affect the mourner's ability to overcome the crisis caused by his loss. That is to say, in the final analysis, the authors go back to discuss the influence of social factors upon psychological processes. No one can doubt the importance of the introduction of social variables into the analysis of the process of mourning, but this cannot serve as a substitute for the understanding of the social components of widowhood in their own right.

In the interim period between the early work of Eliot and the recent work of Glick, Weiss & Parkes, several attempts were made to apply a sociological orientation to the problems of widows (Cochrane 1936; Kubler-Ross 1969; Rosenblatt, Walsh & Jackson 1973). Some researchers have tried to integrate psychological and sociological variables in explaining some of the phenomena connected with the death of a close person. Averill (1968) and Volkart and Michael (1965), for instance, use Durkheim's analysis of mourning rituals as a basis for differentiating between "grief," which is a personal expression of sorrow, and "mourning," which is a normative expression. Both expressions relate to the same event, but are not necessarily identical or overlapping. Spiro (1967) tries to show, through an analysis of Jewish mourning rituals that society recognizes the psychological need of the mourner and creates rituals to meet these needs, thus making grief-work easier.

Much of the work described concentrates on various aspects of the immediate situation of becoming a widow, but hardly deals at all with the state of widowhood as a continuing social condition. Moreover, the literature cited above discusses neither the social mechanisms that control the behavior of the newly widowed nor those that determine the patterns of interaction with her in the future. Therefore Berardo's (1968) critique of research on widowhood, although written many years ago, still holds. In analyzing and summarizing the accumulated empirical and theoretical material relating to widowhood, Berardo makes the following point:

It appears that sociological analyses of death, bereavement and widowhood comprise a minute proportion of the literature in this area and all
too frequently overlap with the psychological in emphasis . . . As a
consequence, we know a good deal about the personal adjustment
process involved and rather little about the sociological features of the
bereaved family. (Berardo, 4)

A concentration on the psychological aspects of widowhood
while ignoring its social aspects leads, according to Berardo, to
distortion in the description of the phenomenon of widowhood.
Speaking of the psychological orientation of such research, Berardo
says: "It needs to be emphasized, however, that this orientation is
characterized by a general lack of concern with the social life of
mourners and with their long-term adjustment" (Berardo, 40).

To strengthen his point, Berardo refers to Gorer's (1965) criticism
on the same subject:

. . . investigators tend to write as though the bereaved were completely
alone, with no other occupation in life but to come to terms with and
work through their grief (and) this implicit picture of a solitary (person)
who has nothing to do but get over this grief has tended to dominate the
literature of the last twenty years. (Gorer, 150)

Bearing this criticism in mind, there are nonetheless a few works
that deserve special attention, since they do deal with widowhood
from a sociological point of view. In *Death, Grief and Mourning,* Gorer
(1965) traces the erosion over the previous half century of the support
system for the bereaved, traditionally dictated by the norms of English
society. The disappearance of part of these normative arrangements
deprived those who were dependent upon, or who had a strong
attachment to, the deceased of both formal and informal social resources to aid them in meeting their problems. Discussing the special
problems of widows of all ages, Gorer concludes: "There is no place in
the British social scene designed for widows" (Gorer, 102). In order to
justify this statement, he describes British pension laws, customary
housing arrangements, the occupational possibilities open to women,
and the stigma attached to any welfare institution to which widows
could turn. All of these, he says, together with the erosion of general
social and familial norms that secured and protected the widow's
welfare, leave her lonely and impoverished—socially if not monetarily,
too—in coping with her new situation.

Research on widowhood took a new turn with the publication in
1958 of Peter Marris's book *Widows and Their Families.* The novel and
welcome aspect of this work was its exclusive and express focus on
comparatively young widows, most of whom still had young children

and who, accordingly, on the death of their husbands, had become the heads of child-raising families. Marris gives a descriptive account of his findings that combines both a sociological and a psychological perspective. These findings are concerned with the meaning of widowhood in different areas of life, such as social and family contacts, economic conditions, and reaction to loss. The main theoretical analysis of his findings appears in his later book, *Loss and Change* (1974). Here Marris analyzes widowhood (as an example of one in a whole series of losses) as a phenomenon that causes change. This analysis is based on the interplay between the set of roles of the wife and those of her husband on the one hand, and of the woman's set of roles and of her self-image on the other hand. Marris contends that, as a result of this double connection, the loss of the husband renders the wife's set of roles meaningless from many points of view, and in this way distorts her self-image and her identity.

Despite the dual sociological and psychological focus of the analysis, most of Marris's conclusions lean towards a psychological interpretation. Clearly, he did not subject his material to a more general and systematic sociological analysis of the state of widowhood, although his material could very well serve for the analysis of reaction to, and conditions of, loss. Despite this flaw in the theoretical analysis, *Widows and Their Families* has great importance for the study of widowhood: it is the first work that presents the social problems of the state of widowhood itself, unobscured by parallel references to the problems of old age.

In her research for the book *Widowhood In An American City*, Lopata (1973A), focusses on questions that are concerned with the social "position" of the widow. This position can be understood, according to her, only with reference to an analysis of her "social role." Lopata's analysis, unlike that of Marris, is not focussed on the psychological aspects of the change of role from wife to widow, but specifically on changes in mutual social expectations that are brought into play as a result of widowhood. Lopata addresses herself in this book and in her later one on *Women as Widows* (1979), not only to the change in that part of the woman's role set that relates to her husband, but to the whole set of roles that she formerly had. This includes roles on which it might appear that the state of widowhood should have no direct bearing. The source of the change in the social position of a widow, according to Lopata's analysis, is in the severing of a "meaningful other" from her network of social interaction. This change will bring with it other changes in the relative position of every other participant in her network. The change of position, in turn, brings in its wake a change in the definition of the relationships and mutual expectations of all the participants to the interaction and, as a result,

8 / ISRAELI WAR WIDOWS

changes also in the different social "identities" involved. This perspective enables the researcher to apply the same way of thinking to a very wide range of social contexts and roles in which the widow participates (Lopata 1970, 1973A, 1973B). It is also apt for an examination of changes in the widow's self-image, for these too may be traced in part to the interaction network of the widow, rather than to psychological changes within herself (Lopata 1973C).

The empirical material to which Lopata applied her approach (Lopata 1973A) was collected from a population of widows ranging in age from mature to old. Since there is a connection between age and a person's set of roles, Lopata's findings are typical for a population of mature, elderly, and old women, but are not necessarily applicable to one of younger women whose set of roles—familial, social and occupational—are different. Therefore, it is clearly difficult to relate Lopata's findings to younger widows, even though her approach and method of analysis might well be effective for, and relevant to, the study of the state of widowhood for young widows.

Gorer, Marris, and Lopata all raise many different kinds of assumptions and questions that relate to the nature of widows' participation in society, not as a one-sided exercise on the part of the widow, but with others having important roles too. This contrasts with the work of most other scholars dealing with the subject who tend to see it in terms of a process of adjustment that the widow goes through essentially on her own, although sometimes with the help of others around her.

All in all, an overview of the relevant professional literature leads to the disconcerting conclusion that the considerable quantity of work in the area is not matched in terms of quality. Certain problems of widowhood have been investigated and discussed time and again without resulting in any real contribution to a theoretical framework that encompasses the phenomenon. Other aspects of the phenomenon have been neglected completely, in terms both of theory and research.

Nonetheless, one must not overlook some important conclusions that can be drawn from this body of knowledge by anyone dealing with the subject of widowhood:

a. From the literature it can be concluded that the loss of the husband (like loss in general) brings in its wake a period of total confusion, of disorientation and disorganization. The expression given to these conditions is called, in everyday life, sorrow and pain, and in the language of psychology is known as the process of grief-work, or adjustment to loss. The social meaning of this period is that during this time a widow is neither able, expected, nor allowed to function in a normal way, even in the most routine areas of daily life.

b. There is no agreement as to the duration of the process of grief-work. Similarly, little attention has been paid to the extent to which both the duration and nature of this period are the result of purely psychological processes, or are influenced by socio-cultural patterns (Caine 1974; Davidson 1968; Palgi 1973). For example, in spite of the many studies of grief-work among "legitimate" mourners like widows, I was unable to find any research into this process among "non-legitimate" mourners, such as an unknown lover of a deceased person—that is to say, in cases where there is no social expectation that one behave like a mourner. Comparisons of this kind might have clarified the meaning of the social struc-tural component in the process of grief-work. Still, the prevalence of these psychologistic theories of mourning among the various professionals who care for the bereaved, and among the popula-tion at large, creates a set of expectations of certain patterns of grief-work. These expectations are directed toward the widow and require her response.

c. The fact that the widow leaves (or is removed from) her set of normal roles requires other people to fulfill at least some of them, even if only on a temporary basis. But this in turn takes place at the expense of the woman's privacy, since comparative strangers in-trude into more or less intimate areas of her life. There is no discussion at all in the literature of such patterns of intrusion, nor of their duration or significance.

d. It is clear that there is an intervening period, a kind of moratorium, between the situation of being a married woman and the change to that of being a widow. This is the mourning period. In the professional literature, I found no distinction made between mourning and widowhood. Nor did I find any discussion of the effect of the mourning period upon the social position of the widow. Some of the issues mentioned above will be addressed in this book, mainly in chapters V and VI.

Family in Crisis

Unlike the state of theory that obtains for widowhood, the sociological literature offers a quite crystallized theory for analysis of the subject of family in crisis. The model for this is based mainly on the work of Hill (1949, 1963), while others have broadened and refined it (Dyk & Sutherland 1956; Farber 1964; Koos 1946, 1950; Morris 1965; Parad & Caplan 1960).

The sociological approach to "family in crisis" is one of the specific derivates of structural-functional theory and its application to the family. Accordingly, this theory views the evolution of family crisis more or less as follows: every family unit maintains a certain degree of equilibrium, otherwise it would not be able to exist. This equilibrium is built on the family's inner set of needs, resources, specific techniques, aspirations, and plans. Within this balanced family unit are created the specific arrangements that determine the way in which the whole unit will function. The unit functions, in turn, on the basis of its needs as a whole, and those of each of its members. The kind and degree of actual and potential resources available to the family, as well as its order of priorities, will determine how the family invests in various goals.

This order of priorities is derived from the norms of society in general and from their interpretation within particular families. According to its values, a family will determine its own particular division of labor and patterns of allocation of resources. In addition, a family will establish its own routines and forms of role specialization. The process of creating such a small but balanced social system is an extended one: it begins with the establishment of the family unit and continues throughout the family's entire life cycle. Any change that occurs inside the family, or in the external conditions of its existence, has to be met by adjustment. A crisis within the family is understood to be any occurrence that upsets this equilibrium to such an extent that the unit is unable to fulfill its essential functions. The greater the number of parts of the functioning unit that are paralyzed, the more serious the crisis; and the more serious the crisis, the more severe are its effects upon the unit, perhaps even to the extent of threatening its very existence.

From this approach to the meaning of crisis it follows that the magnitude and the severity of the crisis do not depend only on the event that is the cause of the crisis, but also on the unit in which it occurs, and on the capacity of that unit to absorb events of crisis without becoming paralyzed completely by them. One can say that the full meaning of crisis may be understood only by examining the conjunction of a particular crisis and the particular family within which it occurs. Various characteristics of the family, most of which were mentioned above, determine the severity and the significance of a specific crisis for a particular family. The following example illustrates this. The illness of a housewife that confines her to bed might constitute a comparatively mild crisis in a family where the division of labor is not very strict, where the manpower resources are sufficient, and where the husband and the somewhat older children also have skills in household management. In a case like this, it only requires a small measure of reorganization to transfer the wife's household tasks to the husband and children, and the family will weather the crisis with comparative ease. By contrast, in a family where there is a very strict division of labor, limited manpower resources, high role specialization, and where all the children in the family are still small, the same crisis can be a very serious one. Even here, however, its severity may be considerably tempered if the family can mobilize available arrangements to provide for a temporary replacement for the ailing housewife. Alternatively, temporary replacement might be available through paid services, in which case the severity of the crisis would be dependent upon the economic resources of the family. Under these circumstances, the family will continue to function with the help of outsiders who temporarily perform necessary tasks, and the family will endure the period of crisis without too much difficulty.

It is clear from this that the theory of family crisis does not offer instruments for the diagnosis of certain events as "crisis-creating" for a family. However, it does provide general guidelines that indicate that the more damaging a particular event is to the family's ability to function, and the less resources the family possesses to cope with the situation, the greater will be the damage to the equilibrium within the family, and the more severe will be the crisis. According to the same theory, overcoming a crisis calls for the reorganization of the family so that it will continue to function as a unit. In the above example, if one assumes that the period of the housewife's illness did not bring about the total disorganization of the family, her recovery and reentry into her set of roles will be defined as "overcoming the crisis." Here, the family in the postcrisis period functions much on the same level as it did in the precrisis period.

However, not every crisis allows a family to function in the same way after it as before. The birth of a child, a crisis that is dealt with at great length in the literature of the sociology of the family (Caplan, Mason & Kaplan 1965; Dyer 1963; Hobbs 1965; LeMasters 1957), is one that most families weather successfully. The organization that replaces the disorganization of the crisis period is not reestablished at the same level and in the same form as had existed before the crisis. In such reorganization the family must adjust itself to new roles, to a different household composition, and to different constraints that arise from the presence of an infant. The theoreticians do not discuss the possibility of a family which does not succeed in reorganizing and functioning in its new composition, and as a result, gives the baby to be cared for outside the household while the couple goes back to functioning as they did before the birth of the child. But in a case such as this, it generally would be agreed that the family had not succeeded in overcoming its crisis. Therefore a return to the same level and form of functioning that had existed before does not prove that the crisis has been satisfactorily overcome. Instead, the overcoming of a crisis is conditional, at times, upon the ability of the family to function with a different composition and in accordance with a new set of priorities.

The theory of family crisis does not deal to any great extent with the period of crisis itself. This is usually thought of as a brief duration for which the family develops a form of emergency organization. The assumption here is that an emergency setup cannot continue to work for a very protracted period since it demands great concentration of effort and resources that would diminish seriously the strength of the whole unit. When the crisis is of lengthy duration, the theoreticians tend to regard it as a series of crises, each of which has the same development and structure as that described above. For example, when the recruitment of a husband/father into the army (Hill 1949) occasions a long period of separation from the family, the theory would define it as consisting of at least two crises. The first is one of separation and of loss to the family of a functioning member, followed by reorganization of the family in various domains. Thus, after a period of crisis and adjustment to changed conditions, the family will go back to a situation of equilibrium. With the termination of army service and the return of the husband/father, the family faces a second crisis—that of reabsorbing him. In turn, this again requires a reorganization of resources, priorities, and expectations in accordance with the new family composition. Each of these events is described as a separate crisis, and the ability to cope with the first will not necessarily mean an ability to cope with the second.

In the exposition of the theory of crisis, the likely duration of the crisis period is never specified, but it is obvious that it is limited. After a relatively short time, only one of two results can occur: either a return to equilibrium, or disintegration of the family unit. As I said at the outset, the theory of family crisis is basically a structural-functional theory that sees a situation of equilibrium as the only one that can exist on a long-term basis. In relation to the subject with which I am dealing, the following conclusions may be drawn from this model:

a. Crisis is not the result of a particular event that is defined as crisis-creating, but of its meaning to the particular family subjected to it. In defining a crisis situation, we should assume that its consequences will be different for each family that experiences the crisis. We cannot assume that crises that are similar in certain respects, will necessarily produce similar results in different families. As applied to the subject of this book, we should expect that different families will be affected in different ways by the loss of the husband-father.

b. Like mourning, crisis is defined subjectively, except that in this definition the "subject" of discussion is a social unit and not an individual. This type of definition draws attention to numerous factors that have a role in the process of crisis and in the adaptation of families to it. The findings of my study show clearly that any attempt to understand the situation of war widows is incomplete if it does not take into account that these women function not only as individuals, but also as integral parts of the families they head, and that these social units are themselves embedded in wider social realities.

c. This model casts doubt on the validity of linking the capacity of the family to cope with crisis to the usual socio-economic status variables, such as ethnic origin, education, occupation, and so forth. Variables of this kind may be important to explain the presence or the absence of certain social arrangements that provide help during crisis. But the fact of belonging to a particular ethnic or educational group still does not ensure automatically that those resources or arrangements, which usually exist in such groups, are actually available to the family during the particular crisis that it faces.

When the model of the "family in crisis" was introduced, it broke new ground and made a singular contribution to the study of this aspect of family life. Yet, although many scholars used this model, in practice they did not succeed in developing its full potential. The empirical studies that were based on the model added only very little to its dimensions, and they reproduced it almost in its original form. The concept of equilibrium, which is central to this approach, was left vague, and no indices to measure it were developed. Therefore, studies that today are based on this model accept that a family which exists without any overt serious crisis, or one that is not on the verge of complete breakdown, exhibits an adequate level of equilibrium. This lack of development of the model has left scholars with many unanswered questions. A family is considered to be in a state of disorganization when it is not functioning properly. Yet how much dysfunction must there be in a family for it to be considered as a disorganized unit? In Jewish families, can "sitting shiv'a,"[2] when the family is proscribed from functioning as usual, be defined as a situation of disorganization? Questions also arise about the criteria by which a family can be defined as not functioning. Are these criteria based on generally accepted norms or do they refer to the level of functioning before the crisis? Are there objective criteria for a minimal level of necessary functioning? And similarly, are there criteria for identifying reorganization that, according to this model, signifies the overcoming of a crisis situation? Still further problems are raised by the need to determine whether the level of functioning achieved by the family after the crisis is more or less similar to their pre-crisis level. Moreover, is it possible to compare levels of functioning in two different families where, for example, both have sustained the loss of the husband/father, but where they differ from each other in every other important respect—in their household composition, in their needs, in their order of priorities, in the resources at their disposal, and so forth?

As they relate to the subject of this study, all these questions crystallize into one central query: when, under what conditions, and by which criteria can a family that lacks a father be identified as not in crisis, or will it remain a family in crisis as long as the widow does not remarry? Chapters III and IV of this book respond to some of these questions.

Social Catastrophe

A personal crisis may be restricted to the individual and the family, or it may be experienced in common with many others as a result of some especially devastating occurrence. But is the individual affected differently by these two kinds of personal crisis? According to the theory of "family in crisis," it is in fact in the subjective perception of crisis, in the experiencing of catastrophe, that the main difference lies. A personal crisis whose source lies within a more encompassing social crisis, frees the individual from feelings of personal failure, of guilt at "being different," and more particularly, provides a reference group by which to measure the severity of the crisis and to serve as an example to emulate in overcoming it (Hill 1949). Personal crises of this kind may be experienced in times of war (Bossard 1941; Shelsky 1954), during periods of severe economic recession, or widespread unemployment (Angell 1936; Koos 1946), or of mass immigration (Shuval 1963). While recognizing the importance of this line of argument, a concentration on the subjective viewpoint of the individual may, at the same time, divert attention from the equally important obverse focus, namely, the likelihood of an objective difference between the two forms of personal crisis. In relation to the subject of this book, it raises the question of whether there is a meaningful and objective difference between the situation of widows, as members of a general category, and that of war widows as members of a more particular category.

Social thought about the significance of calamity and catastrophe received its initial impetus from projected rather than actual events and, in particular, from the pressing prospect of nuclear war. Since the 1960s, there have been several attempts at comprehensive evaluation of the social significance and impact of catastrophe and crisis for communities or whole societies. Since fortunately these are not everyday occurrences, the discussion has relied for the most part upon material evidence, personal testimony, and reports and descriptions of social catastrophes that have occurred in the past. Only a few studies have relied upon systematic, empirical research. The practical aspect of these studies focussed on the impact of social catastrophe on society, with only marginal and incidental reference to the impact on the individual. Despite this, there are conclusions to be drawn from these studies for those who focus their interest specifically on individuals exposed to a state of social catastrophe.

Barton (1970), in *Communities In Disaster*, summarizes much of the evidence and partial research connected with social catastrophe. When overtaken by catastrophe, society changes its way of functioning with a view to helping the affected locales and individuals to cope. The way in which a particular event becomes conceived of as a "social catastrophe" is determined by many different factors. For example, to be characterized as a social catastrophe, it is not enough for a phenomenon to be deemed so by the values of the society in question. This definition must also be supported by the mass communication system that acts in ways expected in a social catastrophe. Thus, the dissemination of information should set in motion activities by formal and informal organizations that are directed towards the needs of the affected region. The ability of a society to cope with a catastrophe depends on a multitude of variables: the magnitude of the disaster, the extent to which it had been anticipated, the resources of the individual, family, and community that are at the disposal of those affected, as well as the technical and organizational capacities available. A society that musters its forces to withstand a catastrophe creates new social frameworks in place of those that had existed before. New leadership comes to the fore, and the old is discarded, at least temporarily. The values of certain roles change, and this alters the prestige of those who fill these roles. Therefore, a society that is coping with catastrophe undergoes very rapid change in many areas of life. Such change seems to be determined by the magnitude and the centrality of the disaster, as perceived by members of the society.

From the foregoing, one can conclude that the impact on an individual or a family of a personal crisis that derives from, and is part of, a social catastrophe is quite different from the impact of crisis where suffering is isolated, and where this is defined as a private calamity. In all cases, it is clear that the social framework within which the victim of a social catastrophe operates is different from that of the victim of a "personal calamity."

The assertion that war precipitates Israeli society into a situation of "catastrophe," as this is defined in the sociological literature, is usually accepted by Israelis without question. Despite this, Israeli sociology has yet to turn its attention to a comprehensive study that deals with changes in the patterns of living during war. However, one can piece together evidence from a number of studies, each with a specific focus that, taken together, leave no doubt that war is indeed a social catastrophe in Israel. This is reflected in the attitude of the press (Goren 1975; Kahane & Kna'an 1973), in changes in role hierarchies, in generally accepted criteria of social prestige (Bar-Yosef & Padan-Eisenstark 1977; Kimerling 1971), and by the creation of voluntary organizations that reinforce the care given by existing agencies to victims of war (Amir 1976). The various activities and organizations that emerge in Israel during war time (such as Yad Lebanim, discussed in chapter II) are all characteristic of societies in catastrophe. Accordingly, war widows must be viewed in their correct context, as victims of a social catastrophe, and not as victims of an isolated personal and familial crisis. This is not just an academic distinction, for it has important practical consequences for the widow herself. As a victim of social catastrophe, she and her family are entitled to benefit from various social and public resources. Had her loss and suffering been defined as "private," neither she nor her family would have such rights. That the category of "war widow" belongs to the wider category of "victims of catastrophe" is an important factor in understanding the situation of these widows. To belong to this broader category determines to a great extent the kind of help available from public sources, as well as the form of aid a member of the category can expect to receive. Being "victims of catastrophe" determines, to a great extent, what they can do to surmount the crisis that has overtaken them and their families. This is the subject of chapter II.

Discussion

The three theoretical approaches discussed above are largely concerned with the same subject, that of reaction to crisis situations. In the first (widowhood), the reaction is that of the individual; in the second (family in crisis), it is that of the family; and in the third (social catastrophe), it is in the wider society that the reaction takes place. In spite of the basic differences in approach, in terminology, and in basis of analysis, there is a similarity in their conception of crisis: in all three, crisis is defined, discussed, and understood as a temporary process. This process breaks the continuity of life at a certain point, and calls for emergency measures of psychological, familial, and/or social reorganization. The emergency organization brings about a concentrated investment of effort and resources for a limited period in which the victims of the crisis are expected to regain equilibrium and capacity to function. The emergency organization disappears when the acute stage of the crisis is over.

And then what?

The fact is that none of the theories mentioned deal clearly or substantively with the question of what happens after the crisis situation has passed. They seem to imply that after the crisis is over, the situation of the individual, the family, or the society returns more or less to its former state, with some adjustment to changes brought about by the crisis. Alternatively, and again only by inference, if the situation does not return approximately to its precrisis state, then it is considered to indicate a failure to overcome the crisis.

My main thesis in this book is that after the crisis situation has passed, nothing (or only very little) returns to its former state. Here this relates only to widowhood, yet it may apply also to other kinds of crisis. This means that after a certain period of absolute chaos, which is how the psychological literature describes the crisis situation of a widow, the war widow finds herself in a completely different social reality from that which she had known before widowhood. This is not to assert that a war widow is a social being entirely different from, say, a married woman, or that there is no similarity between the social worlds in which they live. In reality, the life of a war widow (or any other widow) is made up of components similar to those that make up the life of a married woman, but their priorities, proportions, and prominence differ.

A useful analogy of these situations is that of two scrabble boards, both with the identical opening word—"married." Although the two scrabble sets are composed of the same pieces, it is not likely that the two games played on these boards will continue to be identical, as the alternatives are so numerous. Each game will develop according to the "letters" available to the player, as well as to the player's talents, knowledge, and idiosyncratic preferences. Yet there is a remote chance and a theoretical possibility that, at any point of the game, the two boards will be identical. But were the opening word on one of the boards to be changed in the middle of the game, it is most certainly not possible for the two games to develop identical boards. Changing the opening word on the board would necessitate moving most of the pieces. Some of the alterations would come about as an immediate result of the changed opening word, while others would come in the course of a chain of reactions, and at varying removes from the opening word itself. A change of word opens up numerous possibilities and eliminates others. But it determines the inevitability of differences between the two boards.

The analogy between the situation of a war widow and a scrabble board on which the opening word has been changed is clear. The pieces of the game represent the various areas of life. A rearrangement becomes necessary in order to fit the pieces of the game to the changed opening word. The rearrangement may take many different forms and, in life as in the game, its efficiency and effectiveness depend upon the talents and abilities of the "player." However, the process of changing and fitting must be gone through. And in life, just as in the game, every change brings with it a chain reaction of further alterations that do not necessarily result directly from the change in the opening word, from "married" to "widowed." The analogy can only be drawn so far. The parallel between the game and the subject of the discussion ends with the "rules of the game": whereas in scrabble the rules of play are clear and unambiguous, in reality, rules and norms of behavior differ from one area of life to another, and add greatly to the complexity of social reality.

The changes in the social situation of a woman widowed by war cut across all levels of life—from that of the general social level through to the most personal and intimate relationships in her social network. The implicit assumption in the professional literature—that widow-hood is a condition which affects only the "family situation" of a woman—does not take into account the chain reaction of changes that this crisis sets in motion in her life. It is difficult to follow this chain reaction, since various precipitating factors set into motion a whole variety of different consequences in a multitude of areas of the widow's life. As a result, the various changes in the life of a war widow rarely take the same direction or form, nor do they occur simultaneously or at equal intervals. For instance, the position of a widow in the formal institutions with which she comes into contact is determined by bureaucratic procedures that include legal processes, the compilation of records, and her placement in various settings of rehabilitation. On the other hand, the change in the position of a widow among her friends is a far more covert process that usually finds its course without any conscious intention on the part of those involved, and without direction from the outside. The variety of forms of change in a war widow's life tend to blur, to no small degree, the more general nature of the phenomenon. If variations are disregarded, the character of the phenomenon that emerges is that of a radical change in the position of the woman, and of her relationships and interaction with others. The main aim of this book is to trace, present, and analyze the unique life situation of Israeli women widowed by war.

II

War Widows and State Institutions

The "Fallen Soldiers' Families Law (Pension and Rehabilitation)"[1] was tabled in the Knesset in March 1950, some two years after the War of Independence. This bill was the first attempt to legalize the relationships between the various categories of Israeli population defined as "casualties of war," and society as represented by State institutions. The demand for this legislation apparently originated with those who had been dealing with these families, and who were unable to find within the bureaucratic system either a legal basis for their work or a justification for the considerable expenditure it entailed.

By 1950, the War of Independence was already history, and its casualties no longer "emergency cases." As a result, the Knesset debate on the bill focussed more on the ideological implications of extending aid to persons damaged by the war than on the necessary patterns of assistance. Members of the Knesset were hard put to find expression for practical implications of the law before them, but they did not have similar problems when it came to paying verbal homage to the fallen soldiers and their families. The opening remarks by A. Kaplan, Minister of Finance, are typical of the initial debate:

> This bill expresses the feeling of responsibility and indebtedness which the State, and all those who dwell in Zion feel toward the bereaved families whose dear ones were sacrificed on the altar of independence . . . We know all too well that no recompense or reward can make up for the magnitude of their loss . . . (Knesset Record Vol. 4, 1950, p. 1051)

During the same debate, opposition MK (Member of Knesset) Natan Yelin-Mor (Halochamim) said: "We are not giving these families charity. We are duty-bound to pay them ransom for our own souls, for the fact that it is thanks to their sacrifice that we have attained statehood and liberty and homeland" (Knesset Record Vol. 4, 1950, p. 1057).

19

The nature of the relationship between the "Families of the Fallen," and the State of Israel and Israeli society was first defined in the initial debate on the "Families of Soldiers." The definition reached at that time constituted the basis for all subsequent discussion on the handling of this issue: the families of the fallen were defined as creditors, and the State as indebted to them. This approach was exemplified, years later, in a debate held in 1967, by the remarks of MK Shlomo Lorenz (Agudat Yisrael):

> . . . We must understand that whatever we give is but the very least. It is only a token of our gratitude. For this reason we must compensate them in the only way we are capable of: award them maximum financial compensation, not as a gift, or out of charity, but as a debt repaid. An elemental debt. A sacred debt. (Knesset Record Vol. 49, 1967, p. 2820)

In a similar vein, Rachel Cohen of WIZO (Women's International Zionist Organization), in the context of the initial debate on the proposed bill, said: "In other countries there are honorary citizens. Here that is not customary. But by legislating the law for the families of the victims, those who have lost what is dearest to them will come to feel like honorary citizens" (Knesset Record, Vol. 4, 1950, p. 1056).

From the above, it seems as if there existed a rather broad consensus among members of the Knesset when it came to defining their position vis-à-vis "Families of Soldiers." This held true so long as the definition remained on an abstract plane—"honorary citizens" and "creditors" to whom society owed a "ransom" and a "sacred debt." One would expect that in the light of this broad consensus on the question of these families' social distinction and what they stood for, the law expressing this consensus would grant "privileges"[2] to this group that was so valued. But the law, as formulated by the Knesset Committee on Labor (the legislative body charged with the task), was in fact different. The government, represented by its Minister of Finance, was requesting Knesset approval for turning a number of "emergency measures" used over the two years following the War of Independence into permanent arrangements. A considerable number of those who lost property, jobs, or housing in the War of Independence, and many of those who lost close relatives, coped with their problems either by virtue of their own strength or through the help of resources—material or otherwise—which they themselves acquired through their social-familial network. Others were helped, for a brief period, through the emergency resources mobilized by society in a variety of ways. Two years later, by 1950, only those whose problems could not be solved by the conventional short-term emergency methods remained in the care of the Ministry of Defense. The "Families of

Soldiers" law dealt primarily with the allocation of economic resources, but did not grant privileges to their recipients. Only indigent members of this category were entitled to this economic support. The burden of proving "indigence" rested with the "indigent." "Indigent" people were entitled to assistance only so long as they were unable to provide for themselves: any proof of ability to support themselves through their own efforts (such as holding a job, even on a part-time basis) cancelled, either in full or in part, their eligibility for assistance. The level of support offered by the law was calculated to provide for minimum subsistence. Those entitled to receive aid were defined as "requiring rehabilitation" and, for such time as they received this assistance, they were "clients" of the rehabilitation office and its staff. One was "rehabilitated" when the support of public funds was no longer required.

From their public utterances, Knesset representatives were evidently aware that the law, in its proposed form and content, inevitably resulted in the identification of "Families of Soldiers" with indigent social groups maintained by public assistance. It was the desire to minimize this "indignity" which apparently lay behind the nearly unanimous vote to charge the Ministry of Defense with the implementation of the law, despite the administrative inefficiency involved. It also explains the strong objection to the suggestion that this law be implemented by one of the ministries concerned with welfare and social betterment. It seems that the high status of the Ministry of Defense—particularly as compared with those government offices responsible for welfare—was expected to be conferred also upon the "indigent" among the "Families of Soldiers." Nonetheless, the gap between the identity of an "indigent person" and that of a "bereaved family" and/or a "war widow" could not be bridged. Despite the closing statement of the debate made by MK Yaakov Gil that "The law is a tribute to a progressive state that values the efforts made by its sons" (Knesset Record Vol. 4, 1950, p. 1057), it was apparent that the Knesset membership remained unsure whether the dignity of those entitled to benefits obtained from this law was indeed preserved.

The "Families of Soldiers" law was, by-and-large, an ad hoc solution to the problems it addressed. The content of the law in no way whatever provided for the possibility of change, either within society as a whole, or in the individual situations to which it applied. Not only the law's initiators, but members of the Knesset as well, treated the law as if its sole purpose was to solve the problems of the indigent families of those who were killed in the War of Independence. Although the MKs did not profess to believe that the War of Independence was "the war to end all wars," neither the law nor the debate surrounding it showed any recognition that they considered the possible recurrence of large-scale wars in the region. Even as late as 1967, MKs did not relate to the phenomena of bereaved families and war widows as regular features of Israeli society, but merely as situational phenomena. Witness the words of MK Shlomo Lorencz (Agudat Yisrael), taken from the same speech as that quoted above:

> . . . I would not, perhaps, put forth the proposals I am about to suggest if this law applied to a large number of bereaved families or disabled veterans. But, thank God, we have suffered fewer casualities than we had feared . . . and since, God be thanked, their number is what it is, we need not fear that the financial burden on either the treasury or the citizen will be too great . . . (Knesset Record, Vol. 49, 1967, p. 2820)

Thus, whenever the law was debated and re-formulated, it was approached as a means for an ad hoc solution to current problems.

The structure of the law and its provisions inevitably necessitated its frequent amendment in accordance with situational changes, and over the years many such changes have indeed been introduced. By 1975, there had been nine "Proposed Amendments to the Families of Soldiers Fallen in Battle (Compensation and Rehabilitation) Law." These changes and amendments were of great importance to the population to which the law applied. The standard of living it guaranteed and the various social categories to which it applied became considerably higher. The benefits for "orphans who attained majority" were expanded, and various provisions were made whereby eligible recipients were enabled to meet considerable expenses in accordance with the accepted standards prevailing in Israeli society. Despite these changes, the structure and implication of the law were only slightly altered and it remained essentially a "welfare law." Even after the requirements for proof were reduced and many of the benefits automatically extended to all those defined as eligible, the requirement to furnish proof was not entirely eliminated. The nature of this law was the basis for the complex and problematic relationships between the war widows (and perhaps other eligible groups as well) and the employees of the Defense Ministry's Rehabilitation Department who, for the purpose of implementing this law, represented Israeli society and the State.

The Emergence of the Social Category of War Widows

The "Families of Soldiers" law covered a variety of social categories including the parents, siblings, wives, and children of the war dead. Not long after the declaration of the State of Israel, a new figure of speech was coined which collectively described these categories as

the "bereaved family." Within this bereft "family," the widows constituted the most marginal group of all, and so remained unfamiliar and
unknown to Israeli society as a whole. This fact bears strongly on the
understanding of the situation of the widows of the Six-Day War, as
well as on the patterns of interaction between them and Israeli society
in general, and the formal institutions of the State in particular.

Hand in hand with the process of legalizing the status of the
families of fallen soldiers, an organization called Yad Lebanim (Memorial to the Sons) was created. Yad Lebanim was founded by bereaved
parents, and one of its main aims was to represent the interests of the
"bereaved family" before the State institutions as well as before society
as a whole. It seems that during the period between the War of
Independence and the Six-Day War, this organization actually constituted the chief representative of the interests of those persons covered
by the "Families of Soldiers" law. However, Yad Lebanim was not an
interest or pressure group in the conventional sense. It was founded by
parents of dead soldiers to whom the "Families of Soldiers" law did not
apply since they were not considered indigent. As nonindigent, these
parents were almost anonymous, or as one bereaved parent whose son
was killed in the War of Independence put it: "We weren't even
registered anywhere." The organization enabled bereaved parents to
emerge from their anonymity (or "to be registered somewhere"), and
to constitute a recognized social category without being identified
with the "indigent." Every bereaved parent was eligible for membership and active participation in the organization. Theoretically at least,
this held true for war widows as well. Because the organization was
voluntary, and as such did not pay salaries to members active on its
behalf, active participation, and in particular the holding of key
positions, was confined to those who were not obliged to invest their
time in earning a living. So it was that the majority of the functionaries
in Yad Lebanim were bereaved parents who were not "indigent," while
a considerable number of those requiring the organization's services,
were "indigent" bereaved parents.

Although Yad Lebanim concerned itself chiefly with representing
the interests of bereaved parents, it also took upon itself to represent
war widows as well. In spite of their membership in a common
organization, there were nonetheless extremely sharp contradictions
between the widows and the bereaved parents which surfaced from
time to time, both in individual relationships and in more general
terms. In the context of Yad Lebanim, the most significant contrast
stemmed from the situational definitions appertaining to the parents
and to the widows. The term "bereaved parent" denotes a permanent
state, that is, a bereaved parent remains such under any and all
circumstances. Widowhood does not necessarily denote a permanent

state, but is defined instead as a potentially transitory, temporary situation.[3] The bereaved parents did not see in the widows long-term partners to organizational activity. For this reason, in as much as they were included in these activities, it was for external presentational purposes only. The widows, for their part, hoped that their partnership was for a brief duration only, and were generally ready to leave policy-making in the hands of the bereaved parents. Because the "Families of Soldiers" law related both to bereaved parents and to widows, and some identical criteria such as "income" or "minimum subsistence" were eventually set for both groups, the widows benefited by default from the activities of the parents as a pressure group.

With time, activities of Yad Lebanim became increasingly focussed on representation to various government bodies, particularly on economic issues. At that point, the fact that the widows were not represented on its different committees became more apparent. At a rather late stage, some attempts were made to include them on local committees and on the executive board, but this was largely a formal gesture—a "token widow." One of the widows who served on the executive committee from the time widows were first included in it up until the mid-1970s, related that she was never allowed to represent the widows' interests, that she had not been informed when meetings were to take place, and that decisions reached at those meetings were not made known to her. From descriptions by other widows who attempted to become actively involved in the organization, it is evident that when widows were granted committee membership, they were limited to only one representative per committee. This practice ensured that the widow's single vote did not decisively influence the resolutions passed by the group. Moreover, the representatives of the widows were not chosen democratically, because there was no suitable internal framework for conducting such elections. By the time this study was undertaken, it was difficult to ascertain whether those widows who were members of intra-organizational bodies had joined them on their own initiative, or had done so at the behest of the parents.

This organizational structure of Yad Lebanim was further reinforced in the wake of the Sinai Campaign. The soldiers who served in the military at that time were primarily inductees whose ages ranged from eighteen to twenty-one, most of them bachelors. Those who were killed left behind a larger number of bereaved parents than of children and widows. The public interest, which surfaces in every war in those who have suffered directly as a result of it, on this occasion brought to the fore the bereaved parents and their problems, and strengthened Yad Lebanim in its capacity as the organization representing "Families of Soldiers."

From its inception, Yad Lebanim was funded by the Ministry of Defense. Its standing as the organization representing bereaved families was thereby given official recognition and confirmation. During its initial stage of operation, the organization represented its members in a somewhat independent manner. But matters became increasingly complex, and bureaucratic processes grew more and more obscure. Since it was the organization's view that violent and/or protest demonstrations (of the type resorted to by the Disabled Veterans Organization) were improper and undignified, it was forced to search for alternative means of making its cause known. The solution was to cooperate with the Defense Ministry's Rehabilitation Department. One of the factors that eased this cooperation was the general similarity in outlook between the rehabilitation workers and the active members of Yad Lebanim. With respect to world view, to underlying values, and to social class positioning, there was greater similarity between Yad Lebanim activists and the Defense Ministry personnel than there was between the former and the "indigent" bereaved parents whom the organization's activists were representing before various government bodies.

As mentioned earlier, the original impetus for tabling the "Families of Soldiers" law came from the Defense Ministry staff, and they were the ones who pushed for its passage. Similarly, it was rehabilitation workers who initially requested the amendments to this law in order to facilitate their ongoing work, as well as to strengthen, to expand, and to better establish the Rehabilitation Department itself. The cooperation between Yad Lebanim and the Rehabilitation Department led to their collaboration in the process of introducing changes in the "Families of Soldiers" law, with one organization lending its approval and support to changes proposed by the other (Katz & Eisenstadt 1973). The rehabilitation staff was well acquainted with the ins and outs of governmental administration and bureaucracy, was more familiar with the techniques of formulating issues effectively, and knew how to "get things done." Thus, the demands put forward to the Knesset committees by Yad Lebanim were introduced under the guidance and direction of the rehabilitation staff. In the process of advising the Yad Lebanim representatives as to the issues that could pass in the Knesset, and on the manner in which these should be presented, the staff introduced its own criteria concerning what it regarded as justified (or unjustified) demands by the "Families of Soldiers," and the appropriate way to meet these needs.

This collaboration was advantageous to both parties: the rehabilitation staff achieved almost full control of all matters pertaining to the rights of "Families of Soldiers," as well as the virtually automatic backing of a "pressure group" when it came to presenting their demands to the Knesset and its Committees. Yad Lebanim obtained ease of access to the Rehabilitation Department and a responsiveness to its efforts on behalf of specific individuals, especially those closely associated with the organization.[4] Yad Lebanim activists gained status through their collaboration with the Rehabilitation Department; they developed ties with "high-ups" in the political establishment and the administration (the Minister of Defense, Knesset committee members, and Rehabilitation Department personnel), and they gained substantial support for their organization, both material and administrative. The desire to maintain their ties with the Ministry of Defense and to act in a spirit of cooperation often led Yad Lebanim to be ready to make concessions in the struggle on behalf of its constituency's interests. This process reduced the effectiveness of Yad Lebanim as an organization fighting for a cause.

The number of war widows among the "Families of Soldiers" under the care of the Ministry of Defense was small to begin with, and it was constantly declining, since every widow who remarried and/or whose children came of age was no longer defined as "eligible." Even the relatively small number of widows who came under the Ministry's care in the wake of the Sinai Campaign did not significantly alter this proportion. By contrast, bereaved parents were permanent clients of the Rehabilitation Department's services. Moreover, as they advanced in age and as their problems and needs became more acute, those parents not initially defined as "indigent" sought the Rehabilitation Department's assistance, some on a regular basis, others only temporarily. Thus the widows, as a group with specific and unique problems, received scant attention or social/institutional care. Their weakness, both in terms of power, and with respect to their position within Yad Lebanim, was compounded by the virtual monopoly on the care for "Families of Soldiers" of Yad Lebanim and the Ministry of Defense, in collaboration. As a result, war widows as a group were unknown and unfamiliar to Israeli society, despite the fact that their number during the period between the War of Independence and the Six-Day War was not negligible. After the Six-Day War, members of recognized social categories who were among those affected by the war—"the disabled" and the "bereaved parents"—found orderly and well-prepared groups ready to absorb them without delay. Immediately after the war, the Disabled Veterans Organization announced (through all the communication media) that their members would come to the aid of their "new fellow members." Yad Lebanim called on the newly bereaved parents to join the organization and to avail themselves of its services. Yad Lebanim activists appeared to "forget" that they represented the war widows as well. The widows of the Six-Day War found themselves in a vacuum: no social group or institution considered them its prime responsibility. The only address to which they could turn was the

Rehabilitation Department of the Defense Ministry, and there, their position was marginal. (As a former senior member of the Department put it: "In all the years I'd worked in the Rehabilitation Department, the war widows were actually glorified social cases.")

It was some time after the Six-Day War that the war widows became a recognized and known social group occupying the attention of the Knesset, the government, the press, and public opinion. It is difficult to reconstruct precisely just how this process began. Perhaps it started in the way described by S.E. (No 17),* who was twenty-four years old and the mother of two at the time she was widowed during the Six-Day War.

> . . . friends of my husband's from work went (to the Defense Ministry). They were told that I, as a widow with two children, was entitled to IL 240 (currency no longer in use, at that time about $80) a month . . . I almost had a heart attack when I heard that . . . it's a dreadful insult . . . you are not only left all alone, but no one cares about you. That's when I started to fight the bureaucracy in all of its disgusting aspects.

Not knowing any other address to turn to, S.E. set out by going to the local rehabilitation worker:

> . . . So I told her that a friend of mine had been there and was told that I, with two children, would have to live on IL 240 a month, and that I simply wanted to know if that was true. "I'm simply in a state of shock", I said, "I don't understand how I'm supposed to manage." She told me: "Look, that's the law, and nothing can be done about that. If we can be . of help . . . sometimes we are able to get around the law, and I'm ready to help . . . I understand your sorrow, and I agree that IL 240 a month is not right . . . maybe you should put pressure on the Knesset to change the law."

It is evident, from this exchange that S.E. and the social worker both agreed that IL 240 was not a sufficient sum. They did not agree on the question of whose task it was to act for a change in the law and/ or in the amount of the pension. The rehabilitation workers, at least those in direct contact with the war widows, did not consider it part of their professional duty or responsibility to present this and other concerns of the war widows before the legislative body or the policy-makers (such as the top executives of the Rehabilitation Department itself).[5]

From this single conversation it was apparent to S.E. that the rehabilitation office was not where she would get help in fighting "the bureaucracy." So,

---

*Biographical information on individuals interviewed can be found in Appendix III.

When friends asked me what they could do to help, I told them to write to the daily papers. "That's the only thing you can do to help," I told them . . . Well, it seems they were not the only ones who wrote. A friend of mine, who at one time worked for the paper, telephoned one of the editors and he told her: "Don't worry, there's so much pressure from letters to the editor that this will be written up in two lead articles and an editorial, and there will be pressure on the Knesset" . . . The next day an article on this subject really did appear in several newspapers and there was pressure on the Knesset, and two or three days later Dayan (the then Minister of Defense) announced that the law was being amended.

Another widow in the sample decided to turn to the press herself, and her letter was published in *Maariv* on June 6, 1967, under the heading, "Letter from an Unknown Widow." She wrote:

> . . . I think the public can assist all the widows and orphans of the reserve soldiers and the regular army men who fell in this battle. The attitude displayed by the Defense Ministry, although it may be due to objective reasons, is not marked by either kindness or sensitivity. Widows receive a pension of IL 365 a month for a widow with two children.[6] It seems to me that the catastrophe is great enough, and it will surely take us years to overcome it. They should at least protect us from having to run after a living during the first few years of widowhood. I turn to you, as a military correspondent, and someone who has always known these men who were ready to give their lives for the homeland: Please act to have them come to our aid. The public must be informed of our situation. I end with the hope that you will not let us down.

Eli Landau, the *Maariv* correspondent to whom this letter was addressed, added: "This letter speaks for itself. I was shaken when I read it. Certainly the public too will be shaken . . . The public must express its opinion on this matter, and lend its support to the families of the fallen and wounded."

For the first few weeks after the war, the press was occupied chiefly with the conflict and its consequences. Tales of heroism, descriptions of burial ceremonies and memorial services, debates on the social problems plaguing soldiers and civilians, and other similar matters filled the pages of the daily papers. Amidst these, wide coverage was given to stories about war widows, descriptions of their behavior and their problems. The term "war widows," as designating a social category, made its first appearance in the press only after the Six-Day War, and the press treated "war widows" as if they were a new and unfamiliar phenomenon. Readers were supplied with abundant details on their behavior and problems. This was particularly marked when compared with the other categories—"disabled veterans" and "bereaved parents"—who were treated as familiar and known phenomena.

The press not only "introduced" the war widows to the public, but encouraged public support for their cause, and contributed to it. In the three daily papers I examined *(Maariv, Yediot Ahronot,* and *Ha'Aretz),*[7] I found that twenty-one articles appeared during the period between June 26, 1967 (when the first article concerning assistance to war widows was published), and July 26, 1967 (when the Defense Ministry announced a considerable increase in the widows' pension), all of which expressed support for the war widows in their struggle to improve their lot. Some of these articles were critical of the prevailing situation, others only called attention to the problems: "Assistance for Families of War Casualties—Immediately!" demanded a headline in *Maariv,* June 26, 1967. One week later an article in the same paper stated:

> The apparatus for the rehabilitation of war widows and orphans, as it has been functioning for the past twenty years, is no longer appropriate for present conditions, and the economic reality today is different as well. The entire country must bear this burden, even at the expense of other needs. *(Maariv,* July 4, 1967)

Yediot Ahronot, which in this context generally presented the statements and views of the Defense Ministry Spokesman, made the following promise on behalf of the Rehabilitation Department: "We have cut the paper-work in order to speed up care and rehabilitation" (Yediot Ahronot, July 4, 1967).

"Letters to the Editor" contributed their share to the campaign to improve the material conditions of war widows:

> I was shocked to read in *Maariv* that a widow with two children receives IL365 a month in pension. This seems to me more like a welfare grant than a pension payment. I do not believe—and I'm certain every Israeli citizen would agree with me—that our country is so poor that it must save precisely on expenditures for this purpose" (Hava Weiner, *Maariv,* July 10, 1967).

Or:

> I was shocked to read in Maariv that a widow with two children receives IL 365 a month. I don't know when, why and by whom this amount was determined, but I know it is not sufficient and it must be increased . . . it is our duty . . . to guarantee them a respectable living, and not have them live on charity. (Prof. Zeidmann, Haifa Technion, *Maariv,* July 17, 1967)

It appears that in this sphere public opinion had an impact, and on July 26, 1967, the newspapers reported that, at a press conference one day earlier, M. Kashti (Director General of the Ministry of Defense at the time) announced an increase in payments to families of the war dead, and this increase was to take effect even before a proposed amendment was to be tabled in the Knesset.

The amendment to the "Families of Soldiers" law was tabled for first hearing in the Knesset on August 1, 1967. The amendment included considerable increases in widows' pensions (some 33 percent increase for each category of widow), and smaller increments for bereaved parents and for disabled veterans. This was the first time in the course of forming and formulating the law that the widows were not linked to the bereaved parents, but were considered in and of themselves. The proposed amendment was not sufficiently worked through, and it suffered from a large number of administrative and substantive deficiencies. The Minister of Defense who tabled the proposal, as well as the members of the Knesset who debated it, were aware of its shortcomings and its incompleteness. But time was pressing, public pressure was great, and the Knesset recess was rapidly approaching. As a result, the proposed amendment was debated only briefly before being submitted to the Labor Committee. One week later, on August 8, 1967, the amendment was retabled in the plenary session of the Knesset, and passed on second and third reading without further debate, though with the promise that additional changes would be introduced after the house reconvened. The Knesset's alacrity in this instance was explained in the words of MK Israel Kargman (Alignment):

> The amendment is essential for the families, but it is necessary also for the citizens, whose hearts are aching over this problem. This arrangement (the proposed amendment) which, I understand, is more or less acceptable, will ease our emotional distress too, and we will feel that we are fulfilling our obligation to these families. (Knesset Record, Vol. 49. p. 2821, 1967)

In addition to the amendments to the sections in the "Families of Soldiers" law pertaining to war widows, the growing awareness of the presence of the war widows and the problems plaguing them yielded several other results. The social response to the media messages regarding war widows was very similar in its nature to the kinds of response of voluntary social organizations which help those affected by "social catastrophe." Individuals, voluntary associations, and existing organizations all attempted to enter into the "disaster area" in an effort to extend aid. But, in this case, the "disaster area" was human and not geographic, and the path to it passed through the Defense Ministry which kept the official list of names and addresses of the Six-Day War widows.

In response to the outpouring of offers and suggestions, the Ministry of Defense made a decision, in principle, to the effect that the right to decide on and to supervise any help offered to war widows was to be reserved for the workers of its Rehabilitation Department and for the policy-makers within the Ministry. Any money raised toward help for the war widows was put into a special fund, from which sums to assist the widows were allocated at the discretion of the Rehabilitation Department workers and according to standards acceptable to them. This fund, known as "The Social Fund," was used for specific "rehabilitation" needs not included in the "Families of Soldiers" law. In addition to the financial contributions which expressed public concern for the plight of the war widow, many voluntary organizations offered their services to the war widows' cause. When a proposal to offer a particular service passed the review procedures of the Rehabilitation Department, or when pressure to accept it was heavy, the service was given.

Eventually, some of these services were extended on a permanent basis to all war widows, not only to those of the Six-Day War. When such a service became "permanent," it also became de facto an "accepted standard" for the level of services provided by the State to war widows. When the voluntary organization which had established the service no longer wanted, or was unable, to provide for it, it became very difficult to phase it out. As a result, the continued operation of several services of this kind was financed by the Ministry of Defense. Voluntary activities designed to "help" the widows launched a process through which the standards which bound the State to the war widows underwent a change. The Ministry of Defense, through its decision to retain the right to decide on and to supervise help offered to widows, prevented certain types of assistance from being given, while it gave its approval and patronage to others. In so doing, it adopted standards which had been dictated by public opinion, and eventually it also committed itself to bearing, at least in part, the economic burden of maintaining these standards.[8] In other words, financial contributions and voluntary organizational efforts on behalf of the widows served to change standards of service provided for them, in the same manner that the emergency mobilization of public opinion had effected changes in the "Families of Soldiers" law. But above and beyond the practical results, social concern and interest was instrumental in the formation of the category of "war widows," a category which became familiar to Israeli society and whose affairs and concerns continued to be publicly portrayed in a sympathetic light.

During the first few years after the Six-Day War, the war widows constituted a pressure group whose main forum was the daily press. During this period, the war widows maintained short-term organizations in order to exercise pressure to attain specific goals. Most of these had to do with changes in the "Families of Soldiers" law and with the regulations and arrangements of the Defense Ministry's Rehabilitation Department. In the early 1970s these ad hoc temporary groups began to organize on a more permanent basis and eventually evolved into the "Widows' Organization." In its initial years, this was a "rebel" group of widows—volunteers whose chief aim was to attend to the individual and general needs of the widows. After the Yom Kippur War (in 1973) this group became institutionalized, and for economic, administrative, and organizational reasons, it annexed itself to Yad Lebanim. Although the widows constituted a section of their own within Yad Lebanim, they were nonetheless dependent on it and lacked any real power—out of twelve seats on the executive committee the widows were allotted only one. However, despite what appeared to be the group's return to a lowly position within an institutional framework, the war widows did not regress to the anonymous and marginal place they had occupied prior to the Six-Day War. It seems to me that societal awareness of this category, and the sympathy and support it elicited from the mass media, ensured that widows will not easily be pushed aside again to the fringes of the institutional system.

War Widows and the Defense Ministry's Rehabilitation Department

The Ministry of Defense was responsible not only for the administrative and financial aspects of the "Families of Soldiers" law but also for its implementation. Initially, it seemed that the problems involved were simply administrative, and the implementation of the law, as well as the decisions this entailed, were handled by a "Pensions Office."[9] Over time it became clearer that the problems were numerous and complex, and that they required a much more elaborate administrative system. The functions of the "Pensions Officer" were eventually undertaken by an entire department devoted to this matter—the Defense Ministry's Department of Rehabilitation.[10] The Pension Officers (mainly clerical workers) were not always suited for their task, and it became necessary to find manpower with the sort of expertise appropriate for the care of the "Families of Soldiers." It could well be that the decision to appoint social workers to operate this service was based on the fact that for many years the Ministry's attention had been confined solely to the "indigent" among the "Families of Soldiers."

Before the Six-Day War, the services offered by the Rehabilitation Department, and the economic benefits available to the widow through it, were extremely limited. The monthly pension was paid automatically into the widows' bank accounts. In addition, they were entitled to tuition-free secondary education for their children, and to several small tax exemptions. Due to this, the vast majority of war widows had no reason to maintain regular and/or close contact with the local Bureau of the Rehabilitation Department.[11] Those few widows who required the Bureau's services on a permanent basis were the "welfare cases" among them or, as they were called by the law, the "indigent." These "indigent" widows were described as classic "chronic cases," whose problems did not lend themselves to constructive solution, who were regular clients of the Bureau and were treated accordingly (Weiss 1973). Thus, until the Six-Day War, the experience of social workers, as well as their modes of operation—at least with regard to war widows—were similar to those practiced in public welfare offices.

Following the Six-Day War, and to a great extent as a result of the public's awareness of the social category of "war widows," the automatic payment of pensions as determined by the law was no longer considered "adequate assistance" to war widows. The same public pressure which was directed at the Knesset was exerted also on the Defense Ministry and on the Rehabilitation Department and its employees. In the main, the demand was that the Defense Ministry provide services that would meet the accepted standards of social well-being in the State of Israel of the late 1960s, while giving due consideration to the status and special rights of the war widows. The Defense Ministry's executive framework was required to cope with all the widows' problems and to help them in all areas of life. The Ministry's spokesman declared publicly that the Ministry was ready to assume this mission. In order to realize this promise, the Ministry was charged with finding the most efficient means for assisting each war widow. What was later named the "Social Fund" became the instrument for financing this assistance. During its early days, the Social Fund served as a sort of "petty cash" reserve to cover the immediate and pressing needs of war widows and their children, for which no other source of funding was found. The early records show receipts for expenses such as IL 5 for defraying the cost of a taxi to transport a child to hospital, or IL 39 for repairing a washing machine. In "emergency" cases, a widow's rent was paid by the fund until another more permanent solution was found. Similarly, music and gymnastics lessons for children were sponsored in instances where otherwise they would have to be stopped in the middle of the year, shortly after the death of the father.

During the first three years of its existence, some IL 600,000 from the Fund was allocated to the widows. This sum was not equally distributed among them: to the eighteen widows in the lower 25th percentile (in terms of monies received from the Ministry of Defense), only some 6 percent of the total amount was given, while the seventeen widows who comprised the top 25th percentile, got 42 percent of the total amount.[12] Among the widows in the sample, there were some who received no financial benefits at all from the Fund, while others received as much as IL 18,000 over the first three years of widowhood. These figures indicate that in certain cases (only a few, to be sure) widows were able to double the amount of their monthly pension through additional benefits provided from the Social Fund. It should be noted that a considerable amount of money was involved, and had it been equally distributed, the benefit for each widow in the sample would have been equal to one full year of pension money.

A widow who required financial assistance from the Social Fund had to present her problem to the social worker handling her file. If the social worker deemed the request reasonable or justified, a written request, together with the social worker's recommendation, was submitted to the committee charged with the allocation of the Fund's resources. This committee discussed each request, approved those it judged justified, and then the funds were transferred directly to the applicant. Two elements in the procedure should be stressed. First, since there was no clear definition of the Fund's purpose and/or the widow's entitlement, any item or economic need was eligible for consideration. Second, since the committee did not discuss the application directly with the applicant, the judgement and recommendation of the social worker had a decisive influence on the entire process. This procedure constituted an interesting pattern of dividing responsibility: the possessor of all the information was not a member of the group that decided how to spend the money, while the decision-making group possessed only partial, censored information regarding the applicant and the purpose for which funds had been requested. As a result, no one was fully responsible for the final outcome. This resulted in a situation where the client's complaint about what she considered an unjust decision had no address (Bar-Yosef & Schild 1973).

This system was similar in its arrangements and operating procedures to the manner in which a welfare office serving an "indigent" population operates (Handelman 1976, 1980; Shamgar-Handelman 1975). The client "asks," while the social worker "gives;" the client's rights are defined only in a general way, and the social worker's professional considerations carry a great deal of weight and affect the final outcome of each specific matter. In order to gain support, the recipient must convince the giver of the importance and the legitimacy of the request, and of the degree of neediness. However, in one respect which is both meaningful and important, the system formed in the

Rehabilitation Department differed from that practiced in the welfare offices: the Rehabilitation Department had wide financial backing, and the potential economic worth of its benefits was extremely high.

The manner in which a social worker described the process whereby the initial contact with the war widows was formed, revealed her perception of the system within which she worked:

> I don't know whether you have any idea how we started this work, after the Six-Day (War), when so many cases came to us all at once and we didn't have a staff to cope with the sudden influx? We used volunteers from all sorts of institutions . . . They performed all the initial work—filling out forms, getting the initial details, and handing out superficial information about the services provided by the office. . . . Then, we were able to rest assured that the initial meeting had already taken place . . . and we simply waited for them to give a sign of life, to come and ask for something. (T.T. interview of October 30, 1969)

Major differences in the mutual expectations of the Six-Day War widows and the employees of the Rehabilitation Bureaus were already apparent in their initial meeting: the social workers were waiting for them "to come and ask," while the widows did not want to "ask," they wanted to receive what they felt they were "entitled to" in accordance with the value system, with the public promises made by the government, and with the demands of public opinion as voiced by the mass media. The social workers treated the widows as "cases" (albeit cases with a certain prestige and publicity), while the widows wanted to be treated as "privileged persons."[13] The widows saw the Rehabilitation Department as a bureaucratic institution whose task it was to realize their rights. Therefore, they expected it to operate according to universalistic, as well as specific, standards. They assumed that the principles according to which it operated must be formulated in a formal and objective manner and must be anchored in a permanent system of regulations. The social workers saw the Rehabilitation Bureau as a treatment-providing institution whose task was to find solutions for clients' problems. Determining the client's needs was an integral part of the treatment process, the sphere in which the worker's professional competence was to be utilized and expressed. Thus, the social workers expected the widows to present their problems in a general and diffuse manner, and they considered it their task to translate these problems into institutional and/or treatment language.

It became apparent early on that there was a communication gap between the social workers and some (at least) of the widows. This situation was described by one of the veteran social workers of the Rehabilitation Department:

For two months (after the war) it seemed to me that contact was made with the widows who had difficult problems, who had difficulties managing on their own, or who were ready to involve me. There was a group which was not ready to do so. This group is composed of women with an academic education. . . . These widows came (and asked) "What am I entitled to? What aren't I entitled to? Why doesn't it say that I'm entitled to kindergarten, and why do I have to submit a separate request for that?" . . . They were only interested in rights concerning financial problems, housing debts. . . . (C.N. interview of October 10, 1969).

This pattern of relationship was hard both on the widows and on the social workers. The widows felt that they were being pushed to assume a role they did not want to have, the role of a "welfare case," or in their words: "When I go there I have a sort of feeling that I'm receiving charity" (N.S. No. 60) or, "I felt a sort of humiliation that I had to come and ask" (N.C. No. 6).

The social workers felt rejected and unwanted, and it seemed that they were personally insulted by this. Moreover, they felt unfulfilled in a professional sense. The patterning of contacts, as some of the widows attempted to dictate it, did not enable them fully to express and to meet their professional expectations. The efforts of at least some of the widows, and especially those of high-status, to limit their contact with the social workers to formal matters anchored in the law and in the regulations, and which had to do in the main with economic issues, turned the social workers—in their own opinion—into "cashiers," and "reduced" them to the level of clerks, positions which they considered inferior. The social workers "complained" about the widows. One of them said:

"A.M. is under my care, but I don't know her. She's very—about what the law dictates, provides for. In the beginning she was quite angry about what was not written in the law, or what was written and you have to ask for anyway. She's very closed. She's considered very strong by the widows, and they appreciate her a lot. She's extremely formalistic in her relations with us. She comes only when she has to make arrangements for a car (tax exemption) or such things. (C.N. interview of June 29, 1970)

And with respect to another widow she said:

I saw her altogether some three times . . . she came to see whether she could get a customs exemption. I told her: "Absolutely. Write a letter." No, she's not prepared to write a letter. If it's not according to the law, if it's not exactly what she's entitled to, then she doesn't want it. She always came to me with very concrete things, and over three years she came to me maybe three times (B.M. interview of June 29, 1970)

The difficulties encountered by the social workers in coping with a client population which, at least in part, was unwilling to assume the role of client and to act accordingly, were eased considerably when a new definition of the "client" was introduced. This new definition (which apparently was worked out in 1969) came to replace the vague and outdated definition which no longer stood the test of war widows as "indigent" persons. The new definition, in essence, stated that the war widow was a woman with psychological problems. I did not succeed in establishing how this new definition of war widows and of their situation came into being. I know of no plan or organized framework established to examine the problems of war widows and to redefine their situation and needs. It appears that this definition echoed, directly or indirectly, the prevailing fashion of looking at widowhood solely from a psychological point of view (as discussed in chapter I). In any event, the new definition provided the social workers with a new frame of reference and a new terminology which enabled them to cope, with relative ease, with numerous confusing and difficult questions. From the moment the label of emotional difficulty was affixed to the widows' problems, it became possible to relate any phenomenon and/or undesirable behavior (in the social worker's view) to "emotional imbalance" of one sort or another. Their new armature of terminology and classification gave the social workers the tools to make so-called objective judgements about women who were not "welfare cases," but instead were women who, in many respects, resembled the social workers themselves (in terms of age, education, social class, etc.). The absence of any comprehensive professional training (both theoretical and practical), and the lack of any ongoing and close supervision, "freed" the social workers even from those ethical and professional constraints which are an inseparable part of the occupational values of psychologists, psychiatrists, and others in the helping professions.

During my field-work, I asked the social workers to describe the widows under their care, and their problems.[14] The following is an almost complete transcript of such an interview with one of the social workers, offered here to reinforce the observation made above:

> You want to know about O.? She's a rather limited woman. Her appearance is misleading (O.T. No. 62 was in fact an especially impressive and good-looking woman). Her limitedness is accompanied by serious disturbances in the sexual sphere. She is Kibbutz-born and married an Oriental. Apparently they lived in poverty. She lived in a very small flat in (neighborhood X). Later she bought a flat. Her financial situation is very good now. A little while later (after she purchased the flat), she began forming ties with men, with one disappointment after the other. The men would come to her after her son was asleep. And she

thought—it was some bachelor—that he'd marry her; and he left her, and this was a very difficult crisis. During that same period, in the beginning, she would come to me very often. It was really a little in bad taste—and don't imagine that I represent the ultimate in modesty—(that she'd come) all colorful and painted up, and very . . . well . . . in red slacks, and you can draw conclusions from that. And at that time I didn't know yet what I knew later. . . . She also started working. Now she's having some sort of an affair with a married man—if he's still around. I haven't seen her for some two months. She's so uncomfortable in the company of men that she went so far as to find a driving school where they have a female instructor. I think that's a little . . . (she) covers it up pretty well. She gets confused when she's next to a man. I was pretty amazed by this business with the driving school. I think she's intellectually limited—I won't give her an I.Q. test, but she's not intelligent. She's a very low average. She's working now, and apparently she's quite successful. We arranged for her to be accepted, even though she didn't pass the civil service test. They demand "gurnisht mit gurnisht" (Yiddish for "nothing at all"), but she didn't pass. With the child, she says he's independent, there's a good relationship with the child. Well, I don't know what he sees at home. She's got some sort of problem, I don't know much about its background . . . I don't know whether she needs treatment, but in any event she changes quite a lot of men . . . she shows more enthusiasm about clothes than is appropriate for a woman her age without a husband. She's very childish, and I think she's not too smart. I'm surprised she agreed to see you (agreed to be interviewed for research purposes) because she asked me to tell the Ministry of Defense not to include her in anything to do with widows. She doesn't want invitations, or ceremonies. . . . In an artificial way she closed the door and thought "tomorrow I can begin as if nothing happened. . . ." That is limitedness, or at least immaturity! (B.M. interview of June 29, 1970)

Here, the widow was defined by the social worker as "limited" and as "having sexual problems". This definition did not rely on tests of any sort and apparently stemmed from the social worker's impressions ("I won't give her an I.Q. test but . . . she's a very low average"). The widow's success in her job (even though she did not pass the civil service test), and her good relationship with her son, generally considered in the eyes of social workers as important indices of mental balance, did not alter her "diagnosis." A lack of taste in dress and makeup ("in bad taste," in the social worker's opinion) were grasped as "supporting evidence" for the diagnosis, and she suggested that far-reaching conclusions could be drawn from these external attributes. An attempt to start living again after a two-month period of widowhood was seen as "rather disturbed" behavior, and relationships with men as disturbance due to unknown problems of personal history.[15]

It appears that the social worker's diagnosis was made two

months after O.T. was widowed (at the time she appeared at the Rehabilitation Bureau clad in red slacks). Subsequently, every attributed fact or event in her life was explained by the social worker according to that initial diagnosis. In other instances, social workers considered a readiness to pay attention to details of personal grooming, or an ability to derive pleasure from trivial things, as positive indices of the "widow's condition." But, in O.'s case, "her enthusiasm about clothes is exaggerated for a woman of her age" (she was twenty-seven at the time), and "without a husband." Since she was "limited and disturbed," even her request to be excluded from "anything having to do with widows" was not respected, for I was given her name and address along with those of others, and without any qualifying comments on her reticence.

The "diagnosis" of each widow's condition was different, and so were the components from which it was constructed by the social workers. However, each widow was indeed "diagnosed," and from that there was no escape. Some of the widows sensed the process of labeling which they were undergoing, and attempted, to the best of their ability, to direct it in accordance with their own self-image or their own interests. Others tried to escape the process in its entirety. One of these was A.M. (No. 29). A.M. was one of those whose widowhood did not cause her a serious economic crisis. The war widow's pension, together with substantial financial support from her own family and that of her husband, afforded her considerable material comfort. After one or two encounters with the rehabilitation workers, she decided that all the economic advantages she could obtain through them did not merit the emotional distress they entailed. With the clear knowledge that she was giving up assured benefits, A.M. decided to limit her contacts with the rehabilitation worker to the absolutely essential only. But even this step did not deter the social worker from diagnosing her: "I saw her about three times all told. She's a woman I would not consider strong (a reference to emotional strength). She doesn't turn to (me), she started working. I smell problems there" (B.M. interview of June 29, 1970). With reference to another widow who did not assume the role of "welfare case," the same social worker said:

> She's an extremely un-independent woman, very dependent . . . she's a woman with a lot of fears. Fears about going to the dentist, and very primitive fears . . . she doesn't know how to get herself organized and demand what she deserves. Even from a point of view of treatment, you have to let a person feel they're asking for it, of course that has to be done in a respectful way. It's some kind of lack of temperament. . . . It's something structural, I think. (B.M. interview of June 29, 1970)

When a widow was diagnosed as "dependent" and "primitive," it was difficult of course to "accuse" the social worker caring for her of what, according to other criteria, could be defined as neglect, as a lack of encouragement, or as not providing information regarding existing possibilities, and so forth.

On occasion, the sources of information on which the social worker determined her diagnosis seemed dubious, both with respect to their reliability and from an ethical-professional point of view. An example is provided by the following report:

> She really has difficulties relating emotionally, because she didn't get along with her parents, and she didn't get along with his parents, and now I've heard she's having an increasingly bad relationship with her brother. I know her brother, he tried to help her out in the beginning. He's a soldier in the Air Force, in regular army service. By coincidence, he's the chauffeur of the husband of a social worker I know well, and she told me about him, that he's a nice guy, and I tend to accept that. That's very important information. And now she told me she doesn't get along with him either. It's simply that she's got an unstable personality." (S.S. interview of October 30, 1970)

Information obtained accidentally, which was neither confirmed nor verified in any way, was assessed as "very important" by the social worker, and served as additional evidence on which to build a diagnosis of the widow as an "unstable personality."

In response to my request to the social workers for information about the widows in the sample, I received reports of the type discussed above on some forty widows. (Over time, and in different contexts, I received information on a larger number of widows, as well as follow-up reports on widows who had been included in the first round of interviews.) Of the forty widows on whom "formal" reports were received, only two were not defined as suffering from emotional problems. Discussing one of them, the attending social worker made the following comment: "I'm very fond of her, even though I don't see her often. . . . She's not at all problematic in terms of treatment. She really doesn't make things difficult" (B.M., interview of June 29, 1970). When the basic approach was one of, "I'm fond of her," the interpretation of anything else that happened with regard to the widow was likely to conform to it. The widow's reluctance to visit the Bureau ("she 'phoned me several times and apologized for not coming") was explained by her "wanting to take care of herself." The widow's relationship with a married man was described as "a friend of her husband's took her into the department . . . to give her a job," and even when it "later emerged" that this married man divorced his wife to marry the widow, she did not merit the social worker's moral condemnation, not even to the extent evoked by the "red slacks."[16]

The process whereby the widows were labeled through psychologistic "diagnoses" had little to do either with professional and/or objective models of testing, with evaluation, or with expert opinion: it was based chiefly on the impression formed by the social worker. In light of their limited training in the relevant areas and the small number of meetings between them and the widows under their care, it appears that these "evaluations" were of very dubious worth. There was nothing more to them than there is to that sort of social labeling which resorts to prejudice, to gossip, and the like.

Despite the intrinsic interest of this process of labeling, I would not have discussed it here in detail if, in fact, it had ended with the labeling and sorting of the widows. But the social worker's "evaluation" of the widow—an opinion by the only person in the Rehabilitation Department to come in direct contact with her—turned into a meaningful "fact" which determined her relationship with her "gate keeper" to subsequent dealings with the Defense Ministry. The label attached to the widow affected the social worker's preparedness to listen to her problems, the credibility attached to her statements, and the degree of readiness to respond to her requests. The social worker's psychologistic "diagnosis" determined to a great extent the amount and form of aid, financial and otherwise, which the widow could have received from the Ministry of Defense. For example, when such an opinion stated that O.T. was "limited" and of "very low average" intelligence, there was no chance that her desire for professional or educational advancement would receive the support and recommendation of that social worker. The absence of the social worker's support and recommendation hindered, delayed, and at times prevented entirely, even the initiation of the bureaucratic process which could finance these aspirations. An additional example on the same subject was provided by the social worker's response when asked about the situation of G.H. (No. 10):

Aside from technical problems, I don't know anything. I'm sorry, I didn't handle this case. I know her, and I know her home. First O. (my colleague) handled her, and then that colleague who went on maternity leave. And it came back to me because this is the district. That means that she changed (workers) four times. She's the sort who never saw herself as a head of a family. She was always dependent on the parents. She's also, whatever the brother says, and her father says, and her mother, (dependent on the opinion of other family members). Now she's moving into another flat. And here we really did accomplish something. I'm very glad we are successful. They had an awful flat, very close to the parents', and they were at the stage where they started to build an addition. We went to see the place, and I said I wouldn't put a cent into it, (that is, she wouldn't submit a recommendation for a loan or grant from the Social Fund). For a while there was a big argument, because she could relocate only to a place far away from her parents. But in the end we reached (an agreement that the widow would move to a flat far away from her parents)" (S.S. interview of October 30, 1970).

The social worker's "diagnosis" in this case was that the widow was too dependent. It was not clear what standards she used in reaching this evaluation, but according to her own evidence, it was formed on the basis of superficial acquaintance. Such over-dependence, or insufficient independence, dictated, in the social worker's opinion, that the widow and her children should be separated geographically from parents and grandparents. A different set of considerations could determine that precisely in a case such as this the widow and her children would require the help of a "dependable" person. In order to implement this separation, the social worker withheld a recommendation for financial assistance for completing the construction initiated prior to the husband's death. She could not support her position by her non-professional opinion on the subject of housing construction. However, in the area of "psychology" hers was an "expert" opinion, through which she could either promote or hinder the widow's economic goals.

The process of labeling the widows not only affected their economic opportunities but also, in some cases, forced them to undergo unrequested and undesired "therapy" sessions. As previously stated, it was clear from the outset that a certain category of widows was unwilling to maintain ties with the Rehabilitation Department beyond that minimum necessary to serve their economic interests. These widows were described by a social worker as follows:

> These are widows on such a level that they wouldn't see me as an object for their outpourings. These are widows with education, for whom work was always important and remains important. . . . They are hardworking and serious in every way, and the relationship between them (the widow and her husband) was very beautiful. . . . This stratum, I don't know how to define it, by what name, it's not monied stratum . . . it's more of a cultural thing—they don't want us. (I.S. interview of December 19, 1969)

For some time, these widows were able to maintain the image of being "cultured," "serious," or "on a high level," and it was they who determined the sort of contact they kept with the rehabilitation workers. However, as the practice of defining the widows' situation in psychological terms became more prevalent, the ability of the "serious" and "cultured" widows to limit their contacts with the social workers to the merely bureaucratic and formal decreased. The labeling process was applied to this category of widows as well, and the formerly "cultured" and "educated" or "hardworking" became "closed," "escapist," or "seeking a substitute via her work." The widow's conduct, her reservations concerning contacts with the Rehabilitation Department, as well as her demands or their absence, were all explained as stemming from her "emotional problems" as defined by the social worker. From the moment that the widow's reluctance to form ties with the social worker or to discuss her personal problems with her were labeled as "symptomatic," her behavior was no longer subject to the accepted rules of good manners. Instead it became a target for "treatment" by the social worker. One way by which the social workers broke the widow's resistance to "treatment," was by making meetings and "treatment sessions" on her "problems" a condition for economic assistance. This technique is described as follows by one of the social workers:

> I had a case of a widow who was unwilling to have us intervene. . . . This week she called me (and asked): "Are there supplementary lessons for widows' children?" (is there funding for that kind of need?). I told her, "I don't know, it doesn't just go mechanically!" It's not a question of money, supplementary lessons can be automatic (a recommendation by the school principal or the child's teacher would suffice in order to obtain such funding from the Social Fund), but I'm not ready to do it that way. I think that if there's a problem of lessons, then apparently there are other problems as well. (C.N. interview of November 15, 1970)

In this case, the widow who sought the Defense Ministry's financial assistance was forced to meet with the social worker for a talk. According to the social worker's testimony, there were indeed "other problems." When asked what would have happened if the widow had not inquired about supplementary lessons, the social worker replied: "If she hadn't turned to us on this question, then she would have done so for some other financial help, or some standard approval she would have required, and then, on that occasion . . ." (C.N. interview of November 15, 1970).

Not infrequently, the widows considered the proviso that they attend a "treatment session" in order to receive financial assistance a misuse of the social worker's power. One event, described both by the social worker and by the widow involved in it, demonstrates this point. B.M. was the social worker dealing with B.Q. (No. 50), and gave the following description of her:

> From the first moment she thought she had to be "brave." She never let her feelings show. In the beginning she did not want to come to us, she wanted the army to arrange everything. Afterwards, when she had no choice, she would send her mother or father . . . and her mother knows how to demand what she wants. So I told her (the mother): "Mrs. X., I'm not treating you! I'm treating your daughter. She has to come herself

. . ." I thought it was wrong that she was hiding behind her mother. She herself has children, and she has to live in her own reality. So one day she appeared here all excited and we had a talk and she burst out crying, and then she felt a lot better. Since then, the relationship between us is very good. (B.M. interview of January 1971)

B.Q. was one of the widows who refrained, as far as possible, from assuming the role dictated by ties with the Rehabilitation Department. The technique employed by B.Q., the use of an intermediary, was quite common among widows. In her case, the intermediary role was performed usually by her mother, a well-known public figure, respected in their home town. B.Q. explained: "My mother is very good at these things, you know. She doesn't get excited by these things, she listens, and it just rolls off her." This arrangement worked for more than a year, since B.'s advanced pregnancy and her new-born infant apparently constituted satisfactory "excuses" to permit her mother to represent her, but not forever:

> She (the social worker) began sending me notices that I have to come in person. . . . So one bright morning I decided I'd go. After all, she won't "eat" me. . . . I had all sorts of arrangements to make in town, and receipts for the Defense Ministry. . . . By the time I got there it had started raining. I was carrying the baby in my arms, and I don't know how it happened, as I entered the building, where the guard stands, I slipped and the baby flew out of my arms. . . . I lay there on the floor and everybody was looking at me, and no one made a move to help me. . . . So by the time I got up and calmed the baby down, I was covered with mud and I felt awful. . . . Then I went into her room and she started picking at me and badgering me, and she didn't let me leave until I burst out crying.

After that meeting, B.Q. did not return to the Rehabilitation Bureau on her own. She always took someone along, and even then only when she was not successful in arranging her affairs by mail or over the phone.

It is important to note that this process operated in reverse as well: the widow's openness to "treatment" by the social worker increased the latter's readiness to back her economic requests/demands. There were widows who grasped this principle, and who manipulated it with conscious cynicism: "So what do I care if she wants to know about my sex life; I need her on my side" (O.T., No. 62). Others innocently accepted this situation as the order of things: "So I go there and tell her what she wants to know, how I am, and how my children are, and what I do with the children, and what I have . . . and she gives me what I ask for" (S.L., No. 58).

The definition of the widows as "women with emotional problems" lent the system of relationships between the social workers and the widows the character of "treatment." The rules governing "relationships of treatment" differ from those of other types of relationships (bureaucratic, for example), and so does the distribution of responsibility for attaining the goals for which purpose these ties are established. Many widows complained of having been misdirected by the social workers, or of the workers' ignorance of options available for solving the problems presented to them and, occasionally, even of withholding information which may have been extremely helpful in advancing the widow's economic or other interests. In all such cases, the social worker's behavior was explained by her as part of the "treatment process," while the failure to solve (or solve more effectively) the widow's problem was explained by the widow's "emotional state." It is rather difficult to reconstruct after a period of years why certain problems were not solved, or were not solved more satisfactorily. In any event, the explanation offered by the social workers always laid the blame at the door of the widow and her "emotional state" (Ryan 1971). Several examples of this sort, which at the time of this study were not yet "history," cast doubt on the veracity of the social workers' explanations.

For several years before he was killed, O.X. and her husband were raising an orphaned niece in their home. The Ministry of Welfare, the official guardian of this girl, provided economic support for her. Their official application to adopt the girl was in the course of being processed by the authorities when O.X. was widowed. When her pension claim was being filled out, the social worker registered only O.X.'s two children by her husband. Her niece, who lived in her home and who was being considered for adoption by her, was not registered because—as the social worker explained to me—"she said she was getting (support for the child), so that solved the question." In accordance with the information registered on the claim form, O.X. received the pension due to a widow with two children, while her niece continued to receive support from the Ministry of Welfare in accordance with the arrangement made prior to her widowhood. A clause in the "Families of Soldiers" law, and other information on similar exceptional cases, gave reason to doubt the validity of the social worker's decision that the girl in question was not "supported by" the widow and therefore that the widow was not entitled to include her in the pension claim.[17] The possibility that O.X. was in fact eligible for pension payments for three children instead of two was brought up in the course of a conversation with the social worker handling her case, and her reaction was as follows:

If she had asked, then it would have been possible to find out how much she's eligible for. I think, in a case like this, it is much more logical that the woman should demand this. I think it's a matter of principle. The principle is that a person should demand for himself what he thinks he deserves. (Otherwise) I would have to suggest everything, or every suggestion or all of the motivation would have to come from me, and that, so to speak, leaves the claimant on the sidelines . . . as if we're doing it to him, as if we're not working together with him . . . and then dependence (is formed) and all the side effects.

The case described above, although extreme in many respects, demonstrates and clarifies the subject at hand. The problem raised during the talk with the social worker was undoubtedly complex and exceptional. During the discussion, it was not yet clear whether the widow had suffered as a consequence of the decision. Such an assessment could really have been made only by experts. Moreover, even if the widow had been shortchanged, and even if this was caused by the social worker's unfounded decision, there is no doubt that the mistake was made in all innocence and was the result of a human error in judgement. Nevertheless, the social worker was unwilling to concede that she may have erred, or that her decision merited reexamination. She passed the responsibility for the (as yet unassessed) mishap on to the widow, whom she described as a woman about whom ". . . one couldn't say she is over her depression. She barely smiles, much enthusiasm she doesn't have; perhaps that's also her personality to some extent." The social worker expected this woman to initiate a process with which she was unfamiliar, without any basic information on the law, and in the absence of the tools to examine her options (such as precedents for such special arrangements). The widow's obligation to initiate such a process became a "principle of treatment," while the fact that the process was not initiated was her own "fault," since she did not function according to the principle that "a person should demand for himself what he thinks he deserves." Under existing conditions, there was no chance that a widow would request reexamination of her rights, unless it was explained to her that a mistake may have been made in determining them and/or that there was a possibility that, having boarded this child for five years and having included her in the household, there was a place for reconsidering her rights. The social worker refused, on the basis of a "principle of treatment," to explain the widow's situation to her, and to present the options which perhaps were available to her. Neither did the social worker investigate what, precisely, the legal situation was. It is possible that O.X. raised her three children on a pension calculated for a widow and two children and never found out that she could have done so under more comfortable economic circumstances. But if she ever did discover that it may have been possible to ease her economic burden, and had she asked "Why wasn't I told?," the answer she probably would have received was that given to many widows before her: "because you didn't ask."

The definition of war widows as "women with emotional problems" made matters a great deal easier for the social workers. The dissatisfaction, criticism, and occasionally alienating and hostile attitude displayed by some of the war widows were all conceived as stemming from the widow herself, and not as criticism leveled against the rehabilitation staff. Their economic resources and their authority to make psychological judgements provided the social workers with a great deal of power to manipulate at will the population to which they extended services. Together, bureaucratic procedures and "principles of treatment" served to limit greatly the extent to which the social workers were held responsible for providing war widows with the maximum service and benefits which Israeli society wished to extend to them.[18]

This same "psychological" definition not only failed to make things easier for the war widows, it made their ties with the Rehabilitation Department and its offices all the more cumbersome. The definition rendered ineffective many of the widow's defense mechanisms against her inferior position within the system. A respectable appearance, whether in dress or behavior, adherence to customary patterns of good manners ("if I call her Mrs. L., why does she call me R. or dear?"), and the reliance on status which stemmed from other systems of relationships did not receive the expected reaction within the nexus of "relationships of treatment."[19]

The inclusion of psychological considerations within decisions about the allocation of economic benefits served to make the criteria for receiving such benefits most obscure. As a result, a high degree of inequality was created in the allocation of benefits, and every widow knew of several others who received economic benefits which she did not and/or of benefits which she herself received while others did not. Many widows lived with the constant anxiety that they were not receiving their due, and that they were "missing out" on benefits of which they were not aware.

The "principle of treatment" that the initiative for requesting benefits (of all sorts) must come from the client, required the widows to keep in close contact with the Rehabilitation Department. Only contact of that sort could apprise the widow of information concerning the areas in which requests could be initiated and benefits received. Not only was this sort of contact often contrary to the widow's wish, it occasionally also jeopardized the purpose for which it was actually intended: the higher the frequency of the widow's contacts with the social worker, the greater were her chances of being "diagnosed" as dependent, or as lacking independence. This kind of "diagnosis" diminished the social worker's readiness to provide the widow with the information she needed, since the worker did not want to create "dependence and all its effects." At the same time, the less information the widow was able to obtain during her contact with the social worker, the more contacts she needed in order to collect the information required, and the process repeated itself ad infinitum. Achieving a balance between sufficient but not too much contact, between enough but not too much initiative, and so forth, was a technique which most of the widows acquired to some degree with time, and most of them felt burdened by the need to make use of it. To put it differently, many widows felt that so long as they were either unwilling or unable to give up the economic benefits put at their disposal by Israeli society, they remained at the mercy of the bureaucratic establishment and its representatives—the social workers. Due to the particular structure of this system, they felt helpless, unable to fight for their rights, unable to prevent the undermining of their dignity, or defend their identity, self-image, and self-respect.

The various implications of the ties between the war widows and the institutions of the State are reflected in the words of S.E. (No. 17) who described her connections with employees of the Rehabilitation Department and, in doing so, expressed her feelings and views concerning this system:

Statement of ideological position—the widow as a "creditor" to whom the State owes a "sacred debt."

I really have no criticism against the Ministry of Defense, save for their approach. . . . I am proud of what I gave the country, and I think I have reason to be proud, and I think it makes it somewhat easier for me to carry on. It's a feeling that it's not that a man simply walked down the street and was killed in a car accident, but when he picked up the gun he went to defend what is dearest to him in the world—his home, and this piece of land about which he dreamed all his life. . . .

Statement of the gap between ideology and reality in which the widow is treated as "indigent."

So you stand proud, and you want to fight your battle of survival, and you have a feeling that you gave something, and you are entitled—you're not coming to beg. And you don't feel as if you have come to the point of begging, to fight over every additional lira (Israeli currency, no longer in use) that you need, and for which you have to submit a receipt. You didn't ask for a receipt for what you gave this people; you gave because you thought you had to give, and your husband went because he thought it necessary to fight for this place. But to come and beg, that you're unable to do, it's your husband's blood.

Complaints concerning the withholding of information by the Defense Ministry staff.

For example, there is a (customs) exemption for a TV, there are exemptions about all sorts of things, exemptions for widows—you (Defense Ministry staff) act and run around in order to obtain these exemptions. It's clear to me that a whole legal procedure is necessary—then why do you do us a "favor" (when you give them)? Why not write a circular: "Dear Madam, we have obtained an exemption, and any widow who is interested can come and request the deduction." It's a very big thing and I appreciate the effort that they made. But if you make an effort, don't give the widow the feeling that she's a beggar. The same goes for the telephone, washing machine. . . .

Constant contact with Defense Ministry, the only way to actualize rights.

You have to run after your rights all the time, and be there like a spy, and go three times a week to a place where you don't want to go. It's not true that they (the Defense Ministry) don't give. That's not true. They are very helpful—so why does one have to guard one's rights like a watch-dog? Your rights are because the State values your sacrifice and appreciates your struggle for survival, and it wants to help you—then the help must be given with respect.

Denial of respect in the course of contacts with Defense Ministry social workers.

That (the Ministry of Defense) is the most respected place in the country, and its offices and the way in which they handle (people) is not respectful, and that's a pity. (For example),

The social workers set themselves up as "judges."

I received a 'phone call from a (bureau) director in the Defense Ministry: "Come and see me." So I go . . . and he says: "your file (which was transferred from another bureau) has arrived, and you know, I got a negative report about you from the Rehabilitation Bureau in X. Now I know you, and I can tell you're not like that, that's why I'm telling you this. But you should know, I got a very negative report about you, that you're money hungry, that we should watch out because you're only out for money and you want money—they transferred the file plus a letter.". . . I told him: "Now you know me, you're handling me and you know I'm not that type." So he said: "Yes, that's why I'm ripping up the letter, because I know you, I'm doing you a favor." As if I should say "thank you," and you have to prove all the time that you're not like that. They're giving me grades! That dumb clerk (reference to the social worker who wrote the report) is giving me grades!

The widow as a captive client.

Let me tell you that if I were in a stronger position I'd make a public scandal out of that. Who are they to give me grades! The truth is that I would leave the place altogether if I didn't need it. But I do need it. I need it and he gives me grades—that's preposterous! After my first meeting with Mr. X. (the social worker), and then that meeting where he wanted to punish me, I should have gone to the papers. He wanted to punish me because I cried that I have to live with two babies on IL 240 a month; I only cried there (at the Rehabilitation Bureau) because of that. I couldn't grasp it. So for that they give me a grade, and then he does me a so-called favor and tears up the letter. And he knows me, and he knows I'm not money hungry. This macabre scene, I should have gone to the papers, don't you agree? And I didn't go. Why? Because I have to live with it.

Lack of clear-cut criteria of eligibility for benefits used as a mechanism for controlling the widows.

All the giving by the Defense Ministry is under the table. On the pension I get you can't live or die. So they give me IL 100 more—that is, they set up a committee and they helped me, and they set up a committee and they paid kindergarten tuition, and they set up a committee and they helped me buy a washing machine. For everything they set up a committee and they did it as a favor. Nothing was given by law, everything is under the table, as a special favor to you alone. So they spin cobwebs around you. . . . I would have gone to the papers but I knew that I have to live with it, because the next day I'd want a car, and I knew that if I went to the papers I wouldn't get a car, I'd be punished. I'm entitled to the car (reference to exemptions from import taxes on the car), but I won't get it, and I won't get a washing machine (same kind of exemption) or anything else I'm entitled to because they would punish me. So I didn't go to the papers.

Impossibility of maintaining dignity and self-respect under the system.

I don't know whether you've noticed, but the motto of most of the widows is, "I'm proud, I don't want pity, I want only what is due to me, I want to stand erect." A person can't stand up straight when he's asking for charity and favors.

Just as I can say "that's not right" and "that's not right," I'm also grateful to the State that takes care of my children; I can't say that everything is black, and I am not, God forbid, saying that. (But) you (the State, the Defense Ministry) give so much.

Why this way!

The Household Composition of War Widows

The single-parent family, with a woman at its head, has been the subject of much research in sociology, psychology, psychiatry, and social work. The research generally focuses on the extent to which crime, sexual deviation, poverty, failure in the process of socialization, or emotional disturbance are an inevitable result of life in a family unit without a father (Herzog & Sudia 1968; Marsden 1973; Nye 1957; Peres & Katz 1980; Thomas 1968; Wynn 1964). Although there is no consensus concerning the inevitability of the connection between the one-parent family and emotional or social deviation in its members, there seems to be a generally accepted implicit assumption that the way in which a one-parent family functions is necessarily defective. The basic point of departure of most researchers into the one-parent family is that the exit of the father-husband from the family circle causes irreparable damage which reduces the ability of the whole unit to function as long as it remains without a man at its head. In sociology, the source of this approach lies in the structural-functional school (from which "crisis theory" also derives), but is supported by other disciplines, such as psychology (Freudenthal 1959), psychiatry (Wylie 1959), and social work (Mitchell 1964).

The best presentation of the structural-functional theory as far as it concerns the one-parent family is, to my mind, still that of Glasser and Navarre (1965). The clarity and precision of their presentation accentuate the weaknesses of the structural-functional approach in analyzing this unit. Glasser and Navarre attempt to demonstrate that functional defects necessarily arise from the structure of the one-parent family. According to this approach, in a modern family, the complex of family-related functions constitutes a "full-time job for both adults of the household for most of their waking hours" (1965, 98). Despite the relative flexibility of the modern family in terms of the ability of each

52

spouse to interchange roles in times of crisis, one partner cannot fulfill the functions of both for a protracted period of time, certainly not on a permanent basis. Eventually, limitations of energy and of time inevitably cause a breakdown in the organization of family functions and in the efficiency and quality of their execution. Although not explicitly stated by Glasser and Navarre, the conclusion to be drawn from this argument is that the eventual break-down of the one-parent family unit is inevitable.

Glasser and Navarre's conclusions are based on two assumptions that, to my mind, are neither theoretically based nor stand the test of reality. The first assumption is that the modern family is (always and under any circumstances) isolated. The theoretical and empirical testing of this assumption is the subject of this chapter. The second assumption, that the work-load of a family is too onerous for one adult, is dealt with in the next chapter.

The Isolation of the Modern Family

According to the reasoning behind Glasser and Navarre's assertions, the isolation of the modern family is a condition *sine qua non* (although not in itself sufficient) of their second claim, that of the excessive work-load. The isolation of the modern family obliges it to carry the whole burden placed upon it by the events of its life or the calamities which befall it. Its isolation prevents the absorption of at least some of the added burdens by the extended family group, as happens in societies where the nuclear family is not isolated. A conclusion like this can only be reached provided the definition of "The Modern Nuclear Family" is taken either as a description of the functioning unit, or as a guideline to the boundaries of household membership. Seen from this viewpoint, every one-parent family is necessarily "lacking," "defective," or "broken." In order to avoid this conclusion, which not only fails to stand up to the test of reality, but also does not contribute to an understanding of the way in which a one-parent family unit functions and organizes, it is well worthwhile to examine the family unit as a household group. Looking at the family unit (one-parent or any other) as a household group does not entail an obligation to demarcate its boundaries to accord with the definition of a family. The group may be identical with the nuclear family in its composition, its boundaries, and its way of functioning, but this is only one possibility. The effectively functioning group may be composed of only some of the nuclear family members, while others are active in the framework of another group (family or non-family). By the same token, the effectively functioning group may contain members who do not belong to the nuclear family, but who nevertheless function within the unit and constitute an integral part of it. As such, the composition of the household is one of the factors that determines both the capacity of the family to cope with the loss of one of its adult members and the way in which they cope in this situation. As will be argued in detail in the next chapter, the assumption that a one-parent family is automatically overloaded with chores is unacceptable. Nonetheless, changes in family functioning are only to be expected as a result of such a loss, and household composition can be either a positive or a negative factor in meeting the changed needs of the family.

The household of a one-parent family is often described in the professional literature as composed of one adult and several young, dependent children. This description is contradicted by most demographic survey data, which show that in Western society the majority of one-parent families are composed of one adult and one offspring.[1] But even when the conventional description is accurate, its validity is only temporary. Small children grow older, and their level of dependency is reduced. The sheer change in the age composition of the household automatically alters its set of needs and redefines the limitations on the household's capacity to function. Temporary changes in the composition of the household during particular periods of task overload or a drastic reduction of household functions can be found both in the dual-parent family household as well as in the household of a one-parent family.

Households of War Widows

Before they were widowed, the households of the women in the sample differed from each other in size, composition, categories of members, and patterns of internal arrangements. Although the loss of the husband-father created a common feature in all these families, it did not make them more similar to each other than they had been before. In other words, even immediately after they were widowed, the households of all the war widows were not alike. Moreover, the households which existed at the point that they became widows did not necessarily continue to be the same afterwards.[2] Of the changes which occurred, some were related to the situation of widowhood itself and some were not; some could have been expected as part of the life cycle of the family, while others were not predictable; some occurred voluntarily and some were imposed. But all were significant from the point of view of the one-parent family's ability to organize and function.

A voluntary and planned post-widowhood change in household composition was usually aimed at producing a more agreeable balance between the needs and tasks of the unit and its resources (and as will be seen, in the majority of cases this goal was achieved to one degree or another). The widows changed the household composition sometimes by adding members whose resources exceeded their needs and the services they required, and sometimes by removing members of the household whose needs and service requirements were greater than the resources they contributed to the unit. While voluntary changes in household composition were directed to achieving goals connected with the organization and functioning of the household, changes that were not voluntary (imposed or resulting from the life cycle) brought with them unplanned and sometimes unwanted results. A change in household composition could imply qualitative as well as quantitative adjustments in the way in which the household was structured, the way in which it functioned, and the set of relationships and network of contacts within it. The findings are presented according to the type of household established after widowhood.

The Joint Household

Establishment of a joint household[3] of one kind or another, was an arrangement quite commonly used by the widows in the sample. Just over one-third of them lived in a joint household for a period of at least half a year in the three years that passed between the time they were widowed and the beginning of the research. Some had lived in more than one joint household—in all, twenty-seven widows had established thirty-nine joint households, of varying compositions. A joint household could be created with different partners, and the following discussion pertains to the different possible combinations found.

THE DIFFERENT COMBINATIONS OF JOINT HOUSEHOLDS

Joint households of the widow and her husband's parents. Of all the joint households established, eight were partnerships between the widow and one or both of her husband's parents. Three of these had existed even before the period of widowhood and continued for at least a further half-year after the husband's death. The other five were established after this event. Five of the "new" households were formed immediately after the woman was widowed, within the period of the "shiv'a" or immediately after. From the widows' descriptions of the establishment of these households, it would appear that it was understood from the start that they were for a limited time ("until the child is born," if the woman was pregnant when she lost her husband; or "until the end of the year of mourning," and so on). At the time of the research, only one household of this type was still in existence.

Of the five "new" households established after the woman was widowed, four were formed by the entry of the widow into the household of her husband's parents. In every case, the widow's absorption into the existing household was limited, and her position marginal. She and her children remained an addition to, rather than an integral part of, the household. Most of the household expenses were borne by the husband's parents; the financial participation of the widow was limited, restricted to her or her children's specific needs, to expenditures connected with mourning ceremonies, and sometimes to participation in gifts. The management of the household—cleaning, cooking, laundry, etc.—continued to be carried on as it had been before the widow came to live there. Her participation in housework was usually seen as "help" to those who normally carried out the household tasks, and her role was mainly to care for her children.

The two following descriptions typify the kind of arrangements widows had in joint households with their husbands' parents:

> With us, in the Sephardi community (people who trace their origins back to Spanish Jewry), the custom is to pray every Sabbath for the first year. My father-in-law is now 80 years old and my mother-in-law 60, and I didn't feel it was nice (respectful) for me to take over all the responsibility for the ceremonies and the preparations. So I decided to stay with them for a year, to have a room there and to pay the expenses for everything that I wanted done, so that all the services could be held at the right time. (S.T., No. 43)

> I used to get up every morning and tidy up the room I lived in. Every morning I used to wash all the things of my son, who was very small, and my little girl's as well. And when I was done, I used to help her (the mother-in-law) with the dishes and the floors. On washday she used to wash all the things, mine and hers. I never cooked; she used to do all the cooking. I managed very well. She's a pleasant and good woman and even if I did something that wasn't right, she didn't make any remarks. . . . They didn't want to take money from me and it wasn't pleasant to be there for so long without paying, so I used to go once a week to a department store and buy things—cleaning products if we ran out of them, or a blouse for my mother-in-law. I used to spend about seventy or eighty Israeli pounds and put the things away in the cupboard. (B.I., No. 22)

In each case, the widow's total obligations in the "new" joint household with her husband's parents were minimal and the household routines remained, for the most part, those that had crystallized before the widow entered it. While this arrangement relieved her of many obligations, the structure of the household did not offer the widow the freedom of going out to work or of studying, and it limited her opportunities for forming new friendships and making new social contacts. Dissolution of these joint households occurred between six and eighteen months after the onset of widowhood. In all of the cases this happened without crisis and, it seems, to the satisfaction and relief of both sides. In every case, the relationships in the family remained good, but in no case very close or very binding.

The relationships in the three previously existing joint households became more problematic after the bereavement. By definition, the routines and division of labor in these households were well known to all the members and, for a short time at least, everything continued to function as before. However, in the course of time, the interests of the various partners began to diverge, and the continued existence of the joint household was threatened. The consequent dissolution of these households was very difficult and painful for all concerned.

Only one household was formed by the entry of the husband's parents into the widow's household, and even in this one case, only the mother joined the household. The husband's father and his unmarried brother spent most of their free time at the widow's house, but they returned home to sleep. This arrangement was not convenient for the widow and existed only at the insistence of the husband's family, who wanted to maintain the custom of their community by which the mother of the deceased must sleep in his home for the first year of mourning. But it seems that the community's mourning customs were not the only reason for this demand: the husband's mother was old and sickly and in need of constant care. With her transfer to the widow's home, the household of the deceased's parents (where there were no other women) was relieved of the responsibility of caring for the mother. Since the husband's father and brother spent more of their time and took most of their meals at the widow's home, the additional burden placed upon her was extremely heavy. Her mother-in-law was not able to help with the household tasks, nor did the rest of the members of the family consider it necessary to participate in any regular way in the expenses of the household. The widow herself accepted the burden of the arrangement imposed by the year of mourning. However, when this was over and the family refused to return the husband's mother to her own home, the widow was obliged to dissolve the arrangement by more forceful means. This she did by moving to another town. Similar attempts to exploit a widow and her resources in order to solve family problems, sometimes absolutely against her will, were reported several times.

Although usually a short-term measure, taking the step of entering into a joint household with her husband's parents helped the widow to cope with this difficult period in her life. At the beginning of their widowhood, many of the women evidently felt that it was the husband's parents who were closest to them in their loss. This sense of sharing the loss impelled both sides to seek a closer relationship with each other. One of the ways in which this search for closeness found expression was by establishing a joint household. In the light of this mutual feeling, it becomes clear why all the households of this type were established immediately after the woman was widowed. With time, new interests developed on both sides which eventually began to run counter to one another. In most cases, there was a recognition of the conflict of interests and, at the same time, an admission of the legitimacy of these conflicting interests. The best way of resolving such a situation was in all cases to lower the intensity of the contacts. In the case of a joint household, this meant dissolving it.

Joint households of the widow and her own parents. Of all the joint household arrangements of the widows in the sample, that of the widow and her own parents was the most common form. Thirteen of the widows were partners in nineteen combinations of households of this type. As opposed to the situation of setting up a joint household with her parents-in-law, there was no specific time determining the establishment of a joint household between the widow and her own parents. Some of these households were established immediately after the woman was widowed or were simply the continuation of a joint household which had already existed before, while others were established much later on. One such household was formed after the widow had lived jointly with her husband's parents for the first year of mourning; another about a year and a half after she was widowed. Most households of this type were established by the entry of the widow into her parents' existing household (seven out of the thirteen original households), and only a few by the entry of the parents into their daughter's household (four out of the thirteen original households). Two semi-joint households of a widow and her parents were already in existence before she was widowed. Joint households of the widow and her parents were considered to be, and actually operated as, more permanent arrangements than joint households of the widow and her husband's parents. This was expressed in the careful preparations some parents made to receive their daughter and her children into their home. However, even when the creation of the joint household was totally unprepared, the intentions were to improve the physical conditions at a later stage, with the understanding that this was a long-term, though not permanent, arrangement.

In all these households a clear division of labor developed within a short time. The division of labor in these settings was intended to meet the needs of all the members, utilizing the resources at the disposal of all. In this way an integrated household was formed, and the widow and her children did not constitute simply an "addition" to the existing household. The widow's functions in the joint household with her parents were contingent upon the demands of her daily routine of study, work, or recreation. The personal tasks of caring for her and her children's needs were shared between household members according to their different resources and did not devolve solely upon the widow, as was the practice in a joint household with her parents-in-law. In all the cases in which a widow's mother was one of the members of the joint household, she was the "main" housewife, while the widow herself participated in the household work like any other grown-up daughter. When the father was also a member of the household, the widow left most of the administrative functions connected with it to him. When the joint household was located in the home of her parents, and both her mother and her father continued to fulfill the roles of the "main" adults in this household, the widow felt very strongly that she had gone back to being "a daughter" in the home of her parents. This situation was described by N.T. (No. 63): "Mother is there, so I rely on her and I don't bother about anything; I take a book and go and read . . . (I) am like a young, unmarried girl who knows that she goes home and finds the food ready and she has no worries."

This type of household was certainly not immune to internal pressure, friction, and struggles for power and authority. However, there was here a unity of purpose not found in the joint household of a widow and her husband's parents, a recognition of the legitimacy of the concern for the well-being and prosperity of the widow and her children. This common interest lay at the root of the attempts made to ease the tensions inherent in the partnership and to find alternative solutions to enable it to continue. The solutions most commonly used were either transition to a semi-joint household, or transition to a joint household located in the home of the widow. These alternatives were possible only if the widow's parents were willing to renounce their position of primacy in the household, a sacrifice for which not all parents were ready, but of which not a single case was found among the husband's parents in the research sample.

On the whole, it appears that a joint household of the widow and her parents proved to be a relatively flexible arrangement which served the changing needs of all its members, especially those of the widow. The flexibility of this arrangement, and apparently also the willingness on both sides to see it as long-term (until such time as the widow remarried), would explain the fact that of the thirteen widows involved in one of the variations of joint households with their own parents, ten were still part of the household even three years after they were widowed (when the study was undertaken), as against only one of the eight widows involved with the husband's parents in a joint household arrangement.

Joint households of the widow and family members of her own generation. Six widows established joint households with family members of their own generation. In fact, at different times, some were partners in more than one such household, so that of the thirty-nine joint households in the study, ten in all comprised partnerships of this kind. Only one of these joint households was created with the clear intention and purpose of solving the problems of the widow. In all the other cases the joint household arrangement was, first and foremost, intended to solve the problems of all the participants and, as a result, it also answered the needs of the widow. The partners involved were unmarried young women (in one case, the sister of the widow's late husband; in seven cases, the widow's own sister) who, for one reason or another, wanted or needed to leave the family home. All the cases involved daughters of traditional families where it was not customary for a young girl or an unmarried young woman to live independently. Living together with a widow in her home was regarded as an acceptable and satisfactory solution by all concerned. It appeared that the young women willingly moved over to the widow's home, where they would be considered grown-up and where they would gain a relatively greater measure of freedom, independence, and authority. The widow, for her part, benefitted from the additional "manpower" in the household, and sometimes also from the additional financial resources. Above all, she enjoyed the regular presence of someone in the house with whom she could consult, share responsibilities and daily burdens without losing any of her independence, her seniority in terms of authority, and her position as "head of the household."

This type of arrangement existed only in cases where it offered a solution, primarily, to the problem of the young woman needing a "decent" place to live. In those cases where there was no normative obstacle to an independent life for a young unmarried woman, no example of such an arrangement was found. Quite a few of the widows had unmarried sisters living outside the parental home, often in the same town as the widow. In not a single case did the sister give up her living arrangement, such as a room in a student hostel or a rented apartment, in order to enter into a joint household with her widowed sister. It was accepted by all the parties (the parents, the widow, and the unmarried sister) that a young girl needs privacy and should not be prevented from exercising this right. By the same token, it is easy to see why not one joint household was established between the widow and a bachelor brother, or why a partnership arrangement between the widow and the family of her brother or her brother-in-law was so rare (only one such case was found). That is to say, a joint arrangement between the widow and partners of her own generation could exist only where the advantages for the partners were clear and assured.

Partners to this type of joint household arrangement were found to have similar status/ethnic profiles, a similarity which did not exist in other joint household arrangements. All the widows who were involved in arrangements of this sort came from Middle-Eastern or North African backgrounds and belonged to families who described themselves as traditional or religious, and whose economic and educational status was relatively low.

Joint households of the widow and family members of a generation younger than her own. Only two such households were found in the research sample, and in both cases the young girls (aged twelve and fifteen) were sent to live permanently with the widow. In these instances, the girls were the daughters of the late husband's brother. In both cases, the role of the girls was that of "eldest daughter" in the widow's home, where younger children than they were being raised. The connection thus created between the girl's parents' household and that of the widow qualify this type of arrangement for inclusion under the rubric of a joint household. The girl who became a member of the widow's household formed a sort of bridge or pipeline for mutual communication between her family and that of the widow. Her presence in the house created an "open door" between the two families. The girl herself came and went between the two households with absolute freedom, as did the adults involved. She created a situation in which there was a constant flow, back and forth, of information about what went on in both households, and this exchange of information in most cases served as a substitute for requests for help. In other words, when the girl passed on information about certain difficulties in one of the households, the help needed was almost automatically provided by the other household.

Although this arrangement did not constitute a true joint household nor even a semi-joint household (which usually resulted from the inability to locate the two households in close proximity), patterns of partnership were created which were similar to them in many respects. The family of the girl and the family of the widow participated jointly in all the occasions and holiday celebrations usually marked by a family gathering. The question before every such event was, "Where shall we meet this time?" and never, "Should we meet this time?" The adults in the two families undertook permanent functions each in the household of the other, and there was at least partial acceptance of responsibility on the part of the girl's parental home in matters concerning the household of the widow. For instance, one of the widows involved in this type of set-up lived in a moshav.[4] The widow's brother-in-law, who was the father of the girl living in her home, undertook all tasks connected with the management of the farm and the supervision of the hired workers. On the other hand, the widow was given the full right to decide on matters concerning the girl who lived in her home. Holidays and Sabbaths were spent together by the two families, and they were invited together to the home of their common grandfather, or to visit one of the other family members. Mutual cooperation and help in day-to-day matters were almost taken for granted in these families. At the same time, the two families involved in this arrangement were both very careful to adhere to a strict separation in budgetary and financial matters, and each household served, in the financial sense, its own members only.

Both households of this type had been established at the onset of widowhood and were still in operation at the time this study was undertaken three years later. There was no immediate indication that the arrangements would change or terminate.

LOCATION OF THE JOINT HOUSEHOLD

Theoretically, there were three possible technical-organizational ways in which a joint household could be formed. The joint household could be based in the partner's home, in the widow's home, or in a new home.

Households located in the partner's home. Entry of the widow and her children into an existing household was clearly the least favorable arrangement for the widow from the point of view of her position in the family framework. An existing household has its own customs and routines, and the place of each family member, his power and his position, are established. In this study, the viability of this kind of joint household was found to be dependent upon the adaptability of the widow (and her children) to the existing structure. There were certainly variations in the widow's ability to win for herself some measure of power and authority in the household, and in the readiness of the established household members to allow this. Nonetheless, entry into an existing household diminished, to a greater or lesser degree, the widow's independence, her right of decision-making, and her exercise of power and authority within the family.

Households located in the widow's home. The incorporation of others into the widow's existing household lessened to a great extent the loss to the widow of her power and authority. Even in cases where those added belonged to the older generation, the fact that the arrangement was set in her home allowed her to retain a considerable degree of control over it. The entry of additional members into the household of the widow, and particularly adults of the parents' generation, was possible only if they were willing to share, rather than take over, power and authority within the household. As was shown, the result was a very deliberate selection of additional members to the widow's household, which nearly always excluded men. If a man joined the household, it was invariably either on a temporary basis, or on a basis which did not allow for his full participation in household activities.

Newly-located households. There were no instances in the study of the establishment of one joint household as a result of the dissolution of two single existing homes. One reason for this was clearly connected with the financial arrangements involved in a solution of this nature. When necessary, the Israeli Ministry of Defense would make a financial contribution towards meeting the housing needs of the widow and her children. Under this arrangement, registration of the apartment had to be made in the widow's name and that of her children. Therefore a housing unit acquired with the aid of Defense Ministry funds was always the property of the widow and her children, even where funds from sources other than the Defense Ministry were also invested in its acquisition. This being the arrangement, even the parents of the widow hesitated to give up the housing unit which they owned and invest their money in a unit that was the exclusive property of their daughter. However, this appears not to be the only reason for the unwillingness to enter into such an arrangement. In a situation in which two existing households are dissolved and a new joint household established, there is a strong implication of permanence. Entry into such an arrangement would be possible only if it was assumed that the family status of the widow would not change in the future and that she would remain a widow for the rest of her life. This assumption was not usually acceptable either to the widow or to her relatives. Although there were no cases of such an arrangement, there were a number of cases of two existing households being dissolved in order to establish one semi-joint household. The main difference between these two types of households did not lie in the way they functioned while they were actually in operation but, on the contrary, in what happened when they were dissolved.

A semi-joint household is much simpler to dissolve and does not give rise, while it is being dissolved, to the same complex problems of reorganization as does the joint household. The semi-joint household arrangement is straightforward with regard to ownership of the property. This is important from the point of view both of administrative procedures in its purchase and of the process of dissolving the arrangement. At the same time, it is important to point out that those semi-joint households which were established deliberately and by dissolving two existing households, were very similar to the joint household in their way of functioning. The division of property among household members had almost no bearing on the day-to-day life of the household beyond a general awareness that this was a temporary, mutually beneficial arrangement. It was their outlook on the future, rather than their mode of functioning, that mainly differentiated the two kinds of households.

THE ADVANTAGES AND DISADVANTAGES OF A JOINT HOUSEHOLD ARRANGEMENT

The specific arrangements in the joint households of the widows in the sample differed from case to case. However, in all the cases and in every type of arrangement, the joint household solved one important problem which was, by the widows' own definition, the problem of "being alone." Being alone in this context was not so much what is described in the literature (especially in the psychological literature) as a feeling of loss (Parkes 1972), or as a feeling of loneliness (Fromm-Reichman 1968), but rather the translation of those terms into their practical expression in everyday life.

Immediately upon her bereavement, the widow was faced with the necessity of reorganizing and restructuring her household and child-rearing roles. In addition to familiar roles which either she or her husband had previously carried out, there were new, unfamiliar roles awaiting her. The situation was exacerbated by the fact that in fulfilling this unfamiliar set of roles, the responsibility for making and implementing decisions fell on her shoulders alone. Her husband's death robbed her of the sharing element in the conduct of everyday life, and it was this missing element which the widow had in mind when she spoke about being alone. Entering any of the joint household arrangements solved to a greater or lesser degree the practical problems of being alone, although it did not of course necessarily compensate for the feelings of loss or loneliness. Different joint household arrangements offered different degrees of real sharing of tasks or economic burdens, but all the arrangements facilitated a considerable amount of sharing of the responsibility for the results of the decisions.

In practice, all joint household arrangements almost automatically solved problems such as holding family Sabbath or holiday rituals, or reallocating household tasks during sickness, and they usually eased problems of looking after children while the widow was otherwise occupied. At the same time, however, there were serious strains attached to operating within a partnership which was required to take joint responsibility for making and implementing decisions. Indeed, these efforts were often doomed to failure. Entry into a joint household, and especially continuing in this arrangement, was a kind of admission on the part of the widow that in weighing its advantages against its disadvantages, the advantage of "not being alone" was worth the price of "partnership."

While living in a joint household allowed the widow to take advantage of, and participate in, arrangements for mutual help, and to share in decisions and tasks, at the same time it made her subject to social control within the household. This fact, too, was known and understood by the widows. Almost all of them pointed to one thing or another which could not be done in the framework of a joint household. Depending upon the values and life-style of the family, the widow was subjected to supervision which was dictated by the norms of "what is allowed" and "what is prohibited" for a woman without a husband. In every case and in every form of partnership, at least a minimum of supervision was exercised. The widow was expected to report in considerable detail on everyday occurrences both in the home and outside it: reports on times of leaving and returning to the house, kinds of purchases made, what the children ate, and so forth were requested and received in every type of joint household or semi-joint household. Refusal to give information of this kind was considered a slight. The disadvantages of supervision were perfectly clear, especially when it occurred between categories where it is not customary. Nevertheless, such supervision had its advantages as well: the need to report on her doings, the reports she received in return, the questions asked in this process, even if not always desirable in the degree of intensity and insistence with which they were posed, all gave her a feeling of "belonging" which was the opposite of "being alone."

M.N. (No. 40) tried to leave the family's joint household and establish a separate household for herself and her children at a distance from the poor neighborhood where she had grown up and where her family still lived. Within a very short time, she returned to live with her mother and her unmarried brothers and sisters. She explained the reason for this step as follows: "How can I live here (in the separate apartment) where no one sees me, or sees what goes on here! . . . I realized that here I can die and no one will know . . . I saw that this is no life for me."

Most of the widows living in a joint household recognized both the advantages and the disadvantages of the arrangement. In this, their calculations were arrived at consciously and clearly and, in their frequent use of such expressions as "it pays me" or "it's worth my while," they were referring to the compromises they made, the price they paid for continuing the partnership.

As the study material shows, the attraction of a joint household was greater in the initial period of widowhood than at later stages. With time, the difficulties that attended joint living increased, and this fact, often combined with changing life cycle circumstances and a consequent reevaluation on the widow's part of her own resources, led many widows to reconsider the disadvantages as well as the advantages of a joint household arrangement. The more flexible joint households (partnerships between a widow and her parents) tended to go through processes of change, usually into the form of a semi-joint household, which lessened the disadvantages. In the more rigid forms of joint household (partnerships between a widow and her husband's parents) there was very often a greater tendency to abandon the arrangement entirely.

CONDITIONS NECESSARY FOR ESTABLISHING A JOINT HOUSEHOLD

Entry into partnership in a household may be one of several options open to a woman upon widowhood. However, her freedom to accept or reject this particular option is limited by a number of additional factors which have to be taken into consideration. The first and obvious condition is the existence of potential partners. The research findings demonstrated that only certain categories of relatives were in fact candidates for partnership in a household. Among the widows in the sample there were some who had no relatives (or none in Israel) belonging to categories that constituted a source of candidates for partnership. However, even the existence of potential partners in the establishment of a joint household and the readiness of the widow to enter into such a partnership were not always sufficient. The potential partners had to be ready for such a partnership, and this was not necessarily the case. A typical example of this is found in the description by S.E. (no. 17) of the process of negotiation with her family:

> From the beginning, I said that I wouldn't live with them. . . . I found an apartment, 100 meters away from my parents, quite expensive, and I found myself a maid . . . but—well, I really thought I wouldn't have anything to live on. Only afterwards it turned out that the situation would not be quite so bad. And so I brought up the idea both from the financial and from the practical point of view that, seeing that the

children go to kindergarten and I work and study also, the financial situation, with my having to pay so much money for the maid and at the same time somehow managing to live and with two children and with myself as well—so perhaps I'll eat lunch at my parents. They own . . . (a business which, among other things, supplied hundreds of meals a day), so one more meal wouldn't make any difference. Then a deputation came to me . . . including my brother, who was my best friend, and told me that if I dare to eat regularly at my parents' place without paying for the food I eat here, all my brothers would disown me forever. . . . I couldn't take in the meaning of such a shameful thing . . . I said to her (the mother): "Mother, do you know what they said to me? Do you agree with what they said to me?" She answered: "It's not their business, they shouldn't interfere." "Mother, tell me! Yes or no!" "You have money, but it's not their business, let them not interfere." So I said: "I got my answer."

In this case, there was a desire on the part of the widow to enter into an arrangement resembling that of the semi-joint household. The arrangement did not materialize because of her family's unwillingness to cooperate.

S.T. (No. 44) also met with a similar refusal. The mother of three children, she tried to continue and perhaps even strengthen her close relationship with her husband's family. She found herself confronted by the determined resistance of her mother-in-law, which she described in this way:

I said to my mother-in-law: "Listen, now I am your daughter, you will be living with me . . . you will deal with your pain and I will deal with my pain, and we'll be together." She answered: "That's absolutely impossible." She made it very clear to me that she had lost a son and she was not looking for my help . . . then she left me and went away and I remained with my three children.

Even when both sides were ready for partnership, the necessary conditions for establishing it were not always present. The practical problems involved, and in particular the overcrowded and inadequate housing conditions common in Israel, may well have prevented the formation of joint households, despite all good will and intent.

M.N. (No. 40) described the solution to the problem of overcrowding in her family when, after being widowed, she joined her mother's household: "My mother has a big apartment—two rooms—and on the roof she has a laundryroom. And we slept there with the children, after the laundry was done." This arrangement went on for quite a long time, until a better solution was found.

A similar situation was described by C.N. (No. 36) who, after she was widowed, went to live at her mother's home where, at the same time, her married sister also lived with her four children. In this household, all the kitchen equipment belonged to the married sister, but was used by everyone in the household:

> When I was living with my mother and needed (to use the gas stove or the refrigerator), I used to go to my sister's room. But even a sister in the end got sick of my using her gas and refrigerator, and there was no room with the four children (her sister's). When there is one refrigerator, and with (the widow, her mother and the widow's two children), that's again four)together, eight, ten people using one refrigerator, that was very hard.

The problems of the two joint households cited above, as of many others, were solved by creating joint households based on different compositions and different conditions. At the same time, it is important to stress that no joint household arrangement in the study population was dissolved because of lack of suitable housing conditions until such time as a satisfactory alternative could be found. In other words, in no case was the widow asked to return to her original household because she upset the household she had joined.

The Voluntarily Reduced Household

The reduced household[5] technique is virtually a mirror image of the joint household technique. Through reducing the sheer number of household members, the problem of task overload on the one adult in the family is automatically reduced. Eleven of the widows in the sample reduced the size of their households voluntarily and intentionally.

REMOVAL OF NON-NUCLEAR FAMILY HOUSEHOLD MEMBERS

Out of nine joint or semi-joint households that existed before widowhood, five were dissolved by the widow shortly after she was widowed. Four of these five had been formed in partnership with the husband's parents (one or both), while the fifth was formed by the entry of the widow's grandmother into the home of the granddaughter and her husband. These joint households were of two different kinds and therefore the process of their dissolution differed.

Three of these joint households were formed by the entry of an elderly relative into the household of a young family. In all the cases, this arrangement constituted a solution to the problem of the elderly relative. It appears that the position of these old people in the joint households was marginal and their functions in them minimal. It may be assumed that in the households which existed before widowhood, the old people's needs and the services they required were part of the accepted and crystallized routine. In these cases, the widow wanted to be relieved of the burden of caring for the elderly relative. In two cases, the desire of the widow to free herself from this responsibility was accepted and understood by other relatives and, with the agreement of all concerned, the old person was moved to their household. In one case, neither the elderly relative involved—the husband's mother—nor her other children considered the wishes of the widow, and the process of dissolving the joint household necessitated the intervention of the Ministry of Defense, which undertook the transfer of the old woman to a home for the aged.

Two of the joint households which were dissolved during the period of widowhood were joint households of families in a moshav, where the partnership in the household came about as a result of the partnership in the farm. In both cases, the widow's husband was the son in whose hands the parents had intended to leave their farm. When he married, a second floor was built on to the original moshav house, as a home for this son and his family. In the early years, both generations worked the farm in partnership, the parents' investment in it being equal to, if not greater than, that of the son's family. The cooperation engendered by their working together extended also to partnership in the household sphere. In particular, at the time of the birth, infancy, and early years of the children, one of the women took all the responsibility for management of the joint household, and in this way freed the other woman to help with the farm. As the years went by, however, the nature of the work partnership changed, as the father gradually relinquished more and more responsibility for the day-to-day running and planning of the farm to his son. In both of the cases described, the loss of the husband occurred when the parents had already reached old age and the children of the widow had passed the age of early childhood. Shortly after the younger woman became a widow, only one parent was left in each family, the other parent having died. Although the widows had decided immediately after they were widowed to continue to keep up the farm as it was, they came up against many technical and organizational difficulties in this task. In both cases, they began to liquidate considerable portions of the farm, transferring or renting the rest to be worked by others. The moshav house became a place of residence, and in this situation the old person was an extra burden which the widow was not willing to bear. The widows made their remaining in the moshav conditional on the old person leaving the joint household. The old people were accordingly transferred to homes for the aged, and the contact between them and the widow was completely broken.

In spite of the small number of cases under discussion, it seems possible to draw a number of conclusions from them. In all five cases, a joint household existed for some years before the woman's widowhood; routines were crystallized which, it may be supposed, contributed to the stability of the arrangement. The widow's attitude to the presence of her elderly in-law in the household as burdensome and superfluous sprang, not from any objective change in this person's functional capacity in the household, but rather from the new circumstances in which she found herself, and her own consequent changing aims and purposes. Nor was her attitude affected by the sex of the elderly relative in the household—three of the old people who were removed from the joint household were women and two were men. One should bear in mind, however, that widows entered voluntarily into household arrangements with old people who differed little in terms of age, family relationship, functional capacity, etc., from those who were removed from households. It seems that the decision to enter into a joint household with an elderly partner, or to remove an elderly partner from the household, depended on the relative balance of needs and resources in each household.

REMOVAL OF CHILDREN FROM THE HOUSEHOLD

Of the widows in the sample, seven removed children from the household at different periods and for varying lengths of time in the three years that elapsed between the time they were widowed and the point at which this research was undertaken. The removal of the children from the household took two different forms: sending them to another household or to an educational institution.

Transferring children to the care of another household. Three widows gave their children into the total care of their parents. In these three cases, the widows were very young, having been married when they were sixteen to eighteen years old and widowed within the three years following their marriage. Each of them had only one child who was then transferred to the care of her parents in their household. However, the degree to which they relinquished control of and care for the child differed.

I.B. (No. 3) had a joint household with her parents. In establishing this household, the intention was to enable I.B. to complete her professional education. It functioned in accordance with this plan throughout the period of the widow's studies. During this time, the position of both the widow and her daughter was that of "a daughter in the house"—the widow being "the big daughter" and her child being "the little daughter." When her studies were over, the widow moved into an apartment contiguous with that of her parents; here she slept, worked, and conducted her social life. Her daughter remained in the widow's parents' home, and the widow herself continued to receive most of the day-to-day services of this household (food, laundry, etc.). The position of the widow in her parents' household was similar to that of a grown daughter in the process of moving towards independent living, and this did not affect the position of her child as "the little daughter." In this household the structure of family relationships was kept clear—that is to say, the child knew that the widow was her mother, and that those who took care of her were her grandparents.

N.I. (No. 24) also established a joint household with her parents for a certain period of time after she was widowed. A year after her bereavement, she left her parents' home, rented a one-room apartment for herself, and established an independent household of her own. Her daughter continued living with her grandparents. The widow's contacts with the child, and her obligations towards her, were reduced to one task only—that of bringing the child back each day from kindergarten to the grandparents' home. In this family, it was absolutely clear that it was the grandmother and the grandfather who had the total responsibility for all decisions concerning their granddaughter, and that whenever there was disagreement between the widow and her parents regarding the child, it was the grandparents who made the final decision. On the other hand (and perhaps in compensation for this), the widow's parents did not interfere in her way of life or in what she did. In this family, the little girl called her grandfather "Daddy," and it appears that they were not particularly interested in making clear to the child precisely what the structure of the family relationship was.

I.X. (No. 20) entered into the most extreme type of arrangement from the point of view of the break between her and her child. Almost immediately after she was widowed, I.X. gave her son into the care of her parents who lived in a nearby town. With the assistance of the Ministry of Defense, the widow acquired a new home, a typical "bachelor" apartment. It consisted of a large living room suitable for receiving guests and a small bedroom, and was furnished in such a way that there was no place for an additional person to live, certainly not a child. The widow herself led a semi-bohemian life. She invested a great deal of effort into turning her home into a center for budding artists and intellectuals, and the emphasis was accordingly on those household functions connected with hospitality and representation. Her obligations vis-à-vis her son were summed up in two weekly visits, which apparently were not very strictly adhered to. This widow had only little to say about her son and explained that the care of the child was completely in the hands of her parents. Her parents apparently were also happy with her nonintervention in the way they were bringing up her son.

In spite of the differences between the three cases described, the trends common to all three are worth stressing. In each case, the care of the child was handed over to the widow's parents, and in no case to the husband's parents, even though the objective conditions for this existed. Despite appearances to the contrary, it was in every case clear to the widow (and apparently also to her parents) that the existing arrangement was temporary, that the child was with the grandparents for "custody" only, and that when the time came and the conditions were suitable, the child would return to the mother. It is extremely doubtful whether such an arrangement would be possible with the husband's parents, because the widow would not feel certain that the child would be returned to her. At the same time, the husband's parents would probably be unwilling to undertake an attachment which would commit them to such a great involvement as bringing up a child when there was a considerable likelihood that, in the end, there would be a partial separation. Continuity of relationship between the widow's parents and their grandchild was assured to a greater or lesser extent by virtue of their daughter being a connecting link between the generations.

Another aspect of this arrangement which deserves attention is the type of household that results from it. The three widows who placed their children in the care of their parents set up for themselves very limited households, clearly households for a single person. This type of household is often considered as resulting from the negative aspects of modern society, such as alienation, isolation, or the absence of commitment to mutual help in kinship groups and community settings (Belcher 1967). However, when a single person voluntarily plans an arrangement of this kind, as in the cases described above, it is apparent that, far from resulting from alienation, isolation, or absence of commitment to mutual help, it is rather the result of willingness to cooperate within a kinship group. Breaking away (at least partially) from social relationships which involve obligations and limitations offers at the same time the possibility of achieving a relatively great degree of freedom (Simmel 1964). Under certain conditions and for the sake of achieving certain aims, there are many advantages in freedom, even when it is accompanied by a degree of social isolation. The three widows who set up for themselves a "singles" household directed most of their efforts into areas outside the household and the family—study, work, and social contacts mainly answering leisure time and entertainment needs. The widow's participation in these activities was facilitated by two factors: first, her young age, which meant that she could easily assume the unmarried life-style of her contemporaries; second, freedom and release from her obligations as housewife and mother made it possible for her to join in activities of girls of her own age without being an "exception." In other words, a "singles" household neither limited nor obligated her as would a family household, and it obviated the investment of resources involved in a family household. It thus enabled the widow to exploit her own personal potential in areas which were closed to her before her widowhood and to explore new possibilities which widowhood opened up for her.

Transferring children to an educational institution. Entirely different aims were achieved by the three widows who placed their children for care in an educational institution. In these cases, the widow maintained the home and kept up contact with the child through letters and frequent visits. But from the point of view of the daily functioning of the household, moving the child into an educational institution meant reducing the number of members in the household and, consequently, its functions. However, it was never voluntarily reduced so as to leave less than two children living at home. In two of the cases described, children were removed in turn from the household, so that at any given point in time one child was out of the house. Throughout the whole period, the number of its effective members was less than the number of members in the nuclear family unit. Various explanations were given for removal of the children—some focused on the benefit to the child who was removed from the household, some on the benefit to the children who remained. But in all the cases there was a clear impression that it was difficult for the widow to manage the organizing of the multi-member and multi-problem household. Removal of children from the home for at least a certain length of time was a technique used for transferring part of the household's functions to frameworks outside of the family, and in this way easing the burden upon the widow. In other words, in those situations where the burden was "excessive" (using Glasser & Navarre's terminology), the temporary transfer of certain family functions to an outside agency lightened the burden. With time, the widow's burden eased, thanks to her children's increasing ability to contribute to the manpower resources of the household and to the reduction in household tasks which accompanied the normal family life-cycle process.

Life Cycle and Household Composition[6]

Birth, growing up and leaving the family framework, marriage, aging and death, occurring in the proper order and at the proper time, are usually regarded as normal turning points in the life of a family. When they happen out of phase they may be regarded as crises—for instance, untimely death (Lehrman 1956) or premature birth (Caplan

1960). At the same time, sociologists sometimes also treat normal, timely life-cycle events as crises in themselves (Hobbs 1968; LeMasters 1957). The following discussion will not deal with the vexed question of whether or not a particular event is a crisis, but rather will focus on events which are generally considered as part of the life-cycle of a family and their influence upon the composition and structure of the family of a war widow.

INCREASE OF THE HOUSEHOLD DUE TO
LIFE-CYCLE EVENTS

Sixteen of the widows in the sample gave birth after their husbands had already been called up during the pre-Six-Day War mobilization, which is to say, after their husbands had left the home for the last time. Not all of these sixteen women gave birth after their husbands were killed. A few gave birth before they themselves knew they were widows, and others gave birth knowing already that they were widows. The span of time over which these births took place was from a few days before the women were widowed up until nine months after, but in all the cases, the birth occurred after the last time the father had been at home. From the point of view of the widows themselves, there was a vast difference, emotionally, between giving birth as a widow and giving birth as a wife. Similarly, there was an important difference between a situation where the decision to continue the pregnancy was still open for consideration and a situation where the pregnancy had reached such an advanced stage that this consideration was ruled out. Furthermore, aside from the differences in the emotional significance surrounding the circumstances of birth, each one of these births caused a change in the family composition and in the household of the widow. In this connection, the meaning of the additional child to the family depended to a large extent on the number of other children already in the family.

Of the sixteen children born after the father had left the home, six were first children, five were second children, three were third children, and two were fourth children. The six widows who gave birth to a first child ensured the continuation of the family unit which would otherwise have terminated on the husband's death. Three of the mothers were involved for a certain period in a joint household venture, but at the time of the study each maintained an independent unit together with her child. Already a widow on giving birth, each mother had to function from the outset in the absence of the father's complementary role. The set of functions and tasks in each household was, of course, on a reduced scale compared with a two-parent family.

But, as for any other family, the functions and routines of the household altered and grew with the development of the unit over time, in accordance with its structure and its changing needs and resources.

Mothers who bore their second child shortly before or after being widowed were placed in a different situation from first-time mothers, and the structure of their household was affected in a different way. In all the cases, the widow's firstborn child was still small (under school age). During the period covered by the pregnancy, the birth and the few months following, the widow needed a considerable amount of outside help. In four out of the five cases in this category, the help took the form of establishing a joint household which continued up to the time of this study. The birth of the second child removed the widow from the category of "mother of an only child" (which will be discussed in detail in the next chapter), and created a "fuller" unit. With the birth of a third, and certainly of a fourth child, the family moved into the "large family" category. Four of the women in the sample who gave birth to their third or fourth child after being widowed had only very young children. In these cases the functioning load on the household was particularly heavy.

The increase in a family unit as a result of the birth of children not only added to the number of members in the household or the number of functions and tasks it required, but in certain cases, brought about a qualitative change in its form and its internal structure. The transition from a one-person household (here, the widow herself) to a diadic household, from a diadic to a triadic household and from this to a multi-member household was not simply a quantitative change but also created new qualitative changes as well, in terms of relationships and functions within the household. The significance of the addition of a child to the family was not felt to the full immediately after the birth (and this despite the added burden of tasks which made itself very much felt). However, at the time of the research, when these children were two or three years old, the differences between the household unit with only one child and a unit with two, three or four children were considerable in all areas of functioning, as well as in the interaction among the members of the household.

Birth was not the only life-cycle event precipitating an increase in household size. For instance, in one case (B.H., No. 12), the death of the widow's mother caused an increase in the joint household that the widow had already established with her sister immediately after becoming a widow. Her two younger sisters, left on their own after their mother's death, joined the two older sisters, and became the 'elder daughters' in this joint household.

DECREASE OF THE HOUSEHOLD DUE TO
LIFE-CYCLE EVENTS

Some of the households in the sample lost members as the result of a particular life-cycle event. Both joint family households and nuclear family households were affected by events of this kind. Three joint households were dissolved when the widows' partners left to join other household arrangements. In two of these cases, the widow's younger sister had shared a joint household with her for a period of one to two years, an arrangement which served the needs of the sister no less than that of the widow. One of them was B.H. (No. 12). The increase in her household, described above, was only short-lived. At the time of the study, she was already referring to it in the past: "After it happened (the husband's death), my sister lived with me for a whole year, and after that my two little sisters were with me because mother passed away. And that was good both for them and for me. They helped me a lot." Another widow (I.B., No. 45) said: "My sister works at the hospital and she lived with me until she got married. My second sister as well she studied at (a seminary) to be a kindergarten teacher. She also lived with me. When my sisters lived with me here, it was easier for me." The sisters were all at a stage of transition in their lives. In the course of time, they finished their studies, and took jobs outside the city and/or got married. The joint household was dissolved, its composition was reduced and its structure changed. At the time of this study, there were still two joint households of widows with their unmarried sisters. Presumably, in time, should circumstances so dictate, the younger sister would leave the joint household and the arrangement would accordingly be dissolved.

A third household, semi-joint, broke up as a result of the remarriage of the widow's father. This household had comprised two connecting apartments, with a clear division of functions between the widow and her father; the widow's apartment was the "service center," while the father undertook to provide for the joint household and to manage administrative matters in connection with it. At the time of her husband's death, her father had already been a widower for several years. Joint household arrangements had existed even before her husband's death, becoming still more crystallized after it. The remarriage of her father deprived the household of one of its most important resources: a man knowledgeable and experienced in administration, contacts with institutions, investments, keeping accounts, etc. At the time of the study, the widow's father had been married for only three months, but even in this short time, and notwithstanding his attempts to fulfill his functions in his daughter's household, he was greatly missed.

The joint households described above were arrangements which, for a certain period of time—from one to three years—satisfied the needs of all the participants. Their termination did not stem from difficulties in interpersonal relations or from other internal household problems, but was rather occasioned by a specific event in the life of one member. As a result of the change brought about by this event, the structure and composition of the widow's household were significantly altered.

Among the widows in the sample, there were three whose households, at the time of the study, were going through a process of reduction as a result of the children (or at least one child) growing up and leaving home. In addition, six widows were awaiting the induction of their eldest child (son or daughter) into the army within the forthcoming year, while one widow succeeded in postponing the beginning of the "emptying" process in her household by requesting a special deferment for her eldest daughter.

The significance of the children growing up and leaving home differed from case to case in its effect on the household, the way in which it functioned, and the widow's position in it. B.C. (No. 7) was forty-seven years old when she was widowed. Her eldest daughter had already left home before the Six-Day War in order to study, although she returned frequently to spend Sabbath and holidays with her family. A short time after the war ended, this daughter married, and her younger sister went into the army. When the interview for this study took place, it was already clear that the younger daughter did not intend to return to the family home after her military service, and that she was planning to study in another city. Thus, the widow's household was almost entirely emptied of its members within a three year span, and only the sporadic visits of the daughter in army service filled the void from time to time. The change which took place in the household of this widow was particularly severely felt. Within three years, the household that had served a full family unit became the household of a single person. The functions of the widow also changed accordingly: from a fully active housewife, wife, and mother, she became a widow living alone and facing the same problems that in our society usually confront widows who are fifteen or twenty years older than she.

S.T. (No. 43) was forty-three years old when she was widowed. Her elder son moved to another city to pursue his academic studies immediately after the death of his father, leaving his mother and his younger brother, who was just finishing high school, at home. The changes which occurred in this household were not as acute as those described in the family above. Nevertheless, they were critical enough to place a severe strain on the functioning of the household. It was evident that the transition, in a very short space of time, from a full nuclear family household to a household serving just a diad, which would itself shortly be dissolved, was giving rise to the breakdown of family functioning in every sphere, in particular to the erosion of the widow's own functions.

The case of I.C. (No. 5) was somewhat different. Born and raised in Iraq, she was married there at the age of thirteen, in accordance with local custom. When she was widowed at age thirty-three therefore, she had already been married for twenty years and had four children. Her second and third children were serving in the army, while the youngest daughter was pursuing her high school studies at boarding school and was rarely at home. A relationship between the widow and a divorced man had developed to the point that they were contemplating marriage. The only obstacle preventing the widow from remarrying (which she was eager to do), was the eldest son, a slightly retarded twenty-year-old who refused to leave the house, go to work, and earn his own living. The widow herself tried to find various solutions to the problem, many of which would have required the investment of all she possessed, in order to put an end to her responsibility for this son. She believed that this was her last opportunity to establish a new home and a new family, and the realization of this opportunity depended upon her grown up children being no longer her financial responsibility, nor under her care. In other words, the widow estimated that the emptying of the household was her only hope of not finding herself at a young age (under forty) in a situation and under conditions similar to those of an old widow.

Although at the time of the study only three households had actually been affected by their children leaving home, the widows in the sample were highly aware of this eventuality. Even the mothers of very small children were conscious of the empty home awaiting them in the future, and every stage in their children's lives which signified a process of maturation (starting kindergarten, school, scouts, going to camp, and so on) aroused in them a fear of the moment when the house would be empty and they would find themselves alone. The fear of this moment played no small part in the widows' interest in remarriage (Shamgar-Handelman 1982).

Crises, Calamities and Household Composition

Some households were affected by a calamity or crisis which befell the family unit, over and above the death of the husband-father. In no case in the sample was a household constrained to increase its composition by the enforced addition of another member. The instance most closely approaching an imposed increase was described earlier in this chapter. In this case, the arrangement which began as a voluntary increase eventually became a constraint upon the widow, and she found a way of dissolving it, even in the face of opposition by the other partners. In the sample households, crisis events which affected household size always resulted in its reduction.

Within a year of being widowed, two widows each lost a child as the result of a malignant disease. There was obviously no connection of cause and effect between the widowhood and the death of the child. Nonetheless, because these two calamities occurred within such a short space of time, in each case they were perceived by the widow as being one single calamity, leaving her with a totally different household from that which she had known before. In one such case, the widow and her four-year-old daughter were left after the double calamity as a diadic unit, with no experience or knowledge of how to function in this strange and new situation. In the second case, the widow spent much of the year following her husband's death at her sick son's hospital bedside. On his death, she was left with her two small daughters in a home which had been run for a prolonged period by strangers, in a way foreign to her. She, too, found herself in a totally unfamiliar household situation, with a whole new set of needs and problems to cope with, completely different from those which had existed before widowhood and before the death of her son.

The experience of a widow living in a moshav took a different form. Her fourteen-year-old son had for many years been a problem child. Presumably, the combination of reaching adolescence and the loss of his father exacerbated his situation to the extent that he had to be sent away to a special education school. Bearing in mind that a fourteen-year-old boy in a farming community is already an active member of the labor force, it is hardly surprising that the death of her husband and the departure of her son gave rise to severe problems in the running of the farm. In this case, the imposed reduction in household composition and, in particular, its reduced work force, not only altered the way in which the household itself functioned, but also brought about a definite change in the whole way of life of the family. The widow went to work outside the moshav, the farm was neglected, the moshav became simply a place of residence and the household functioned like an urban household.

The history of changes in household composition described by B.I. (No.22) illustrates the power of manipulation a widow could exercise, the importance of the partners to the meaning of the arrangement, and the effect of the household composition on her day-to-day life.

Before widowhood—
nuclear family household

I'm the youngest at home. I have an older brother. He has three children and they live here. Another sister lives in (Town A), and a second sister lives in (Town B).

Before, I lived in (Town C). There I had a very small flat of one room and I couldn't manage there with two children. Before it happened (the death of the husband), we had only one small girl and even so it was difficult, so we were considering building an addition (to the flat).

After widowhood—joint
household with husband's
parents, located in their
home.

But when it happened, I couldn't stay in this flat anyway, so I went to live with his parents. They live in (Town D). I lived with them for a year and a half, until I bought this flat. At the time we joined them (the household of the husband's parents), they were all (the late husband's siblings) still unmarried. They (the parents) have quite a big house—they have three quite big rooms, a big entrance hall, and quite a big kitchen.

Overcrowded conditions
not a barrier to establish-
ing a joint household.

I had a room for myself and the children and my sister-in-law slept with me so that I wouldn't be bored by myself.

Widow not an integral
part of household.

Financially, this is the way it worked. At the beginning, they didn't want to take money from me and it was very unpleasant for me to live with them for such a long time and not to pay anything. So I used to go once a week to the department store and I would buy some cleaning material or some tinned foods that were missing, or a blouse for my mother-in-law. I would spend some 70 to 80 Israeli pounds and put everything I purchased in the cupboard.

Voluntary increase of
family size within joint
household.

When the girl was eleven months, I found myself pregnant again. We didn't want it, and I contemplated having an abortion, after he returned from the army. But once it happened, it was already impossible ("impossible" here refers to the emotional commitment to her husband, since medically an abortion would have been possible at this stage). I was just hoping that it would be a son and I would call him after his father. And that's exactly how it was.

Dissolving the joint household to the satisfaction and relief of both sides.

I left because I wanted to have a home of my own. I didn't want to be there all the time. I wanted the children, when they grew up, to know that it is their home and not their grandmother's. They (The husband's parents) didn't want to let me go. They wanted me to be with them all the time, but once I left, they accepted it very nicely. Every Saturday night they come to visit us. My brothers-in-law also come every few weeks. Sometimes I take the children to visit them—I have very good relationships with my husband's parents. They love the children.

Creation of new nuclear family household;

Recognition of joint household advantages.

I moved here a year and a half ago. When I moved to my own flat it was totally different. It was not the way it used to be when they (the parents-in-law) used to help me. Then I didn't spend a lot, but on my own—I missed it (the help) a lot. After I moved to my flat, if not for my parents—where we went to eat sometimes, and sometimes they brought us some fruit—I really couldn't have managed on what I get from the Ministry of Defence. I couldn't do anything to fix the house. It would really be hard. If my parents didn't help me a little, I couldn't live on the 500 pounds I get. My parents are in my place almost all the time.

Joint household arrangement with widow's parents, located in her home.

Now I don't have any special problems, but a few debts. My parents sleep at my place at night, they eat wherever is more convenient, sometimes at my place and sometimes at theirs. Sometimes they are here all the time, exactly as though they were in their own home—they do the shopping and everything. Either I'm in their house or they are in mine. I'm the youngest and they have no one at home any more.

Refraining from dissolving the parental household emphasizes the temporary nature of the joint household.

Joint household arrangement as a solution to "being alone".

Integrated division of labor within joint household.

In my flat I have a living room, two bedrooms, kitchen, bathroom and two balconies. My father sleeps in one bedroom and my son has a bed in the room with my father. My mother and my daughter are together with me in the room. They keep their clothes here and I have two special drawers for them in the cupboard. If they need something more, they go to their house and take it. If they are here and they need something, they go there and fetch it and if they are there and they need something, they come here to get it. That's the way they manage, so that I should not be by myself. In the morning, they eat here. My father, who works in the municipality, has a break between 8:30 and 9:00. So we all eat breakfast together. When my father leaves for work, my mother goes shopping and I fix the house. My mother cooks lunch and dinner here in the kitchen. But there (in the parent's house) it is good, because there is a back yard and the children can play. So we go there for them to play.

IV

Household Functioning

The previous chapter cast doubt on Glasser and Navarre's assumption concerning the isolation of the nuclear family. In fact, the data of this study show a considerable variety in family structures, all based on strong ties between the nuclear family and its extended kinship network. Glasser and Navarre's second assumption concerns the supposed excessive workload in the one-parent family. Their claim, that one spouse cannot bear the additional burden of tasks caused by the loss of the other partner, would seem to be based on two implicit assumptions which are worthy of further examination.

The first implicit assumption is that the total set of functions in a family is static and permanent, despite changes which may take place in a family's situation or structure. The logic of this assumption is questionable, and does not hold in the light of reality. Every stage in the life of a family, as well as change in a family's circumstances, composition, and needs, brings with it accompanying changes in the set of family functions and roles. Each such change will also bring about a new distribution of time and energy, as well as of other resources, in order to meet the new demands of function and role. There is a great deal of evidence in the sociological literature of the variability in the set of family roles as part of the life cycle of the family: birth (LeMasters 1957), growing up (Bossard 1953), aging (Townsend 1957). These changes are usually also related to changes in the composition of the family and household unit. In much of the research, there is a tendency to view the one-parent family from the perspective of a dual-parent family. From this point of view, it is a "broken," "incomplete," "fatherless," or "motherless" family, and not a family with its own unique composition determining its own set of roles and arrangements.

When the point of departure of the analysis is the family as a functioning unit, the loss of one of the spouses will inevitably reduce the functional capacity of the unit, but it will also bring about changes in the set of family tasks to be carried out. As the literature dealing with the functioning of the one-parent family has mainly ignored the latter aspect of change, some elaboration is called for.

1. *Disappearance of family functions*
   With the loss of a spouse, those functions which were contingent upon the set of relationships and mutual services between the spouses cease to exist altogether. At the same time, other tasks which the family unit may have performed in connection with the activities of its members outside the family or household (such as business entertaining) may also disappear, or at least be considerably reduced in scope.
2. *Decrease of functions*
   The absence of one member of the family automatically reduces the burden of tasks and services in the family unit and in the household. Thus, for example, less time and labor now need to be expended on household services, such as cooking, laundry, and cleaning.
3. *Introduction of new functions*
   The loss of a spouse creates new functions within the family unit. For the widow, they may include responsibilities for involvement in memorial occasions, tending the grave, contacts with military and rehabilitation authorities, etc. Although these new functions obviously devolve upon the remaining spouse, they are definitely not functions of the deceased spouse which are now transferred to the survivor.

The implicit assumption that the set of family functions is static not only ignores changes in these functions, but also makes no reference to the dimension of time, and in particular to the family life cycle. It is as though from the moment a family becomes a one-parent unit, it loses the characteristics of development and change which are surely found in every family unit. This aspect is vital to the understanding of functional patterns in a family for two main reasons. First, the stage in the family life cycle at which the unit becomes a one-parent family is significant both from the point of view of its ability to function and in the kind of internal functioning dictated by circumstances. A one-parent family bringing up infants and small children, for instance, must solve the problem of its continued existence by means different from those available to a unit which becomes a one-parent family at a point where the children are teen-agers or older. Second, a one-parent family has its life-cycle just like any other family—children are born and grow up in it, mature and leave the home, the parent ages and becomes old. These life-cycle changes determine, in the one-parent family as in any other, the kind and the order of priorities of functions which must be carried out, and therefore also the ways in which its needs are best met.

The second implicit assumption of Glasser & Navarre is that as time and manpower (energy) are human resources, the loss of one parent will inevitably bring about a lack in the resources of the family unit. However, no such a priori assumption of significant lack of resources in the one-parent family should be made. Since work capacity and time are human resources, they are, by their very nature, limited. However, not everyone possesses these resources in equal quantity, and certainly not when they are measured by the yardsticks of ability to use them and skill in their manipulation. Furthermore, in a modern society where both time and labor can be bought, such assets as financial means, education, social and family connections, can be exchanged for the necessary human resources. These assets are certainly not shared equally by all people. The various resources at the disposal of the one adult in the family may successfully replace the time and the energies of the missing spouse.

The conclusion that the loss of an adult family member will necessarily bring about a drastic decrease in family tasks and the disintegration of its functions is not well founded. The loss of a family member, like any other significant change in a family, will bring about changes in the arrangement of the set of functions, in the distribution of resources and in the way they are used, as well as in recruiting potential resources that had not previously been put to use. The specific solutions for each family unit depend upon its needs, on the one hand, and its resources on the other. Disintegration of the family unit is only one of the many and varied possible outcomes of dealing with a one-parent situation.

Functioning of the Widow's Family and Household Unit

The needs, internal arrangements, and patterns of functioning of any family household are to a large extent determined by the different elements in its composition—the number of members, their ages, the nature of their participation in its activities, and so forth. To this extent, the household of a war widow is no different from any other family household. However, the one-parent family has to function in the absence of those socially accepted norms which guide the two-parent family in determining its household arrangements. As a result, the war widow has to draw heavily upon her own skills and resources and rely upon her own judgment as she sets the pattern of her specific household arrangements.

It is usual in the sociological literature to divide the set of functions of a family unit and its household into two types: instrumental functions, whose purpose is to ensure the maintenance and physical well-being of the individuals in the family and of the whole unit; and expressive functions, whose purpose is to strengthen the unity of the family, to give expression to its values, and to meet the emotional needs of its members (Parsons 1955; Zelditch 1955). This classification of family functions is drawn from the theories on small groups and is intended to explain the pattern of specialization of functions in a family according to the criterion of sex. Whether or not this classification serves the purpose for which it was intended, it is not appropriate for classifying the activities carried out in a household since, in most cases, these activities display both instrumental and expressive aspects and meanings. Actions which are carried out for the purpose of maintenance and well-being of household members have at the same time a vested expressive value significance and commitment. Feeding household members is a clear example of this and was, in fact, mentioned by many of the widows interviewed. The need to eat is a basic physical need. Many instrumental activities and tasks are connected with providing food for members of the family. However, besides satisfying the physical needs of those partaking in it, the family meal (in all its variations) fulfills expressive value functions which are of great importance in a family unit. The relative weight attached to the instrumental or expressive significance of specific functions will differ at various points in time. So too, the question of which household members are available to participate in carrying out those functions differs, as well as the kind of emphasis attached to their contribution. On ordinary weekdays, work tends to be routinely divided according to different skills, applying the yardstick of sex. These routine functions are largely concerned with the process of maintaining the family unit, and the emphasis in carrying them out is accordingly instrumental. At special times, however, such as holidays and occasions of particular significance for the family unit, the emphasis is largely upon the expressive aspects of functions, and the composition of those performing these functions tends to stress the expressive-cohesive aspects of the family unit. The level of cooperation is raised in the performance of functions at special times, even in those specialized tasks which are normally carried out by separate members of the family. The combination of instrumental functions, and the expressive significance attaching to them, creates the special life-style of the family, its ambience, and the nature of the relationships within it.

Insofar as this could be reconstructed after a time lapse of three years, the impression was gained that before the advent of widowhood in the great majority of the families studied, there was a division of labor in essence similar to that described in the literature as being usual in a modern family. The woman was responsible for, and/or carried out, most of the tasks connected with the services provided by the household for its members, as well as most of the tasks involved in the physical care of children; the husband was the principal breadwinner, and it was usually his task to attend to most of the administrative matters of the household and to tasks requiring technical know-how. In the great majority of cases, husband and wife cooperated in decisions involving their children's upbringing, major purchases, and important issues of family concern. Within this broad framework, there were many individual variations in the execution of specific tasks, the nature of cooperation between spouses, the extent to which each partner deputized for the other in task performance, and in the degree of rigidity in sex-typing specific tasks.

From the findings presented in chapter III, we know that even three years after they were widowed, nineteen out of the total of seventy-one widows preferred not to maintain a separate household for themselves and their children. Those who preferred, or who were obliged, to maintain an independent household had to devise a method of organization and functioning to meet the changes in its needs and composition resulting from the bereavement it had sustained, and also to cope with any additional changes which the household had undergone during the period of widowhood. When the widows talked about their present household arrangements, they almost always compared them to those they had maintained before widowhood. The presentation of the research findings will follow this pattern. Because of the great difference between the way a household ordinarily operates and the way it operates at special times, the findings of each of those forms of functioning are presented separately.

FUNCTIONING OF THE HOUSEHOLD ON REGULAR DAYS

Areas of functioning specific to the wife. The decrease in the number of members in the widow's household unit reduced both its needs and the services it provided. As a result, it also reduced the functions of the woman who had borne responsibility for them in the past and continued to carry them out after widowhood. However, the set of services was not only determined by the number of household members; the absence of the deceased husband from the unit had a significance far beyond the numerical value of a single member. The importance of the presence of the husband in dictating the set of services in the household was, to a considerable extent, a function of the accepted norms regarding the respective duties of husband and wife in the family framework, the concept of the "privileges" and "needs" of the male head of a family, and the constraints imposed as a result of his activities outside the family framework. But above all, his approval and esteem were highly meaningful rewards for her efforts and thus provided an important motivation for performing these tasks. With the death of the husband, the routine service tasks of the household lost part of their significance, especially as an important source of rewards and esteem for the woman responsible for performing them. Thus, the loss of the husband to the household eliminated both the raison d'etre of certain of the daily routines, and the reward for their accomplishment.

On this point O.X. (No. 21), mother of three children, said:

> I, for instance, at the beginning, loved to bake cakes and, for the Sabbath, to try out something new, make some new dish, because I knew that he (the husband) liked it. And after . . . (her husband was killed), for maybe a year and a half, I didn't touch the baking oven and I couldn't do it. . . . And in the kitchen I had a very bad time for a while, because I had the feeling—here you are making . . . but for whom are you making it, if he's not here? . . . and even doing the washing or ironing, or in every corner of the house.

On the same subject, U.M. (No. 34), mother of two children, said: "When there isn't a man in the house, the kitchen is automatically different. The expenses are smaller. And besides, I hate cooking. So, when there is a man, it's a different thing—and one does it (cooking). But, when he's not (in the house)—you just eat something light."

The absence of a "reason" and the lack of a "reward" resulted in a reduction in those household functions which the widow saw as meaningless after the death of her husband. This seemed to be the case for both large and small families, but the situation in the latter was particularly acute, especially in those cases in which the widow was left with a household comprised only of herself and one child. N.C. (No. 6), who had an only son, said: "As far as my home itself is concerned— I feel I have no desire to do anything. I don't cook, for instance. I simply don't feel like standing for an hour and cooking for (her son) who doesn't even know what he's eating. I look after the house very little."

Widows who had run a big, full household felt its dwindling functions and significance mainly by comparison with patterns they had known in the past. I.O. (No. 39), whose household after the death of her husband was still further reduced by the departure of her elder son to do his academic studies in another city, expressed her feelings about her shrunken household in this way:

A home where there is a husband and a family is entirely different from (what I have) now that I am alone. One son is in (City H) and one son, although he's here—but I don't feel like cooking a lot and I no longer want to buy this, or something else, that I would have bought when my husband was. . . . I used once to want to sit down and serve at the table properly, but now I say, "Oh, it's not worthwhile just for me and for him alone."

B.C. (No. 7) echoed these sentiments, expressing them in an even sharper vein. Her two daughters left home after their mother was widowed and she was accordingly running the household purely for herself:

Look, I don't say that I neglect the house, but I've nothing to do. Wash the floors again! I have no laundry to do. I once had a lot of work. In summer, (the husband) sometimes used to change his undershirt twice a day. And I had a garden. I got rid of it. I have a heart problem and I'm not able to—I had all the fruit trees pulled up. I'm not saying that my husband used to do these things (like gardening)—we used to get someone. Now (after his death), to have to pay money for it, it's not worth it, and to do it myself, *geit nischt* (Yiddish for it doesn't work). There was a time when the children used to help. That's all I can (do)—I left myself the lovely garden in front of the house, it was beautiful. . . . For instance, on Sabbath, then of course I cook a proper meal in any case—my big girl (daughter) comes, or the little one, or sometimes someone just drops in. But then until Monday there's no reason to cook . . . although it's always the same food. For instance when I make meat, I don't make it just for one day—I make enough and I eat the same thing half the week, but at least I do eat some hot food. At the beginning (after being widowed), when I was eating I used to lock the door. I used to cook for myself, but I never laid the table for myself! . . . Then, I used to eat standing. Now, I sit down and I eat. . . . Sometimes I ask myself, "What are you doing it all for? So that you can think you're alive?"

It can be seen that, faced with a loss or reduction in certain of the service functions she had previously performed, a widow could withdraw still further from fulfilling them. The need for these services may have diminished, or disappeared, the normative pressures on her to perform them no longer applied, and the rewards and esteem which their performance had previously brought her no longer existed to prompt her to carry them out. Given this situation, she generally opted for one of two solutions. The first was to transfer these service tasks to an agent outside the household. Most commonly, among the widows studied, this involved arranging for the main meal of the day to be taken outside the home. Usually, in such an instance, the children took their main meals at the educational setting where they were studying, while the widow herself either paid for an outside meal, or had her meal in some other household (perhaps in her parents' home). Alternatively she may have managed without a main meal altogether. Accordingly, in households such as these, the preparation of food was limited to sandwiches or omelettes and hot drinks, so that the tasks involved in the purchase, care and storage of provisions, as well as the cleaning connected with cooking and food preparation, were greatly reduced. The second option the widow could adopt to enable her to reduce her household service tasks was to pay others to come to her home to perform them in her stead. In so doing, she shed responsibility for her housewifely tasks, and allowed the service agent to assume this aspect of her role, often even to the extent of transferring control of the way in which the household was managed and run. However, even where no attempt was made to reduce the services of the household, some reduction of services inevitably took place in every case.

Areas of functioning specific to the husband. In many households, certain maintenance and administrative tasks had always been considered to fall within the husband's special sphere of functioning. In the case of maintenance tasks, there were many variations between households, both in the maintenance tasks required in general, and also in the number of these tasks undertaken by the husband. The life-style and patterns of organization of certain families were so dependent upon the husband's function in household maintenance that, after his loss, no way could be found to continue to maintain even the basic framework of the household. In other households, although this framework was retained, it was nevertheless necessary to transfer to others some of the tasks performed in the past by the husband. These functions were carried out in one of the three following ways, or by a combination of all three: a. the widow herself (or her children) acquired the knowledge and the skills to perform the tasks formerly carried out by the husband; b. tasks which were formerly the husband's were performed voluntarily by persons not belonging to the nuclear family; c. professional workers were paid to perform the tasks formerly carried out by the husband. The choice of method to ensure the performance of such tasks depended on many factors: on the widow's financial resources and her ability to obtain the services of professionals; on her social and/or family connections and her ability to find, within this set of connections, people who would replace her late husband in carrying out tasks which had been his; on flexibility of sex role images held by the widow herself and her readiness, therefore, to learn new "men's" skills; and, of course, on her objective capacity to perform such tasks. However, in addition to all these factors, and especially with regard to tasks which required contacts and negotiations outside of the family unit, the possibility of the widow's taking upon herself the former tasks of her husband depended upon the readiness of "significant others" to accept her as qualified to carry them out.

The problems posed by the maintenance tasks confronting the widow came particularly to the fore as she made a decision whether or not to move to another home which she perceived as easier to maintain. In some cases, both the life-style of the family and its social network were related to the place in which they lived. In order to continue living in the same place, the widow had to secure the ongoing performance of many maintenance tasks which in the past had been the husband's. If she failed, she was forced to move. A situation of this kind was described by I.O. (No. 39):

We had a rented house . . . we really loved the house, although it was old . . . but it was old and needed repair. . . . We had a tiled roof which was in bad condition, so while my husband was alive, he took care of it. I wouldn't have been able to. And when the winter came, it leaked and I just left it, so it got worse. We had a garden and the winter was over and the children didn't want to look after it. . . . We were terribly sad because it was spoilt and there was no one to fix it up and the garden was neglected and everything together. So we thought we would move to another place—that it would be easier for us . . . that there would be a new apartment in an apartment house, and if anything was out of order, there would be the house committee. . . . It (moving to an apartment) was a real crisis, for me and for the children . . . it was about two and a half years ago. Until today, the children have not become adjusted. The little one has no friends; he's too lazy to go down . . . he keeps telling me: "Mother, you know, it's a pity that we left the house." Although I did have friends, but all of them are actually in Tel Aviv; they stayed there, but the distance became enormous. And those who were in (the town near Tel Aviv where the widow lived) weren't really such good friends, but I could, if I felt like it, get to their place on foot. But to go down specially (from the new place where she lived)—for that, they aren't friends enough. I can't say that I've remained all alone because of this, only that it became very hard for me.

A problem of a special nature confronted widows living in a moshav. In moshav living, the distinction between the family household and the family farm is unclear. The continued care of such a mixed enterprise called for a rather complicated interplay of resources and manpower, reflected in the words of K.L. (No. 55), who was one of the few moshav widows who continued to work the farm, even though on a reduced basis:

We have an orchard plus a poultry house. That's what remains for me (after the two tractors, owned and operated for hire by her husband, were sold). I look after it. In the season, that is during the harvest, I get Arab workers and they do the harvesting. I also go out. I look after the poultry by myself. When there is heavy work, cleaning out manure or deliveries (poultry to market), I get a laborer and pay him. Before my husband fell in the war, he used to go out to work (with the tractors), and I always looked after the poultry. . . . The children were small then, so I didn't go out to the orchards . . . after the war, I took in a girl, monthly. For almost a year and a half, there was a girl working here monthly—helping in the house, and the children were small. Now, there's help only once a week, and if I need it, then I take a laborer (for yard work, as distinct from harvesting). Usually, I go to my brother-in-law. It's his worker and I can take him . . . and the worker knows that my brother-in-law is supervising him, because with this worker a woman has nothing to say. I said to him (the laborer), "Perhaps you should make the path wider?" So he answered, "It's O.K. this way." So I told him, "Good, I'll speak to Moshe"—that's my brother-in-law. "If Moshe says so, then that's the way."

In order to continue to maintain the household and the farm attached to it, K.L. made use of all three alternatives mentioned above to substitute for her husband in carrying out the tasks that had been his. She undertook some of the tasks herself, such as hiring workers for the harvest and going out to the fields with them. In order to be free to carry out these tasks, she transferred some of her own "traditional" tasks to a hired employee. As for those of her late husband's tasks which she herself could not carry out, she again hired outside help. One of her husband's tasks, which she could neither do herself nor hire someone to do, was that of exercising authority over the hired workers. Her brother-in-law took responsibility for this (voluntarily) and it is clear from her description that he invested a great deal of effort in it. It seems that had there been no one to perform this function, the widow would have been unable to continue to maintain her farm as she did.

Another widow, Z.T. (No. 68), also from a moshav, could not cope with the problems of carrying out her husband's former tasks. She described the situation thus:

I came to the conclusion that, really, I would not be able anyway to hold out on the farm for many years. Perhaps I began to feel this when all sorts of technical problems started to come up, problems that men solve very easily and which, for me, were mountains. Like, for instance, a broken faucet, a burst pipe in the middle of the night, and water that must be closed off in the field and you have to go out by yourself to do it. . . . And I had to get help from people, and people were less and less willing (to help), as compared with how it was before (right after she was widowed), and I started more and more to call in experts and pay them and it wasn't realistic (financially worthwhile), and so I arrived at the point where I decided that it really isn't for a woman.

Z.T.'s attempts to find substitutes to take over her husband's tasks met with failure; volunteer helpers were not forthcoming, and she did not find it financially worthwhile to pay for services which she herself, neither objectively nor subjectively, was capable of performing. At the time of the research, she was planning to sell the farm and leave the moshav, the only solution she viewed as acceptable and reasonable in the light of events and circumstances.

In urban households, maintenance and administrative matters tend to be less complex, and some wives in the sample had had experience of them even before widowhood. The husband of U.M. (No. 34), for example, had served in the Permanent Army, and was accordingly away from home for several weeks at a time:

> I was alone for many years, all the years that I was married. So that managing by myself and running around myself (to attend to matters), that I always did . . . doing things myself (technical things) is only a small part of the problem. At the beginning it was hard for me to deal with all the financial matters, and the insurances, and the accounts, since I had never done this before. Bills for electricity, water, telephone, the municipality . . . my husband was very well organized and he left everything in order, indexed and in files . . . and I sat down one day and learnt it. It doesn't take much to learn.

Among widows in the sample, there were those whose experience at tasks formerly performed by the husband was minimal. Nevertheless some of them succeeded in overcoming this barrier, as was described (with some satisfaction) by O.T. (No. 62):

> I did all the administrative work myself, and it fell on me like a thunderbolt . . . things that in all my life—on my kibbutz—in all my life I never knew . . . and even my parents couldn't help me, as they also lived on the kibbutz—they really knew nothing. No matter how much they wanted to (help me) they didn't know how. . . . When my husband was here, I didn't know what it was to pay an electric or water bill; today it's really no trouble for me.

Faced with the necessity of carrying out technical tasks, usually considered to be strictly "men's jobs," the widow would again explore the three alternatives described above in an attempt to find a substitute for her husband in this sphere.

S.H. (No. 11) recruited men from her kinship network and from among her neighbors to carry out these tasks: "If a venetian blind was broken, I asked a neighbor and he did it for me. When people insisted on my buying a television, my brother-in-law went and ran around and bought me a television, and my other brother-in-law—my husband's brother—did the antenna for me. That means, I paid only for the materials and he did the work and all the rest." But S.T. (No. 42) was obliged to pay to have the tasks of her late husband carried out: "When my husband was alive, I never used to call in the plumber, and the carpenter, and the glazier. He (the husband) did it. Today I have to pay for everything with good money. I'm even lost when it comes to knowing how much to pay." On the other hand, B.C. (No. 7) overcame the barrier of the "sex image" and learned how to do these jobs herself: ". . . if there's no choice, then I get the help of a trained person. But lots of little things, I've learnt to do myself. I sometimes think, 'how do I dare!' "

In certain cases and for certain tasks, the widow's willingness to "dare" and to carry out the tasks which her husband formerly did was not sufficient. Sometimes, the people in the "complementary roles" refused to enter into "role contact" with her. T.E. (No. 18), for example, recalled that she was obliged to leave her apartment immediately following the end of the "shlosheem" (thirty days' mourning period): "I had no choice, since this man from whom we rented the apartment wanted it back. I don't know why, maybe he was afraid that I wouldn't pay him." And in the same vein, W.H. (No. 15) said: "Yesterday Shalom (the widow's brother-in-law) went to the man who does the tiles and the man told him that he doesn't want anything to do with a widow—if she's not able to pay, he wouldn't take her to court, and he doesn't want anything to do with her and will only deal with Shalom and that he, Shalom, is responsible for the money." In both these cases, a widow was not considered to be a "safe customer" and she was deprived of the possibility of filling the role of "lessee" or of "customer," roles which in the past were filled by her husband, or by her in his name. The widow was obliged either to renounce this role for herself and for her family, or else to find a man to represent her in such transactions. In the majority of the cases, there was one such man, usually a relative, who played the part of "guardian" and who represented the widow in business transactions and in other matters in which she was not considered a "legitimate" participant. In those few cases where the widow was not successful in finding a substitute performer to carry out her husband's tasks, it posed a constant problem in the conduct of everyday life.

S.H. (No. 14) described some of the problems with which she now had to cope:

Before (being widowed)—I never overstrained myself, I didn't even go to do the marketing. He (the husband) used to stock up the house. There were no worries, everything was fine, and he used to mend things and arrange. (After his death) and until today—I've no light on the balcony, and the plumbing is not so good, and there's no one to fix it.

Among the specialized functions of the husband, in most cases, were certain tasks connected with the education and upbringing of the children, even though most of the physical aspects of these functions, together with the supervision of the children, in fact, usually fell within the special area of the woman. The functions of the husband-father in the upbringing and education of the children were connected with the "male image" and with the functional expectations to which this image gave rise, as well as with the specific areas of his knowledge and expertise. Thus, the husband-father often assumed the role of the person in authority, the one who punished, the one who decided and determined what was allowed and what forbidden, the adviser and the guide in "masculine" areas such as choice of a profession or study "track," or participation in "masculine" recreational activities like football or adventurous outings. These functions were predominantly the specialized domain of the man in those families where the masculine/feminine images were the main yardstick by which the division of labor was determined. In families where these images were less ingrained, the father's roles coincided more with his own particular areas of competence, skills and talents, which he would draw on to supply information and technical help. In these cases he would invariably also consider it part of his role to put the children to bed and read them stories.

Many of the functions performed by the husband-father in this area are by nature temporary, and three years after his death had, in any event, lost their significance. At the same time, the development of new functions which would normally arise with the continuing interaction of parent and child was automatically curtailed by his loss. It would appear that in a considerable number of cases, the main value of these functions lay in the opportunities they afforded for cooperation between the father and his children. In cases where this was the main significance and value of the function, the person who performed it was irreplaceable. However, the widow quite often attached a value to the performance of this function over and above its aim, even when the special significance inherent in the cooperation itself between a father and his children was lacking. She therefore tried to find someone to substitute for the father in the performance of this function, particularly when she did not consider herself as a suitable substitute. Because of the changing nature of these types of functions, it is hard to identify precisely which tasks performed by the widow in the education and upbringing of her children would have been performed by her husband had he been alive. Nonetheless, it seems clear that in this sphere of activity, as in other spheres, not only did she herself take over some of what presumably would have been his responsibilities, but she also looked to options outside the nuclear family for help where she felt in some way inadequate or unable to cope. Again, there were two major alternatives open to her—she could either turn to volunteers recruited from her kinship or social network, or she could pay outsiders to perform these tasks.

When she chose the alternative of paying, the widow would most usually place her child in some form of recreational setting, special interest, or sports group. Her rationale for so doing, if the child was a boy, was his need for masculine-oriented pastimes. One widow even went so far as to pay a young man to spend some few hours each week exclusively with her six-year-old son, since she considered that she must provide some masculine form of contact for him. In any event, and whatever the sex of the child, the widow reasoned that had the father been alive he would most certainly have been involved in these kinds of activity with his children. It seems, however, that the value for the widow of paying for professionally supervised facilities went beyond these stated considerations for, in having the children taken off her hands for a given period, she was temporarily relieved of the duty of care and responsibility for them, and given a few hours of relative freedom such as she would have enjoyed had her husband indeed taken his children out for sport and recreational purposes. It was apparent from the considerable sums of money that the widow was prepared to invest that these few hours of freedom were very precious to her.

In many other cases, the widow would recruit the help of family or friends to substitute for functions that she felt had been part of her husband's realm. In some instances, the non-performance of a given function would come to symbolize the orphaned state, for the mother and for the child, and the mother would then encourage the men in the kinship network or in the circle of friends to perform this particular function, at least for a time.

U.G. (No. 51) recalled the help given by a couple who were neighbors and friends. "The man came in regularly twice a week to put the children to bed, to play with them and read them a story . . . and what was very important, like clockwork . . . and for a pretty long period of time." A similar description was given by O.X. (No. 21):

> There was a period of a whole year when (her son) didn't want to go to sleep until my brother came and talked to him a bit and told him some story, and that's the way it was for a whole year, that I had to phone him to come . . . until slowly he (the son) stopped of his own accord.

In the cases described above, the need for this function to be carried on passed with the maturing of the children and, in these and other cases not cited here, the function had already ceased to be carried out by the time the research was instituted. On the other hand, in some cases the widow felt that, as the children matured, it became more and more difficult for her to fulfill functions previously performed by her husband. This was described by I.O. (No. 39), the mother of two boys, both in their late teens:

> . . . and there's another problem, that the little one (aged 17) is very jealous of the big one (aged 19) and this makes for problems . . . this existed even when my husband was here. But when he was here, then— as we say—my husband spoke, and that was it! Nothing more to argue about. . . . I wouldn't hit such a big child, and I wouldn't shout, because if I shout he will shout still louder . . . they need a father to convince them about things where I can't. And if I can, well then it's not the right kind of convincing—they accept it because they want to do it for Mother, but they're not convinced—they don't believe in it.

Her conviction that only a man could handle the problems of teenagers made her try to impose this function on one of the friends of the family, apparently against both his will and the will of her children:

> My husband was . . . a battalion commander, and the man (in question) was third in command. He's an engineer by profession . . . and he always tried to keep up a relationship with us, and we really have a relationship. But I wanted to transfer it to the children . . . I wanted there to be a relationship with our big son, and with the little one. He actually did try, but it's really very difficult.

B.B. (No. 1), was one of the widows who deliberately did not deviate from any of the areas of "women's functions," and she maintained this attitude with regard to parental functions as well. Because of this, she recruited help from two sources in those areas which she considered important to the children's "masculine" activities. Describing her relationship with a couple who were an important source of help, she said:

> The husband, there, although he is a very busy man, he's a professor at (institute of higher learning), he knows that the child needs a man, and sometimes he comes in the middle of the week. He leaves work and comes and takes the children to things (activities) that I can't do. For instance, when I bought the bicycle, he came and took my son to all kinds of open spaces where he could ride. . . . Here, there are army people who aren't really friends, who are younger than I am but served with my husband, and they take the trouble—on the Sabbath, they come and take the boy to the football game, because that's something I don't do.

In spite of all that has been said and exemplified above, three years after the women in the sample became widows, only a few were able in any regular way to recruit substitute males for authoritative, advisory, or informational functions. In the great majority of cases, when it was necessary, there was some friend or relative who was ready to help with a particular subject; however, only very rarely was this a man who had an on-going relationship with, or a regular function in, the family. Exceptions to this were those grandfathers who, even when there was no joint-household with the widow, undertook a regular function vis-à-vis her children, and in this way maintained a continuing functional relationship with them.

Areas of role-sharing. The areas of role-sharing between husband and wife were evidently mainly focused on decisions concerning *family policy* (that is, determining family arrangements, and arriving at important decisions in the life of the family), on *family representation* in the framework of the household (receiving and entertaining guests), and on *joint family activities* (educational and recreational). These areas of role-sharing, like the other areas of functioning, called for a certain degree of skill. Here too, in the course of time, routinized patterns of operation were formed. However, the main skill in such activities was actually that of "pulling together," that is to say, of willingness to share rights and obligations, to show consideration for the needs and the limitations of the participants, and to develop techniques to achieve desirable results for all. There was an inherent difficulty in substituting in these areas of joint activity because the specific function was itself of less importance than the participation in the whole.

The life-style of a family is determined by its patterns of distribution of resources (economic, manpower/time, skills, and knowledge) in order to achieve various family aims, and by the priorities it attributes to these aims. This is expressed in the daily life of a family through the decisions it makes concerning the family budget, major purchases, how leisure time is spent, the pattern of education of the children, and so forth. It appears from the descriptions by widows in the sample that, in most families before widowhood, decisions of this sort were jointly arrived at and often jointly carried out, at least in part. Choosing an apartment, making major purchases, and disciplining the children, for example, were almost always joint functions, while in some families, even routine chores such as weekly food shopping were done together.

The transition from thinking in terms of "two" to thinking in terms of "one" is very clearly expressed in the areas of decision-making and of determining family policies. In those sets of social relationships and contacts which involve diffuse obligations and sharing of responsibility, it is not possible to find a substitute for the role of the deceased male spouse in setting family policy. At the same time, and despite the absence of a partner in carrying out this function, policy decisions regarding the future of the family unit and the way it operates must be made. In the words of I.M. (No. 28):

> When I married, I hardly knew, and until I got used to being a housewife—it takes time until one gets oneself settled into married life. . . . Yes! Until you begin to think "as two, as a couple," and afterwards you have to think about everything "as one"—that's a very difficult crisis . . . you begin to get used to your situation and (to the fact) that you are alone. Before (at the beginning of widowhood) you simply go on thinking "as two"—for a long time, you think "as two." Afterwards you understand that you are alone and you must think "as one." This transition from "two" to "one," this is very difficult.

According to I.M. (cited above), for a certain length of time (and as regards certain matters for quite a long time), the widows continued thinking in terms of "two." That is to say that some decisions were made under the assumption that the husband's views on the matter were known, and the widow's decision was arrived at as a result of her agreement with this view, or as a compromise between her position on the matter and the supposed position of her husband. The story of K.I. (No. 19), illustrates this situation. She was twenty-three years old when she became a widow. The couple had been married for nine months and, for reasons connected with the individual plans of each of them, they had decided to postpone having a child for a number of years. In spite of this decision, and without planning it, K.I. became pregnant and was in the first weeks of pregnancy when she was widowed. She thus found herself in a situation where she could still (and must) decide whether she wanted the pregnancy to continue, or whether she preferred to end her condition. This decision would determine both the future of the family unit (terminating the pregnancy would mean the end of the family unit) and the future life of K.I. herself (continuing the pregnancy would mean the creation of a new one-parent family unit, and all the long-term obligations this would imply). K.I. decided to continue her pregnancy. From her words, it would appear that a major consideration in her decision was what her husband's view would supposedly have been:

> There were several things that entered into it . . . it's not only my child. I decided that this is the way (continuing the pregnancy) that my husband also would want me to choose, and this was certainly a consideration. . . . After all, my husband knew that I was pregnant and this, at least, was a great comfort to me. Even though the child wasn't planned, but once it

was there, both of us were very pleased. (At the same time) to go through childbirth without a husband and without a father (for the child) is a truly shattering thing.

However, it is not possible, for a protracted period, to continue going through the process of determining family policy in every area on the basis of the supposed views of the husband. Most widows found the transition from the process of decision-making by "two" to that of decision-making by "one" a difficult burden. W.H. (No. 15) said of this, simply: "It's hard for me, as I always have to decide alone." This applied particularly when the decisions concerned the children, because, ". . . the child is not only mine," and the "partner" in the child was not there. This was explained by S.H. (No. 14), who had to decide about what kind of school her six-year-old son should attend: "For me it was a heavy burden. If I had someone with exactly the same responsibility as I have, then we would decide together. And if it was a wrong step we took, the responsibility would have fallen equally on the two of us."

With time, most of the widows learned to think in terms of "one" and take on the function of determining family policy. When this function was performed by one person, the way in which it was done changed. As long as the function was being carried out by both spouses, it involved a process of negotiation aimed at reaching an agreement and/or compromise acceptable to both. Upon widowhood, this process of negotiation was no longer possible. On the other hand, having to reach a decision on their own responsibility caused many widows to become exceptionally cautious in the decision-making process. This caution was expressed in the attempt to gather all the information they could before coming to a decision. This involved consulting many people, if possible professionals, with the clear aim of making "safe" decisions, that is, choosing the least hazardous alternatives. This was taken to its most extreme form when the decisions concerned the welfare of children and/or the future of a whole family. In such cases, the widows would opt for a "safe" course even when it involved additional investment of resources. A typical example of this was the kind of medical care the widows tended to choose for their children. H.N. (No. 37) said:

> I have a private doctor, definitely not a Kupat Holim (Sick Fund) doctor. He knows me and knows how to handle me. For me, myself, the Kupat Holim is good enough, but for him (the child) . . . at Kupat Holim they would have told me, "It's nothing. Take him to the nurses' room—they'll take care of him." And the child vomited and vomited. I went to a private doctor and this private doctor behaved so nicely . . . so I go to him for every little thing, at least twice a month.

S. T. (No. 42), who was well aware that she tended towards the "safe" decisions, described her feelings in this way: "There are things that I normally (not being a widow) wouldn't do . . . for instance, ordinarily, a child gets dental care at school. So I went privately and paid a lot of money. I'm sure that, had my husband been here, I wouldn't have done this."

Even three years after becoming widows, for most of these women the necessity to make decisions on their own in matters of fundamental importance to the functioning, well-being, and future of the family, was the most difficult of the tasks they had to bear. However, quite a number of them recognized that the right to decide by themselves also gave them a considerable amount of freedom.

The functions connected with receiving and entertaining guests are the practical expression of family representation in the framework of the household.[1] Social life centered on the home is a widely accepted facet of Israeli society, particularly so for married people. The unit participating in this type of social life is usually "the couple," that is to say that one couple are hosts, while other couples are invited as guests. These social contacts are mostly based on rotation of the roles of "host" and "guest" among the couples—sometimes this rotation is rigid and regular (each week a different couple is the host), and sometimes it is more flexible and is based on the assumption that, as time goes on, each of the couples will take its turn at being host. This function is both the host's contribution towards meeting a need of the social group as a whole, and a way of presenting the home of the family unit to the social group. In home-based hospitality, a pattern of role division, sometimes almost a ritual, for receiving guests at home evolves, covering all the different aspects of entertaining—serving food and drink, conversing with guests, and so on. Regardless of the specific pattern adopted by a couple, the tasks are integrated so as to create a single, cooperative host team.

The scale of entertaining at home was generally rapidly reduced after widowhood (see chapter V). But even in the relatively few cases where the social contacts of the widow offered her opportunities to fulfill the function of hostess, most widows found themselves unable to carry out this function because of the lack of a partner in the host team.

T. B. (No. 2) was pregnant when she was widowed. She recalled (almost nostalgically) the period immediately following the birth of the child during which there was a nurse in the house (partly paid for by the Ministry of Defense, as part of the assistance given to widowed mothers of newborn infants): "She was there all day—all day she was there. It was nice, because then I could sleep a lot and receive guests the way it should be and everything." When asked what she meant by "receive guests the way it should be," she could not explain. On looking into the position and functions of a nurse in the household, it was found that this woman took responsibility for all the service tasks in the home, including serving guests. In this way, T.B. was free to devote herself to conversation and entertainment. This is doubtless what she meant when she described this situation as an opportunity "to receive guests the way it should be."

In contrast to the widows cited above, some of the widows in the sample were able to identify exactly the source of their difficulties in fulfilling the "hostess" role. C. M. (No. 27) said: "If a few couples come, or maybe two couples, then at least the two men have something in common to talk about. But when one man sits here and we are two or three women, I understand that it can't interest him, and if it does—then maybe only for half an hour." This widow obviously felt the lack of a man in her host team. For her, his presence was essential for entertaining their married friends, where the conversation customarily divided along masculine and feminine lines.

Among the friends of Z. Z. (No. 26), separation of the sexes in entertaining guests was less important. Nevertheless, despite all her efforts, she too had difficulty in carrying out the hostess functions:

> With good friends, the relationships are entirely mutual—like before. If they take my children (for some pastime), I try in return to take someone else's children. If I'm invited I also try to invite—although it is uncomfortable for me to invite people to supper and I run to the kitchen and can't produce a meal and talk to them at the same time. It's simple—I can't divide myself in two."

There were many widows in the sample who, because of the change in their set of social contacts, were prevented from forming host-guest relationships. Others, who might have been able to form such relationships, avoided it because of the difficulties of entertaining guests without a husband. Those widows who did continue to entertain guests felt that, in spite of the effort they invested, this function was performed on a low level.

In every family (as in every group), there is a need to share information, exchange views, express family unity, and arrive at a consensus in matters related to norms and values. For the families in the sample, part of this need in the past was met as a by-product of various activities of the family unit and its household; the other part of this need was filled and emphasized through activities reserved for the Sabbath, holidays, and special occasions. However, in many families the daily routine also included activities, the main significance of which lay in the fact that they were an instrument for meeting the need of the family, or the couple, to communicate and to express its unity. In the absence of the husband-father, these activities (often amusements or pastimes), tended to lose their communicative-cohesive significance, and sometimes even became a symbol of the deceased partner. In such cases, even if it was possible to find someone as a substitute, the widow tended not to carry on this activity.

The description given by O. X. (No. 21) related to an activity that lost its significance when it ceased to serve the communicative-cohesive needs of the family unit: "We used to go out of the house . . . and so we could wander around even for two or three hours, and sometimes together with the children, and sometimes in the evening, before going to some movie. Then mostly we left the house about half an hour before and just looked around, sat down in some cafe and had a cup of coffee or an ice-cream—this I can't do today." And, in the same connection, K. I. (No. 19) said: "I don't go to the movies. (Since becoming a widow) I went only once, after a lot of pressure (from friends). I don't want to go. I used to love it (going to movies) and I went often. It's uncomfortable for me. First of all, the knowledge that part of the enjoyment, and all my pleasure, was that I was with my husband, and now I don't . . . it doesn't attract me any more."

Widows' responses to questions in this area yielded a picture of family-based activities which was very different after widowhood from that which had existed before. In the past, the focus had been on joint activities of husband and wife in which the children participated, according to their ages and the type of activity. Whether this activity consisted of an outing, a conversation in the family living-room, a visit to a museum, or working on a joint hobby, it was the parents who gave tone and direction to the activity. It was the cooperation between the parents that created the framework into which the children were absorbed. After the loss of the husband-father, general family activities were mainly dictated by the needs (real or supposed) of the children. Before widowhood, as I. H. (No. 13) described, it was common for the family to take a stroll in the main street of the little town where they lived. Now, her changed circumstances had altered her feelings about this activity: "I'm not able to go for a stroll alone with the children. Our town is different from a big city. . . . I don't feel comfortable when I'm by myself with the two children in the street . . . I take them to the sea, or sometimes there's a children's show." G. M. (No. 37) had similar problems: "If I go out, it's for him (the son), on the lawn. I take along some embroidery or knitting, sit with him—neighbors also sit together and talk and the children play." N. S. (No. 61) also faced a situation like this: "Although it's not the kind of thing where I'm with him all the time, but whatever we do, we are doing it together."

The joint activities of the widows and their children provided the needed opportunities to communicate, to exchange opinions and information, to guide the children and give expression to feelings of family unity. But in these joint activities, the ability of the mother-widow to find companionship and to express herself was extremely limited because of the lack of age-status balance within the group. S. H. (No. 11) explained this situation as follows: "I always have to sit and play with him . . . I sit like a little girl and pretend to be a dog or a cat and play with him . . . I wanted to go a bit, see people (adults), talk a bit." Within the nuclear family unit, the widows could not find the contact they needed with "equals," the possibilities of sharing experiences and so forth, and they were forced to seek these in the context of other relationships.

FAMILY AND HOUSEHOLD FUNCTIONING ON THE SABBATH AND ON HOLIDAYS

Sabbaths and holidays constitute focal points of confrontation between the widow and her widowhood. At these times the fact of widowhood is given symbolic and technical expression, the source of which lies in a combination of factors.

First, Sabbaths and holidays are times, both in Jewish tradition and in Israeli culture, when the whole family comes together and all its activities are directed and organized accordingly. With this background, the absence of the husband-father and of his contribution to family activities makes itself more strongly felt than on ordinary days. Second, because spending Sabbaths and holidays in the framework of the family is a general custom in Israel, the arrangements made and substitutes found (whether paid or voluntary) for ordinary days are only rarely available at these special times. Third, the ceremonies and rites of the holidays, particularly of Passover,[2] and of the Sabbath, are family-oriented, and the role of the male head of the family is central. This applies both when the family is religious, and where the performance of the ritual is purely a symbol of ties with tradition. Fourth, the importance accorded in Israeli society to the Sabbath, to holidays (especially the major holidays), to the rites and ceremonies which accompany them, and to the family's way of celebrating them finds expression in many areas of life in Israeli society—in the atmosphere of the street and of the stores, in the mass communications media, and in the subjects studied in school and kindergarten. These normative expressions exert a pressure on the widow to find a way of celebrating the Sabbath or the holiday in an accepted way.

As a result of this combination of factors, most of the widows found themselves helpless and unable to "make a holiday" in their own homes. Yet the majority saw it as one of their most important commitments to assure their children's participation in these ceremonies. They were therefore constrained to look for partners to share in Sabbath and festival activities for their children's sake, rather than their own. Generally, the holidays and Sabbaths were not good days for the widows in the sample who frequently referred to their occurrence as some kind of misfortune that befell them. The social norms and the prevailing atmosphere on those days only served to emphasize the difference and marginality of the widow and her children.

O. X. (No. 21), for example, reported that: "In our situation (widowhood), all celebrations are actually mourning." And E. M. (No. 32) (who lived in a moshav where it was customary for friends to celebrate holidays together) explained: "Holidays are altogether different (from ordinary days), because then people always gather in families, each family together. Even for me, in my own circle, it's much harder. If I had to look for something (find a way to celebrate) or stay at home—I wouldn't be able to."

According to the widow's own estimate of her ability to create a holiday atmosphere in her home, there was an inverse relationship between the number of children she had and the "size" of the holiday: the "smaller" the holiday and the more children she had, the more she felt herself able to "make a holiday" in her own home, together with her children; whereas the "bigger" the holiday and the fewer children she had, the less she felt herself able to create a holiday atmosphere at home. Among widows who had an only child, many found it difficult to create what was, in their eyes, a "minimum" Sabbath atmosphere, and they tried to find an arrangement whereby they and their children would be able to spend at least part of this day in the company of others. But even widows who had a number of children (three or more) found it difficult to organize a Passover Seder ceremony on the customary festive scale with their children alone.

S. H. (No. 14) who, with her only son, spent every holiday and Sabbath at her mother's home, had this to say on the subject: "I can't give my house a holiday feeling like there is at my mother's. There, when the whole family is around the table and the house is full and everyone is sitting together, it's both a holiday feeling and a family feeling." The description by N. S. (No. 61) exemplifies the difficulties in creating a holiday atmosphere, even for a "small holiday" in a family unit consisting of a mother and an only child: "Once at Shavuoth (the Feast of Weeks—Pentecost), we were just the two of us. At first, I really thought of calling my sister and inviting her, but afterwards I decided it was impossible always to be dependent on others. So I prepared the table with all sorts of things (ceremonial dishes) and the two of us sat and it wasn't much fun, but I tried to sing some songs and. . . ." The inability, objective or subjective, to give their home the special atmosphere of a Sabbath or a holiday lay at the source of the widow's great dependence on others for keeping these occasions in a way which they considered desirable. N. S.'s awareness of the situation as quoted was accentuated by the happy ending to her tale: "I tried to sing some songs, and suddenly the bell rang, and a few of my students came with flowers and fresh fruits to wish us a happy holiday. They joined us at the table, and. . . ."

In the light of the family-related significance attached to the celebration of the holidays, there was an expectation, perhaps even normative pressure—both on the widow and on her relatives—for her to spend the holidays within the kinship framework. A review of the frameworks within which the widows in the sample celebrated the Passover, for example, during the years of their widowhood, revealed a very strong tendency for families to come together to celebrate the holiday. Of the total number of widows in the sample, only twelve did not celebrate this holiday together with their relatives. All the others (fifty-nine) took part in the Passover Seder in the company of relatives of varying degrees of closeness. Among the twelve who did not spend the Eve of Passover with their relatives, one widow and her children celebrated it at a public Passover Feast (these are held in commercial establishments—hotels, restaurants, etc.—with participation paid), three spent the holiday in the company of friends, while nine of the widows, for lack of other possibilities, spent the holiday at home alone with their children. Other holidays also (concerning which no systematic investigation was undertaken) were more often celebrated by the widows and their children in the company of their families than in any other manner.

The availability of an appropriate resource—in this case a kinship network—to a large extent determined the way in which the widow met the problems posed by the Sabbath and holidays. The kinship network itself varied in the kind of relationships that existed within it, in the kind of services it was prepared, or felt obliged, to extend to the widow and her children, and in the price demanded from her for such services. Very often, the kinship network offered to include the widow and her children in Sabbath and holiday activities but it "demanded" in return that the widow and her children make a commitment not to fail to participate in these occasions. (This type of relationship was formed principally when there were others in the kinship network who required help in order to create a festive atmosphere—usually aging parents with no other children or whose other children were far away.) Frequently, in large kinship networks, the widow and her children were assured of participation in holiday events without such an obligation on the widow's part. However, the kinship network did not automatically assure this participation, in which case each holiday and sometimes each Sabbath called afresh for the renewal of "negotiations" between the widow and members of her kinship network concerning her participation on the particular occasion. That is to say that different kinship networks offered different degrees of assurance that there was, in fact, a suitable framework for celebrating the holiday and demanded various forms of "payment" in return for providing such a framework.

Permanent or temporary as the arrangement may have been, the widow was always the one who was invited, and was rarely allowed to play the role of host. On these occasions, whereas in Israeli (Jewish) households there is a great deal more activity going on than at ordinary times, in the widow's home the activity was diminished, and often actually ceased altogether. This was particularly the case in small family units of a mother and an only child. Such family units are easily mobile and are not hard to accommodate as guests. Quite a few widows with one child stayed with relatives for the entire period. In the households of these widows (even more than in those of others), activities were considerably reduced on the eve of a Sabbath or a holiday. The special activity of a household in preparation for the Sabbath or the holiday is an integral part of the festive atmosphere, and the "bigger" the holiday, the more the preparations in readiness for it make themselves felt. While widows who spent most Sabbaths and holidays in the homes of their relatives were indeed relieved of the burdens of preparation, at the same time they lost the sense of belonging and of sharing which was all around them. The lack of a role in the tasks of preparing for the holiday increased the widow's sense of being different and an outsider. The removal of the Sabbath and holiday celebrations away from the household emptied and diminished the home and increased still further the widow's feeling of being dependent and out of place. Many widows described their homes as "a house without a Sabbath or a holiday" or, as I.O. (No. 39) put it: "Once we had a home, and we saw to it that the holidays should be at home. We took care that the 'Festive Board' should be laid and that it should be as beautiful as it's supposed to be. Now, it's really, some-how, finished."

Sabbaths and holidays are times of increased social activity. In many social groups, it is assumed that on these occasions either everyone in the family stays at home and is ready to receive guests, or else they go out with friends without any long-term planning or advance notice. Widows who left their homes for the duration of the holiday, or even for part of it, or who were absent from their homes for many hours on the Sabbath, were dropped almost automatically from the visiting programs of their friends and relatives. As a result, there was a still greater decrease in their social contacts, which in any case tended to dwindle with widowhood, and the process of "emptying" the home was accelerated. Most widows in the sample, but more particularly those who had a regular arrangement for spending holidays and Sabbaths in the homes of relatives, felt that they were "paying" for this by eroding their potential social contacts which, because they were relatively rare, were so important to them. Thus a conflict arose between the widow's desire to retain the arrangements that assured her and her children a pleasant way of spending holidays, and the desire to free herself from the commitment attached to such arrangements. This conflict was expressed mainly when the holiday arrangement limited in some way the widow's freedom to operate in forming social contacts. The comments of A.M. (No. 29) illustrate the problem:

> I remained in (town K) really because of the pressure from my mother-and father-in-law. Then (after the death of the husband-son) it wouldn't have entered my mind that I could leave them . . . the advantage in it is that this way you have a family. They are very attached to the child and I'm attached to them. I have always been attached to them, more or less. At the beginning (when she became a widow), you're very depressed and more attached and dependent on them. And as time goes on, they become more dependent on you, and with you it's the opposite—you want to be free and more independent, and it's a sort of paradoxical situation. . . . For instance, we (the widow and her son) eat lunch there on Sabbath . . . you can't arrive there and tell them that you don't want to come. You have to give at least two weeks' notice in advance that you won't be coming on a particular Sabbath. If it hadn't been a kind of obligation, it would be much pleasanter for me to come. It's really not so convenient . . . especially if someone asks me in the morning (Sabbath morning) if I want to join in something (some Sabbath pastime), then I can't come along on that Sabbath morning and say that I won't be coming for lunch.

Only two of the widows in the sample, neither of whom shared in a joint household arrangement, succeeded in establishing patterns for spending Sabbaths in the company of others without thereby "emptying" their homes or losing their part in the social life of the Sabbath. In addition, alternative arrangements entered into by them changed the position of the widows, moving them from a marginal place in Sabbath events to a central position. These two widows described the arrangements in their families for the main event of the Sabbath and the holidays. Before widowhood, it had been the custom for the family of T.L. (No. 57) to spend the Sabbath Eve at the home of her husband's parents and she described the changed situation: "Usually on Fridays, there's a family visit—I have a sister and she comes to visit me with her family. They are the regular basis, and almost always other friends come and it usually includes supper."

N.S. (No. 61) was also able to change the arrangements for spending the Sabbath and the holidays together with her kinship unit:

> On holidays and Sabbaths everyone comes here. The custom used to be that on Sabbath Eve or on holidays we went to mother's, all of us. Since the war, I said to my mother, "Everyday (I'm ready to come to you), but on the Sabbath to come home at 9:30 when it's already dark, that's impossible." And everyone started coming here. Sometimes twelve, sometimes eighteen—and sometimes we are only eight. They always come, and I prepare (the meal) and it's no problem.

The two widows cited above succeeded, with the help of their relatives, in transferring the "main event" of the Sabbath (and one of them also that of the holidays) to their own homes. This arrangement involved a great deal of work for them and a considerable expense. Such an arrangement was possible only if there was a clear commitment on the widow's part to make it permanent. However, in return, the "emptying" of her home was avoided and the Sabbath and the holidays again became occasions when the widow participated for her own sake and not "only for the children."

With the acceptance of the widow's home as the regular center for such gatherings, it became also a focus of other kinds of social and family visiting. A household in which there is a festive meal every Sabbath Eve (or every holiday) can, with comparative ease, absorb additional guests at these meals. The existence of this permanent arrangement made the regular participants an integral part of the household on holidays and Sabbaths and in this way solved, to a great extent, the problem of entertaining without a partner: the widow and the regular participants in the Sabbath and holiday meals constituted a host team for invited or unexpected guests who were not part of the regular arrangement. In this way the widow remained an integrated part of a network of special family contacts.

The following extracts from the interview with N.T. (No. 63) encapsulate the changes which took place in her household after her husband's death. While no one specific example can represent all the possible changes which may occur, it does give a general picture of the dimension of the changes.

	What are the difficulties in organizing the household?
Lack of partnership and of sharing	It's not so pleasant to be alone, but I can tell you that it isn't difficult. If I had thought about it a few years ago, I wouldn't have imagined that I could

manage, because my husband really helped me a great deal—with everything, in the house, with the children, with everything. But we manage very well—only that it's not pleasant.

The wife's specialized functions: Diminished functions due to change in family life-style.

I always worked, even before I married. I always ran the house while I was working. Now I have much more free time. I don't know how, but it's a fact. First of all, the children got bigger and that changes a lot, it's an important factor. When they were smaller, there was more work with baths and food. And secondly, I hardly cook, one could say not at all. Not that I used to spend such a lot of time in the kitchen even before, but still, I did give it some time.

Altogether, the kind of meals, children's meals—I don't give it the same thought as I used to. Today, most of it is done by the woman who comes (housekeeper). From noon and until I come home, a woman looks after them (the children), and it's the same woman who has been here all the time (even before widowhood). The woman stays until I return at about five.

Due to transfer of tasks to voluntary helper

Generally there is less work and besides my mother helps me. She comes almost every evening. She doesn't stay long, sometimes it's for half an hour, sometimes an hour. She comes and goes. She comes to see (if everything is in order), and at the same time, she does some things also, for instance, the supper.

Do you get help in other things?

In the area of care and supervision of children

A great deal. For instance, I leave the house at seven-thirty (A.M.) with the two bigger children, and there's another small child who has to be taken to the kindergarten. My father does that. My father comes early enough so that the child doesn't stay alone. If I want to go out in the evening, I have a baby-sitter—my big daughter. When she goes out— Grandpa (the widow's father) comes. Besides, I

Cessation and/or renunciation entertainment of guests.

don't entertain guests and before, I used to. Still anyone who comes is welcome, but I don't do everything (connected with official or semi-official entertaining). That's also the reason why pretty soon even those who now invite me will stop. At the beginning (after being widowed) I didn't feel like it, and now—it's no longer that I don't feel like it, it's— I just got out of it. I keep thinking that it's foolish

Dwindling of household tasks on the Sabbath (and apparently also on holidays).

and that this is not the way to keep up relationships with people. But anyhow, at this moment, it gives me free time. There are very few friends who come to me and to whom I go. My Sabbaths are actually even freer. The rest of the time is not much freer. The truth is that even before this, I thought about it—otherwise I would not have been able to tell you at all (discuss the subject)—it seems to me that I have far more time on the Sabbath. Perhaps—then (before widowhood), everything that I didn't manage to do during the week I put off till the Sabbath and now, because I've got time during the week, I'm free on Sabbaths. For example, I go to concerts. I took a subscription to the concerts, something I wouldn't have been prepared to do (before widowhood). I was always so terribly tired. And also gym (gymnastics), that's new (only just begun)—it's one evening a week.

Increased functions and new activities.

Specialized functions of the husband: some are transferred to the widow.

Dependence on others to carry out certain tasks

Apparently it's possible to do everything if one wants to. For instance, I thought that I would never know how to drive, and now I drive. And they are all things of that sort. Of course, if he (the husband) had sat with the child in the evening and explained to him about the stars, it would have been better. But if he isn't told about the stars, he'll learn by himself in a few years. And I'm also not an ignoramus and I can also answer. But naturally, there are some areas where I can't help, especially the boys. Now, I'm terribly dependent on other people. I'm not really dependent as I told you, I manage very well, but there are things that I can't do alone. For instance, what has really changed—if I want to drive somewhere (for amusement or to visit), I'm dependent on someone else. I don't get up and go by myself or with three children.

V

Social Life of War Widows

The study and discussion of the informal social contacts of the individual in modern society stem from different theoretical domains and cover many types of social contacts not organized on an institutional basis (Brain 1976; Boissevain 1974; Lazarsfeld and Merton 1954; McCall 1970; Mitchell 1969). Characteristically, the individual's network of acquaintances, social connections, and friends changes frequently, and on a voluntary basis. This frequently shifting network of social contacts, a function of the social, geographical, and occupational mobility which typify modern society, may serve to weaken, strengthen, or sever the different kinds of contact. At the same time, the different social frameworks within which the individual fulfills various roles do not necessarily overlap, and this allows for a high degree of freedom in choosing social contacts. Within each individual's general set of contacts there is a wide range of types, varying in degrees of closeness, structure, and organization; some contacts are mainly instrumental and partial in nature, while others may be more general and diffuse. But whatever their specific composition, the totality of all these contacts gives the individual a feeling of belonging and of social support, as well as a framework for self-expression. At the same time, they constitute an important source of information and of social approval upon which one can base the criteria for testing one's own opinions and attitudes regarding many aspects of daily life (McCall & Simmons 1966). The main characteristics of friendship contacts of different kinds are their voluntary nature, the free choice of those participating in them, and the freedom to enter such relationships and to leave them without incurring social sanctions (Suttles 1970). These characteristics mirror the value stress in modern society upon individualism, self-expression, and freedom of choice. The level on which these values are expressed differs from one type of social contact to another, but ideally it is the friendship relationship which most fully corresponds to these values (Cohen 1961). Informal social contacts (on different levels of closeness) are considered a basic human need, and

112

the lack of such informal contacts is considered to be the cause of one of the maladies of modern societies, namely, social alienation.

Where the point of departure of discussion and research is social expression of values like individualism, self-expression, and freedom of choice, it is not surprising that the most common unit of analysis in dealing with social contacts or friendship relationships is the individual. As a result, certain areas of research into this type of contact which are relevant to the subject we are dealing with have received little attention:

1. Sociological discussion of and research into the place of the individual in different social settings has been largely male-oriented (Acker 1973). Not surprisingly, therefore, much of our knowledge on informal relationships is derived from studies focused on males and only in a small minority of cases on females, and even then, only on the limited aspect of the social contacts of married women. Still less knowledge has been accumulated on the subject of social relationships and the place of unmarried women in various social contexts.[1] In the last few years, however, the increasing interest in the social place of women brought with it a not inconsiderable body of research pointing to the differences in the pattern of participation of men and women in various areas of life, including those where the variable of sex was not considered relevant. These studies show the limitations in the analogies that can be drawn between the findings concerning male samples and the situation of women in the same areas (Safilios-Rothschild 1972).

2. Research findings show that certain social groupings are made up of social contacts among family units (the couple usually participating as a unit in the grouping), rather than of social contacts between individuals. Yet very few studies deal with the social contacts and/or social life of the family as a unit. As a result, little is known about the structure and content of this type of social contact and the way in which it is initiated and develops.[2]

3. Significant life changes—for instance, those resulting from geographical and occupational mobility—affect social life, too (Boissevain 1974). Changes occur not only in the overall set of social contacts, but also in the composition and structure of the social network (Litwak & Szelenyi 1969). The impact of family life-cycle events, such as marriage and the birth of children, on friendship networks and social contacts has, however, been the focus of little study. The importance of this subject is frequently raised in discussion of the process of family break-up, whether caused by divorce or death. Most studies in divorce or widowhood do deal, to some extent, with the changes wrought by these events in the friendship

networks of those involved in them, but even in this area, the number of systematic studies is very limited (Cain 1974; Goode 1956; Hart 1976; Lopata 1969, 1973B, 1979; Miller 1970). Little is known, either, about the way in which new contacts, if any, are created for those people who are defined as "formerly married" (Hunt 1966).

In general, we know that at least part of the social life of married people tends to take place with other family units, and each individual participates as a member of his particular unit. The set of social contacts thus forged is built, to a great extent, on those contacts formed by the husband in the course of his life outside the family (work, political activities, and so on); only a minority of them stem from the activities of the wife outside the household (Babchuk & Bates 1963). This is especially the case where most of the functions of the woman/wife are connected with keeping house and rearing children, with very few activities outside the family. Social contacts generally, and social contacts between couples in particular, tend to exist between people who, according to relevant criteria, are similar or equal (Paine 1969; Suttles 1970). According to this general trend, women tend to maintain their sole social contacts with other women in the same neighborhood (Whyte 1956). This tendency is particularly pronounced among women who are housewives. In a situation of family break-up (resulting from divorce), husband and wife engage in a process of dividing their "social property." However, just as their other assets may not be equally split, so too the "social property" is not necessarily equally divided. The break-up of the family, whether by divorce or death, brings with it a loss of part of the social property acquired by the family, and this part ceases to be available to either partner, or, in the case of death, to the surviving partner. Thus, changes in the social contacts of a person as a result of losing a spouse are to be expected.

Changes in the Social Network

There is no way of understanding the rapid changes of social contacts following widowhood without taking into account the customs derived from religious codes of behavior and their influence on the mourners and their friends. War widows, like other mourners, are influenced by the restrictions concerning the mourning period. In order to understand the inner dynamics of the changes in the social contacts of war widows, the influence of the restrictions concerning the mourning period should be stressed and clarified.

Engaging in social relationships and pursuing a social life are generally conceived as pleasurable and entertaining activities, and therefore participation in them, and to some extent the enjoyment of social contacts of any kind, is considered to be unsuitable for a person in mourning. Jewish tradition recognizes three periods of mourning— the "shiv'a" (the first week after the funeral), the "shlosheem" (the first month after the funeral), and the "shana" (the first year after the death). Each of these periods calls for a different kind of expression of mourning, and the customs attached to them differ from one social group to another (Spiro 1967). The absence of clear social norms to dictate suitable behavior is again evident in this sphere, as in so many others already discussed. Furthermore, there is no agreement as to whether behavior befitting widows in general is seemly for a war widow. For these reasons, the widow's participation per se in social life, and how and when her participation is socially acceptable, are very often questions which cause inner conflict for the widow herself and tension between her and those around her. The confusion caused by this lack of normative clarity evidently prompted this response to the Readers' Letters section in Mrs. Bavly's Column, "Manners and Customs," which appeared in the daily newspaper *Ha'aretz* on March 17th, 1968:

> I am astonished by the behavior of my friend whose husband, not long ago, was killed while on active service. She began to appear in public, went to the theater, dressed and made up in the latest fashions, even before the "shlosheem" was over. I remarked on this and her reply was that her emotional stress is so great that she tries to avoid sitting at home alone with her thoughts, fearing a mental collapse. Should I agree with her and help her along these lines?

Mrs. Bavly's reply reflects an acknowledgement that, in the area of "manners and customs," there are no clear rules of behavior befitting a widow in the first months of her widowhood. Mrs. Bavly had recourse to the very general principle of what is in the "public interest." Her response was as follows: "To my mind, we have no right to dictate to anyone how he should behave or how to react to what happens to him, as long as his behavior does not go against the public interest; and your acquaintance is not harming anyone."

As part of the outward expression of their mourning, many widows refrained from appearing in public, participating in various kinds of commercial entertainment (movies, nightclubs, and so on), or even in informal social gatherings considered as happy occasions (parties, for instance). Other widows were excluded from social contacts of this sort on the assumption that it was "not nice" to invite them out during their mourning period. A few widows tried, with varying degrees of success, to break away from the social fetters which bound them.[3] In all cases, however, the prewidowhood pattern of social life ceased, either by or against their own volition, and their participation in social life became limited to those areas relating to the condition of widowhood.

The widow's exit, or her exclusion, from her set of social contacts for a period of time, from a few weeks to a year or more, caused considerable damage to those contacts and to her social life. Her renewed participation in them after an interruption usually occurred under conditions which differed, at least in part, from those which obtained before her widowhood, and the form of her renewed participation was, therefore, also different.

In the course of the interviews, some three years after the sample group had been widowed, most of the widows reported significant changes in their social life and in the type, content, quantity, and quality of their relationships. A comparison with the past was an integral component of the widows' own evaluation of their social contacts in the present. Following the widows' own train of thought, the ensuing discussion will deal first with prewidowhood social relations and the changes which occurred in them after widowhood, and second, with the creation of new social relationships.

The widows' accounts of their prewidowhood social life pointed to considerable variation with regard to the kinds of social contact they had established. The source, extent and density of their former social networks, as well as the place of the couple within them, were evidently closely related to the general accumulation of roles and to the life-style which each family had maintained before the husband's death. From the widows' descriptions, it was evident that their social life had revolved both around "social events" and gatherings, and around social activities with friends. The friends were usually classified by the widows themselves according to the degree of intimacy in the relationship; generally, they were either "acquaintances," "friends," or "close friends." In addition, social contacts were often maintained with a "group." These main types of social contacts will be discussed in turn. They differed from one another in the extent to which they were institutionalized and structured, in the number of people included in each category, the aspects of life they covered, and the content and level of personal involvement demanded in them. Most of the women did not maintain all types of contact; all had acquaintances, many had friends, but only a minority had more than one of the remaining types of contact.[4]

SOCIAL EVENTS AND SOCIAL GATHERINGS

These were generally characterized as "social obligations" and very often arose from the husband's political or occupational role. They included social occasions to which women were also invited, such as a festive gathering of high army officers, a picnic for factory workers and their families, a reunion or a graduation ceremony held by the husband's class at university, or a reception in honor of a friend's promotion at work. To a certain extent, participation in the celebration of events like the wedding or birthday of an important public figure would also be included in this type of occasion. Being invited to such events was a token of belonging to an exclusive social circle, and accepting the invitation was part of the obligation that devolved upon a member of the circle. Events of this kind always conferred prestige on those who participated, although its level might differ according to the prestige of the circle invited. Even in cases where both spouses had connections which generated invitations to social events—through their work, political activities, membership in voluntary organizations, and so forth—the social events deriving from the husband's activities generally commanded higher prestige, since his status was usually higher than that of his wife. Such social events facilitated the renewal of social contacts which, for one reason or another, had been broken, as well as the strengthening of existing contacts and creation of new ones. In certain ways, these gatherings offered a relaxed ambience for informal negotiations of various matters which would otherwise have had to be negotiated through more formal channels. They also afforded an opportunity to acquire up-to-date, and often confidential, information which could not be obtained in other ways. Some of the widows in the sample had often participated in social events of this sort, and they formed an integral part of the couple's social life. Others had participated in such events rarely, if at all. As the husband's occupation was the key for entry to these kinds of event, after his death the widow's access to them was almost totally cut off. Where the events or gatherings were clearly related to the husband's work (for example, a party for project or factory workers), invitations ceased immediately upon her being widowed and were never renewed. Most widows expected that this would be the case, and found that they could accept it. However, they found it harder to come to terms with the fact that even invitations to events and gatherings that had no connection with their husbands' occupation ceased immediately after they were widowed, and were only rarely renewed after the year of mourning. T.L. (No. 57) recalled: "As it was before, it can't be now. Most of the meetings (social gatherings) we had before, almost all—80 percent— were through my husband." These kinds of gathering figure prominently in the lives of Permanent Army personnel. Participation of wives in these gatherings, and sometimes of children as well, is a measure of compensation for the protracted periods of absence of the husband-father from the home. Being cut off from this type of contact created a great gap in the widow's social life. N.I. (No. 23), the widow of a Permanent Army man, said: "I miss it a lot. I was so much a part of the army—it was my family."

To some extent, these events and gatherings were replaced by social events and gatherings related directly to the state of widowhood. In the first years of widowhood, the war widows were invited to public events connected, directly or indirectly, with war. These were generally military memorial ceremonies, like the military exhibition of August 1968, in which the first evening was dedicated to "The Thousands of Families of The Fallen and War Invalids." It was not uncommon for war widows, especially those whose husbands had been high-ranking Permanent Army officers, to be invited as honored guests to events of this type. For example, at the beginning of 1968, a party took place at the Officers' Club of the Southern Command to celebrate the publication of the Album of the Six-Day War. "The General of the Southern Command, General Yeshiyahu Gavish, gave an inscribed copy of the Album to each of the officers at the party. The first Album was given to Mrs. Aliza Alton, the widow of Colonel Shlomo Alton, who was killed in action in the Gaza Strip. She sat on the General's left, at the head of the table" (*Ha'aretz*, September 18, 1968). Initially, war widows were invited to all the memorial ceremonies held by the battalions in which their husbands had served, as well as to State ceremonies marking Memorial Day and Independence Day. However, within five years of becoming widows, many of them had been dropped from the invitation list to State affairs, particularly to the more prestigious ones. In most cases, the social events to which they did receive invitations were related to ceremonies in memory of those battles in which their husbands had fought. On occasion, they and their children were invited to social events organized especially for them, such as parties on religious holidays organized by voluntary religious groups, or collective birthday and bar mitzvah parties for war orphans.[5] However, these types of social event, organized solely for war widows and their children, carried little prestige. Those who had been accustomed to attend more prestigious social events avoided participating in them, or did so only when the former were completely closed to them. War widows whose social life in the past had not included many social events were the ones who tended to participate in those events organized especially for them. There they sometimes met people whom they considered to be important or influential. However, many widows were loath to exploit these contacts, even though they were often given telephone numbers and visiting cards and encouraged to make contact if help was needed. Whether for practical reasons or for reasons of prestige, most of the widows who had previously participated in "social events" felt that they had suffered a serious loss in being deprived of access to this part of their social network.

THE GROUP

This was the term used to describe a permanent, fairly structured and organized social group to which the women had belonged before they became widows. The group usually crystallized around a few couples that formed its nucleus and directed its regular routine of social activities. Intermittent or temporary participation in a group of this kind by persons not belonging to it was always possible, and the permanent members could bring a guest to one activity or another. The activities of such a group consisted of entertainment and leisure-time projects, particularly the types of activity mostly pursued on weekends and holidays, or in the evening. The group's cohesiveness was usually attributable to their common enjoyment of a particular activity, often playing cards, or going to movies or to other places of entertainment, or going on picnics, swimming, etc. In most cases, the group also gathered regularly to spend time together in the home of one or another member, sometimes according to a fixed sequence of hosts, and sometimes by a less routinized, ad hoc arrangement. The practical arrangements for group activities were also divided (although not always equally) among the permanent members (buying movie tickets, organizing transportation for those without cars, organizing food for picnics, and so on). The group usually developed a sort of routine as to times and places of meeting and/or techniques for passing information on planned activities and on the various members' roles in preparing them. Only those considered "full members" of the group were included in this communication and preparation network. In addition to the regular activities of the group, its members joined in the family celebrations of other members and in special festivities, such as New Year or Hanukkah (Festival of Lights) parties given by one of the members. Within the group, there were members who had closer mutual contacts and others whose contacts were limited to group activities. There was only partial overlapping between members of the group and each member's circle of close friends and acquaintances. A member often had close friends who were not members of the group, nor were all the group members his close friends.

The socially accepted norm proscribing participation in entertainment and leisure-time activities in public automatically prevented the widow's continuing involvement in the group. The kinds of activity it pursued were out-of-bounds for her during the period when she defined herself, or was defined by others, as a mourner. In most cases the group did not offer to include her, nor did she ask to go with them to the movies, on trips, or on picnics. During the "shiv'a," and sometimes for a few weeks after that, members of the group paid her condolence visits but, after a short time, the contacts between her and the group became attenuated. One or two members of the group might become her friends or close friends, but contact with the others generally ceased.

The process of returning to social activity after the mourning period was usually gradual, and the widow did not, for the most part, return to full participation in the group. Where the widow did reenter the group, however, her place and her participation in it were marginal and usually mediated by those members who had become her friends or close friends. If, for instance, the group went to a movie, the widow was included only if one of these friends took the initiative of asking whether she wanted to participate and saw to it that a ticket was bought for her. Again, if the usual activity of the group took the form of rotating hospitality in the home of one or other of the members, the widow would be invited only if the hosts were her friends or close friends and not otherwise.

A form of screening system operated to determine the suitability of various activities for a widow, and she was not invited to those considered unsuitable. The "reasons," the "standards," and the "screening processes" differed from group to group, so that in different groups different activities were considered unsuitable. For example, in a group where the norm was that "you only go to a discotheque in couples," a widow who had no partner (temporary or permanent) was not asked to participate. Sometimes, the lack of knowledge as to what the norm was and what behavior was called for was the reason for excluding the widow. The common activity in one of the groups was an outing to a restaurant on a "dutch treat" basis (that each couple should pay for itself). Members of such a group, aware of the position in which the widow would be placed by this arrangement, did not know how to handle it. The members would usually have been willing to pay for her meal, but this would have created an awkward situation. It was equally unpleasant to let her know that each couple was paying its bill separately, for then she would have been the only woman to be paying a bill. So it was preferable to avoid unpleasantness and simply not invite her. Sometimes the widow would be invited by members who were her close friends and, on leaving the restaurant, her meal would be on their bill. But here, again, her participation in the group was by courtesy of her friends, rather than in her own right.

The screening process also manifested itself in other areas of the group's activities, such as those dependent on technical facilities and arrangements—going to the sea meant that friends or close friends must find a place for her in a car (if she had none), and the driver must be willing to fetch her and take her back home. If the arrangements did not work out, the widow was dropped from this activity. Not all the widows in the sample were members of a group of this kind before they were widowed. Of those that were, only a few returned to the group after the mourning period. In some cases, particularly where the group was very small, the loss of one couple destroyed the group as a whole, so that there remained no group for the widow to return to had she wanted to do so. In other cases, where it did continue to exist, the gap which had formed between the group and the widow was so great that there was no way of bridging it. Even in those cases where the group continued, retained contact with the widow, and tried to draw her back into it after her mourning period, her position remained marginal and her activity only partial.

The following are some of the descriptions the widows gave of the contact they had with their groups before and after being widowed:

As is usually the case in Israel, there is always some kind of group and you always find yourself with more or less the same people. So we also had a group like this. But of course the majority was made up of my husband's work contacts—his co-workers. I simply don't see them any more, except for one or two. (T.B., No. 2)

The moment I met my husband, I met his group as well. They were his friends—quite a big group—and we always went out together, spent time together, met often—until the day he was killed. Since that day, there is no friendship and no group. (I.H., No. 13)

We had quite a big circle (group). We used to meet every Friday at somebody's house, and the relationships among us were such that, even if I did not see one of them for a few weeks, the contact was still kept. This friendship didn't begin here—we went through the concentration camps together, through the ghettos, through the displaced persons camps in Germany. We went the whole way together. With one of the couples we got a flat in (city T.) when we arrived as new immigrants. After that, we brought the others here to live, because this is where we were. Others who were our friends also came from the old country. So, that's the way it is with friends. I have one friend who has children. Her daughter has a boyfriend. When her daughter and her boyfriend go along, obviously they don't take me too. It's the same with other friends of mine, a couple—the same situation. There are five seats in the car; if there is a vacant seat, they take me along. We had many friends, and I have friends. But friendship is a good thing under good conditions, under normal conditions. When you can invite them, then they invite you. So I'm telling you—the way it used to be on Fridays, even now they come to me—but much, much less. (B.C., No. 7)

Two of these quoted passages typify the way in which widows experienced severance from the group, and require no explanation. The third quotation clearly expresses the ambivalence of the widow towards the group: on the one hand, she felt deeply anchored ("this friendship didn't begin here . . . we went the whole way together . . . we brought the others here"); on the other hand, the widow could not but see, and give expression to, her marginality in the group. With considerable insight and rationality, another of the widows in the sample realized just how unequal her position in the group was:

> I have very good friends—to be more exact, one good friend. I see her quite often. Whenever she has guests on Friday night, she lets me know and invites me. I go. And it is perfectly obvious that I am out of it, because this is a group which meets also in various other places. I am her "case." Everyone has his case and I am hers. I know she has the best intentions and I never say anything to her about it—she's really a good friend. She can't say to her other friends, "invite her too," and I'm sure it never even entered her mind. (T.N., No. 35)

CLOSE FRIENDS

The widows used this term to describe people whose relationship to them was informal and very close. The level of intimacy here was higher than that in any other social relationship, many more areas were touched upon, and the relationship itself was more far-reaching, intensive, and enduring in character. Close friendships usually demanded mutual trust, openness, freedom in exchanging information, concern for each other's interests, and readiness for mutual help. The nature of the many different elements in a relationship between close friends depended upon the needs of both the parties, but a high degree of involvement, emotional and practical, was always expected. Close friends were expected to help in a crisis and to participate in family joys and sorrows.[6] The way in which a close friendship was maintained changed according to the circumstances of those participating in the contact. Sometimes it was maintained through frequent meetings or through correspondence, and sometimes by meetings especially planned in order to surmount the problem of geographical distance (Litwak & Szelenyi 1969). Most of the widows in the sample reported that friends of the family were initially the husband's friends. Through him, they also became friendly with the wife.[7] In a fair number of cases, the common friendship was established by husband and wife together (at parties, vacations, outings, etc.) meeting people who in time became their friends. Only in a small number of cases did the wife's friends, mainly from before her marriage, become friends of the family.

Most of the close family friends were married—of all the widows in the sample, only three had maintained close friendship relationships with unmarried people (men or women) before their widowhood.[8]

Irrespective of the source of the relationships, three types of friendship were maintained by each family: close friendships between the husband and his friends, close friendships between the wife and her friends, and close friendships between the couple and other couples. The separate close friendship contacts the husband and wife each had tended to be unisexual, the wife having female, and the husband male, close friends, although there were exceptions to this pattern (Booth 1972).

Close friendship between the husband and his friends. The wife's level of involvement in this type of friendship was different in every case. Generally, her position was that of "the wife of a close friend," and not that of a close friend in her own right. In extreme cases, the widow met the close friend of her late husband for the first time when he came to pay her a condolence visit. With the relationship as tenuous as this, most of these contacts were broken immediately after she became a widow. Even in those cases where the contact was not completely cut off, it continued only in a sporadic and superficial way, exemplified by the opening sentence of Baruch Nadel's article, "The War Widow" (*Yediot Aharonot*, May 5, 1968): "As about ten months had passed since we buried Colonel A., I thought that I ought to go and visit his widow again." Only very rarely did a widow report that the close friend of her husband subsequently became her close friend.

Close friendship between the wife and her friends. Before widowhood, this type of relationship was clearly limited and organized so that meetings between the women did not hinder or clash with the social relationships and arrangements of the family. The women usually met either in the mornings, when the husbands were not at home, or during working hours if the women had the same place of work, or in the course of activities together while caring for the children. This type of relationship generally continued after the death of the husband, and it was not uncommon for the content of the relationship and the types of activity together to increase—the widow and her children were often invited to take part in the leisure-time activities of her friend's family. The friend's husband was willing to accept such functions as advising and giving technical help in the widow's household problems. Sometimes she was invited to join the friend and her husband at a movie or a theater. Nonetheless, the center of the relationship usually remained between the two women and did not develop into a triad; the widow's relationship with her friend's husband continued to be peripheral.

The quartet friendship relationship. This type of relationship was usually described as a relationship where each of the participants was considered a close friend of each of the others. From the descriptions given by the widows, it appears that it was considered desirable to try to develop every friendship into a "quartet" friendship. The quartet friendship was formed when it was possible to evoke enough positive mutual sentiment in those spouses who had not been part of the original friendship relationship. Lack of this sentiment frequently caused the original relationship to be destroyed. However, the kinds of activities and contacts described indicate that, in some cases, what they were talking about was two subsystems: the two women maintained a close friendship relationship, and the husbands likewise. Each subsystem mutually encouraged the other in their close friendship, and the quartet functioned as a unit when a given activity required the participation of all four people (Babchuk 1965). But even in such cases, the self-image of the quartet was that everyone was a close friend of all the others.

After the death of one of the husbands, the quartet relationship could develop into one of two forms: in the first, the relationship between the two women became the center of the friendship and the husband remained on the periphery; in the second, a triad, or triangular relationship, was formed in which the widow was a close friend of each of the spouses. The first form is, in many ways, similar to the continuing friendship between the two women, as described above, but with one important difference: the continuing friendship relationship between the two women was based on a pattern and techniques which were formed before widowhood, while the transfer of the core of the friendship from the two-couples relationship to the two-women relationship required the creation of new patterns and techniques to maintain it. In this situation, the content of the relationship was usually dominated by "feminine" interests, such as spending time together while looking after children, shopping together, or meeting in the afternoons at a cafe with women only. When the widow was invited to take part in activities in which her friends—the couple—participated, this was usually a family activity which included the children, both hers and those of the couple. In this type of relationship, the widow dropped out of the adult social activities in which she and her late husband had previously participated together with the other couple.

Descriptions given by the widows illustrate the changes in the content of the friendship relationship, and the techniques developed to maintain the contact after they were widowed:

> Now it is quite different; it goes on during the day, because they (the friends) have children and I have a child too. So this is the way we

see each other (through contacts centered on the children) and remain in touch. . . . I really enjoy having my friends who have children around me. The way it happened was that I became friendly—not because of the children, but because I became friends with them, and since it turned out that they have children, it is even better. (T.B., No. 2)

I have close friends where the husbands don't like the movies. So I go with the woman and there is no problem. (I.O., No. 39)

We used to meet more in the evenings—just the grown-ups. Now, I meet them often, but mostly with the children. (C.H., No. 16)

When the quartet had originally included two subsystems of unisexual friendships, the tendency later was for the relationship between the two women to develop further, and for the man to exclude himself from it. The general framework of the relationship accordingly broke up. The following quotation was typical of many widows who recognized the inevitability of this process and felt the deprivation keenly: "Let's say a man comes to visit—what would we talk about? I understand them (the men who ceased social contacts with her).There's nothing to say, and I miss it a lot" (N.I., No. 23). When the quartet relationship dwindled to a dyad between two women, its importance for the married couple, vis-a-vis other friendships, also diminished. As far as the couple—or the wife—was concerned, this relationship became comparatively marginal, and so was their investment in the relationship. To the widow, however, this relationship still retained its importance, and accordingly she was prepared to invest in it far more than was the other woman (Boissevain 1974, Chapts. 2 & 4).

The second form into which the quartet relationship could develop was that of the triad. In this form, all three remaining participants, who in the past had been part of the quartet, continued to maintain a close friendship. This type of relationship was found to present considerable problems, and only by a great deal of sensitivity, awareness, and careful handling on the part of all three was it possible to maintain the triadic relationship for any length of time. The transition from quartet to triad brings about a disturbance in the inner balance of the system of relationships. The shift in this balance is the factor which makes it so difficult to maintain the triadic relationship for a long time. This shift stems from three sources—the number of participants, their sex, and their status. In a triadic relationship, every disagreement among the participants creates a situation in which one of them is "odd one out;" and every alliance between any two of the participants constitutes an exclusion of the third one. This happens in any close contact of three people.[9] The triadic relationship between the widow and the "friendship couple" was bound to be even more delicate owing to its specific structure. The spouses were bound by a primary obligatory tie by virtue of the marriage relationship. In so far as this tie expressed itself in the friendship relationship, the triad consisted, in fact, of two separate units—one composed of a couple and the other of an individual. Because of the constant alliance between the spouses, the widow found herself external, or marginal, to the contact, or excluded from it more frequently than did either of the other two participants. This situation was often described by the widows in the many variations they employed of the expression "fifth wheel to the wagon," which indicated that they felt themselves an unnecessary "appendage" to an existing set of relationships. Even when the friendship-couple participated in the contacts with the widow as individuals and not as a couple, there were nevertheless difficulties in balancing the relationship. As previously stated, a close friendship relationship is characterized by trust, openness, free exchange of information, and concern for each other's interests. Basically, these are also the characteristics expected in the relationship between husband and wife (Lopata 1979, chapt. 6). As long as these relationships existed within the framework of the quartet, it was possible to maintain a balance. The level of close friendship between the wife in one couple and the husband in the other was balanced by a similar level of close friendship between the two others making up the quartet. The social norms that apply to the rights and obligations of marriage supported the convention that such a relationship would not go beyond that of friendship (a convention honored as much in the breach as in the observance). When the set of relationships changed from a quartet to a triad, this balance was destroyed, and the close contact of the widow with one of the spouses inevitably caused the remaining spouse to become external to the system. When the main contact was between the widow and the woman of the couple, the husband would, with time, drop out of the relationship, and it would be limited to a close friendship between the two women. Where the main focus of the relationship was between the widow and the man of the couple, and if the mutual trust and closeness between them exceeded a certain level, the wife was liable to feel hurt or threatened in her marriage.

According to the widows' accounts, even where there was no change in the pattern of the actual relationship from the prewidowhood to the postwidowhood period, the change in her family status placed the widow in the role of a threatening factor in the life of her friends. The social image of "the eternal triangle" (as it appears in stories, folklore, and jokes), and the popularized psychological and psycho-analytical interpretations of betrayal in family life, as well as the social-moral norms concerning the uniqueness of the relationship between husband and wife, contribute in no small degree to the image of a widow as a threat to the family life of her married friends.[10] The widows themselves were well aware of the social image of "the eternal triangle," and most of them accepted the social-moral norms which apply to married life. As a result, most were careful that their close friendship relationships with married couples should not go beyond what was "permissible" and "accepted." Many of them went along with the popular notion that an unmarried woman endangers the marriage of her friends and close friends, and a good number of them believed that it was in fact in their power to do so. One of the widows in the sample (S.E., No. 17) summed up the relationship with married close friends in a sort of general caveat to widows: "You are alone and you must learn to accept the fact that you are alone. You must not get too close to a married couple for fear that you will destroy something there—without your ever knowing it."

The avoidance of such unacceptable relationships with married close friends did not stem from altruistic motives alone; it lay no less in self-interest than in moral considerations. In most cases in which the type of relationship between the widow and the husband in the friendship-couple deviated from the accepted relationship, or even when there was only a suspicion of any such deviation, the result for the widow was the loss of both of these friends. Quite a number of widows in the sample reported the loss of friends as a result of the wife's suspicion (whether founded or unfounded) that her husband was courting the widow, or that the widow was chasing him. Once a widow was labelled a "husband snatcher," even those close friendships where there was no suspicion of any exceptionable relationship with her were endangered, and married couples (especially the wives) would be wary in their contacts with her. Of all the widows' social contacts and relationships, a close friendship with a couple was far more rare than either a temporary lover or a passing affair. This is why the widow often felt that a "romance" was not worth the sacrifice of an enduring friendship. This kind of consideration was what motivated many widows to avoid becoming involved in contacts or in activities which might raise suspicion or gossip.

The description by S.E. (No. 17) illustrates very clearly the weakness of the widow in her friendship relationships with married couples.

There was nothing between me and the husband, except very real and deep friendship with both him and his wife. They were my best friends and they helped me—it's impossible to describe how much. He was a very good friend of my husband and all that. One day he came to me and said, "I'm going to divorce my wife and I want to marry you—you are everything I've dreamt of all my life." I said to him, "Tell me, do you know what you are doing to me? If you want to divorce your wife, go ahead and divorce her, but don't get me mixed up in it. You want a divorce—get a divorce, but don't get two things mixed up together. You know that I am constantly under social scrutiny and a sort of social pressure. They will say that I am a widow who gets every man into her bed, who destroys families. And in such a small and closed society, it's a terrible thing." I told him, "Go home. You ought to know that you have a nice wife and two children, and if you weren't such a good friend of mine, I wouldn't have talked to you at all. But I am a mature woman and you are a very good friend, and I have to tell you." Anyway, he went home and told his wife he was leaving and she, of course, asked if there was another woman, and he said, "Yes, I love S. She hasn't talked to me about it (the relationship), but it's already a year that I have been thinking about it." It was obvious that his wife didn't believe him. She came here and caused a big scandal. All the neighbors heard, and they stopped speaking to me—it's easy for people to think ill of you. It became a general social scandal and all the friends knew about it. I let her scream, because she was my friend, and then I said to her. "Ask him what I told him—whether I opened the door of my house to him, or whether there was anything between us. I don't know what is happening." He also told her there had been nothing between us. Then, apparently, she understood that that was the truth; but she found it very hard to swallow, because it meant that he did not want her. It was easier for her to say that I dragged him into my bed and took him away from her. Of course, he remained at home. And she went around telling everyone that it's easy for her to forgive him and take him back, because I am a whore. So the whole city decided that I am a whore and people stopped greeting me in the street and I kept quiet—I wasn't going to defend myself. Anyway, what could I do—go out in the streets and scream? In any case, two months after it all happened, my third floor neighbor came down and said, "I've come to apologize. I should have apologized two months ago. We know you are not the one to blame, and it's simply an ugly and sick society." I said, "Thank you—but go home, so that your wife shouldn't say that I'm trying to get you now." In the gossip circles of the city, they already had something to talk about—about the war widow with two children who wanted a ready-made university lecturer. Obviously, with this couple I cut off all connection. But with the rest of the group (the neighbors were part of the group)—well, they began slowly recognizing me again, greeting me again and other things of this sort. But as for friendship—there was certainly no question of that.[11]

From this description it is clear that, as a result of all the social accusations, judgments, and sanctions levelled against her, the widow lost many of her social contacts. We may assume that the fact that the husband remained with his wife was accepted as repentance on his part and a return to the social norms. The couple as such, and even the husband himself, did not suffer social sanctions to any great extent, and most of the damage caused by the incident was borne by the widow.

Of course, not all the quartet relationships which became triad relationships passed through such severe crises as this. However, in all the cases, there was a definite awareness of the change in the inner balance of the relationship. As a result, the qualities of relaxation, openness, and trust which had characterized them were marred, as the participants in the relationship became more suspicious and more cautious in their contacts with one another. These strains and tensions made some of the widows give up at least in part, if not entirely, their contacts with friendship-couples. In several cases, the widows reported that it was the friends who had cut off the relationship, and the likelihood is that this had resulted from similar feelings of unease on the part of the friends. C.H. (No. 16), for instance, said: "There are many (close friends) who broke off the relationship altogether. There are some where I broke it and it is 100 percent my fault. But I did it knowingly, intentionally. It was uncomfortable with them—it was just uncomfortable to sit with them for a whole evening." K.B. (No. 46) made it clear that, in her case, the initiative came from her when she described her reactions to invitations from married friends: "They treated me with a lot of consideration. But for me it's a bit difficult—I just can't. Sometimes I go, and sometimes I say I have other things to do—all kinds of things. It depends on how I feel. It's awkward and unpleasant for me to go and see them." In this type of situation, every superfluous word, a remark out of place, a change in behavior, was interpreted by the widow as a sign of rejection. O.X. (No. 21) described how a remark considered by her to be offensive broke up a long-standing friendship:

> I had a very good friend. I used to go to her house and I felt as good there as she did in mine. So one day she says to me, "You know, I have an uneasy feeling that maybe it's painful to you that mine (my husband) came back and yours (your husband) didn't." And that broke me completely and that was enough for me. I said nothing to her—I just left. But it hurt me terribly, because it shouldn't have happened. They were our friends—really close friends.

In the light of the structural fragility of the triadic relationship, it is not surprising that no widow reported having more than one or two friendships of this kind. Since the number was so limited, the few they had were in danger of being overloaded with expectations, demands, and dependency on the part of the widows. The widows themselves were aware of this danger and tried to guard against it, as may be seen from the description by B.C. (No. 7):

"Here, in this street, I have two friends where I can go and sit, even in a housecoat. But—and not only once—I left my house, went down the stairs, and when I got down, I decided to go back home quickly. I suddenly remembered that I'd been there the day before and perhaps they didn't need me there again. And this in spite of the fact that, as I told you, we are very close friends. Sometimes there is a feeling that even to them you can't go every day.

The life-span of a triad relationship which originated in a quartet relationship was in most cases short, and many of them were already dissolved when this study took place. Some of the past triads dissolved apparently because the friendship-couple were fearful of such a relationship, or perhaps did not wish to carry the heavy load put upon them as "the only friends" of the widow.

FRIENDS

This term was applied to people who took part in the social life of the widow's family, but with whom the contact was not as strong or as intimate as between close friends, and who were not members of the group. The types of contact with people defined as "friends" varied from case to case. Often the contact was maintained for its own sake, and the pleasure lay simply in being together ("they are interesting people," "they are amusing," "it's pleasant to be with them"). Widows also described as "friends" people with whom contacts were exclusively limited to a particular activity ("it's nice to go walking with them—they know the country so well," "they enjoy western movies and so do we, so we go together"). The definition "friends" also applied to coworkers with whom there was some contact beyond the work place, as well as to people with whom the relationship was instrumental or based on cooperation engendered by mutual interests ("when I want to buy something, I ask his advice, because he knows about such things," "we prepare for the exams together, because we study well together").

Contacts with friends were flexible, both structurally and in content. Meetings with friends were not usually organized as a matter of routine—they might cease for long periods and then be voluntarily renewed. The content of the relationship might change and be more varied at one time and less so at another. It was not unusual for friendship contacts to become close friendship contacts, and this kind of change would be considered as a welcome development of the relationship. Change in the opposite direction, that is, where a close friendship became only a friendship, was seen as a loss, and was usually accompanied by feelings of disappointment. The widows were aware of the subtle twists and turns in the life of a friendship and noted the different levels of closeness in a relationship, for instance, that a friend might be considered "friend enough" for one thing, but "not enough of a friend" for something else. The mutual obligations that friendship imposed on the participants were also somewhat ambiguous and were usually a matter of negotiation between them. At the same time, however, there was a considerable degree of exchange of services of various kinds within the friendship network, as well as a good deal of mutual help. Friendship did not necessarily imply having a relationship with both spouses and, particularly if the friendship had an instrumental focus, the contacts would take place outside the family and just with one spouse.[12] In cases of this sort, the relationship with the friend was quite clearly limited in time, location, and content ("a friend at work," "a friend in the army reserve service"). When the scope of the relationship was expanded, the tendency was to bring the other spouse into it. As in relationships with close friends so, here too, relationships among friends which exceeded the defined space, time, and content borders were usually among married people. Since contacts with friends were not anchored in a group, they did not provide even the minimum set of rules of behavior of a group, nor its norms which would have dictated the rights and obligations of its participants (Paine 1969).

Because of the nature of the friendship relationship, it suffered the weaknesses both of the group relationship and of the close friendship relationship, without enjoying the strengths of either. In many cases, contacts with friends were impaired because the activities in which they were anchored were considered, either by the friends or by the widow herself, as unsuitable for a widow or for any unaccompanied woman. This was particularly so when, in the past, the contacts had involved going out to places of entertainment, or joint activities planned for couples. Where the husband had been the focus of the contacts with friends (for instance, when the activities together usually centered on the hobby of the two husbands), the contacts became irrelevant and broke down very soon after the woman was widowed. But even where the husband had not been the center and where the contacts had not come to a complete halt, they retained mainly their instrumental character and significance in the new situation. Thus, work or study colleagues would often maintain contact with the widow within this framework without expanding either the activities in common or the content of the relationship. The uneasiness of the triad situation was often the barrier which prevented the relationship from developing into a close friendship. The most vulnerable of all the contacts with friends were those based on the expectation of mutually derived benefits. In most cases, rightly or wrongly, the widow was not considered to be a worthwhile partner in this type of contact, and it was accordingly broken. From the widows' reports, it appears that there was a definite tendency for "friends" to break off the contact with the widow immediately, or shortly after, she was widowed. Whether by past experience or by a kind of "foresight," in all probability the friends realized the difficulties that would beset friendship with the widow, and many decided to avoid problems by breaking off the relationship while the level of involvement was still low. The fact that these contacts did not take place within a group framework ensured that breaking them, sometimes even in an insensitive manner, would not evoke social criticism or sanctions. In the following descriptions, widows recalled the behavior of their "friends" after they were widowed:

> All those who had been our friends stayed our friends until he fell in the war. The moment he was killed, no one knew me any more. (I.H., No. 13)
> All those I had contact with in the past—almost all of them—I don't see them any more. At the beginning, I asked why they don't come, and everyone had an excuse—busy, can't manage it, children, don't feel well—there was always some pretext, and that's how the contact broke down. I'm still in touch with some friends, but it's not the same kind of contact as before. (T.E., No. 18)

As noted earlier, there was considerable variation in the type and number of the family's social contacts, even prior to widowhood. Quite a number of the widows had maintained contacts only with "friends" in their married days; in these cases, the vulnerability inherent in this kind of contact caused a marked attenuation in the widow's set of social relationships after the death of her husband, sometimes even to the point of her total isolation:

> We had a wide circle of friends. Now, they see me from a distance and . . . I'm used to it by now and I'm not hurt. Now I just shut my eyes to it. But at the beginning, when I saw them turning and running away . . . (at this point, the widow stopped speaking and began crying bitterly, unable to continue. After a while, she went on): My husband had a friend. They arrived in this country together. He always used to call out to me when he passed in the street. Today, when he sees me on the balcony, he doesn't stop, but drives on. I don't know why. Both he and his wife stopped coming to see me. Only if I bump into them face-to-face in the street and they have no choice, they ask me how I am and how the children are. Nobody comes to me—nobody! (I.C., No. 5)
> There were so many friends, but since the war they see me in the street and turn off into another street. They came during the week of mourning and, after that—finished. No one invites me. If I'm walking in the street, they cross over to the other side. (I.B., No. 45)

I have nothing left of my former contacts. It's quite hard. I
remember how, in the beginning (immediately after she was widowed), I
had nowhere to go but to my sister. (I.B., No. 3)

Even when the thinning out of the social contacts did not reach such
an extreme point, there was nevertheless an attenuation in the relationships and, with time, even the widow's own expectations faded, Z. T.
(No. 69) expressed it this way:

You asked if I have a lot of friends. It's quite a complicated problem with
friends. I think I have friends, but a lot of friends—no. It may be because
our social life before was quite active—even more than that. Not that I
blame anyone, but there is a problem here. At first (after the husband's
death), when you were invited, you didn't feel like going. And then,
when you already feel like going out, you're not invited. So, to tell the
truth, I hardly ever go out. Only when I go to (another town), I go out.
My friends there are closer in this sense. So there are really evenings
when I don't know what to do with myself. Maybe, at our age (she was
thirty-three at the time of the interview), one doesn't have many friends
anyway. (Z.T., No. 69)

But feelings of unease in relationships with friends were apparently not always one-sided. In the same way that some of the
widows had taken the initiative in ending close friendships, a number
of them reported that they themselves were instrumental in breaking
off contacts with friends, particularly with married friends, as described by N.S. (No. 60).

If I tried today to have the same contacts as I once had, it could be
done—it's only for me that life has somehow changed, it's because I
somehow went backwards and not forwards. Today, for me, those
couples can't be my social group. They come to me, but I hardly ever go
to visit them—I don't like visiting them. I don't like just going to visit
people. But maybe it's also because, in some way, I find that I'm very
uncomfortable. Because, for them, everything continues as it was; but,
for me, everything was broken somehow. Maybe that's why I don't keep
up my contacts with them. But I believe that, today, if I really wanted to,
I could bring back all of the relationships—perhaps not exactly as they
were—but I'm the one that made the relationships weaker, and that's
because I was uncomfortable. There was even a period when I was, in a
way, envious that somehow, for them—though it's not a nice thing to
say—everything was fine, and for me, everything was finished.

The widows, like most people, had a wider circle of friends than of
close friends. At the same time, because of the lower level of commitment involved in a friendship relationship as opposed to a close

friendship relationship, the chances that friends will make the widow feel unwanted and rejected were higher than the chances that close friends will do so. Far more widows advanced this feeling of lack of belonging as a reason for breaking friendships than those who gave it as a reason for breaking with close friends. It is not possible, on the basis of the widows' reports, to decide whether they were describing two different processes by which the relationships were severed, one where the initiative came from the friends, and the other where it stemmed from the widow; or whether they were, in fact, talking about a single process only, in which the friends rejected the widow who, feeling this rejection, then severed the contact with them. I lean toward the assumption that it is actually one process which different widows tended to present in different ways.

ACQUAINTANCES

These were defined as "not complete strangers," but neither could they be counted as "friends" or "close friends." The degree of closeness and familiarity in acquaintance relationships varied considerably. A person with whom an evening might be spent in the home of mutual friends could be considered an acquaintance, as well as a person one met at work, in the course of studies, or in one's neighborhood, where a few courtesies or remarks about the events of the day were exchanged. On the other hand, people with whom the relationship was a good deal closer than this would often also be defined as acquaintances. In acquaintanceship, no mutual obligations are imposed, nor is any investment demanded in order to maintain the status quo in the relationship. In the main, the accumulation of acquaintances is a kind of reservoir of potential social relationships which can be developed and made closer. The process by which the relationship of acquaintanceship is transformed into friendship or close friendship, and the extent to which the reservoir of acquaintances can be tapped to meet the social needs of the widow, is discussed below.

Social Life as a Widow

NEW SOCIAL RELATIONSHIPS

The great majority of widows in the sample wanted to establish new social relationships to replace the "old" social relationships which had been severed and to satisfy new needs which had arisen as a result of their situation as widows. Their ability to create and make a success of new social relationships constituted one of the ways whereby widows could judge their capacity to function independently (not as part of a couple), and gave them the opportunity to assess their own worth, as well as society's evaluation of them. Last, though by no means always least of their considerations, widows who wished to remarry knew that by increasing their social contacts they were at the same time enhancing their chances of finding a suitable candidate for marriage.

Many widows found that their circle of acquaintances widened considerably after their bereavement. Widowhood, and the services and arrangements connected with it, brought most of them into contact with people they had not previously known: representatives of the public, of institutions, of the army, voluntary communal workers in various fields of "assistance to widows," and other war widows whom they had not met before. As a consequence of being widowed, many moved to new houses and/or new towns, many began to work, or changed the place and the type of work they had been doing before, and quite a number began short- or long-term studies in various educational settings. The widows tried to establish social relationships, friendships, or close friendships, in all those areas of life where this type of contact is customary: in the neighborhood and at work, with the parents of their children's friends, in places of entertainment, through family members, and within various frameworks specially designed to provide places of meetings for people seeking new social contacts.

Two main difficulties prevented the widows in the sample from forming new friendships or close friendships. One was that of finding "suitable" partners. The yardsticks by which suitability was measured differed from widow to widow. For some widows, age and marital status were the principal (although not the only) factors by which suitability was assessed. Other widows were more selective and measured suitability by more complex and personal criteria in which class, education, common interests, etc. played an important part. Most widows, in addition, were anxious not to feel different or set apart from their fellows, and therefore gauged suitability according to how comfortable they felt in the company of the people in question. The second difficulty lay in penetrating existing, well-established, social networks suited in form and numbers to the needs of the participants (Boissevain 1974, Chapt. 4). For the most part, the attempts of the widows in the sample were neither very successful nor really satisfying. Despite a considerable number of new acquaintances, they succeeded in forming only a few friendships or close friendships, and even in these cases, the criteria of suitability were often not met to the full.

T.N. (No. 35) was a senior member on the staff of an institution of higher education. In the course of her work, she had many social contacts and a big "collection" of acquaintances. In spite of this, according to her account, the number of her new friendships was extremely limited: "1 have a few new friends. Actually, one family, one could say. I don't think he (the late husband) even knew them. I work with this fellow. They have two little girls the same age as my small children; so we go on trips and to the sea together. There's also a neighbor here with whom I'm quite friendly. But it never came to the point where I went out with them anywhere, or took a trip anywhere with them." H.N. (No. 37), a housewife and mother of an only child, did not have many acquaintances and was chiefly occupied with her home and her son. When asked about her friends and close friends, she replied: "I really only have one friend here—the mother of Sarele. We meet every day and fetch the children together from the kindergarten. I visit her." Another widow, U.M. (No. 34) said:

> I have new friends that I met at different places, some here, some there. If you are nice, you are invited. It's not really active social life, but it's quite comfortable—there are no obligations. But of course, there are evenings when I am alone, stuck at home, and nothing can help. For instance, there was a lieutenant-colonel—I called him "the Commander of the Widows," because he was in charge of matters concerning the widows. So he became a kind of "friend of the house." He used to visit us a lot, and he was the children's best friend. But now he's out of the country.

At the beginning of the quotation, U.M. gave the impression that she had quite a number of new friends. But when she tried to give an account of her new friendships, she barely came out with one—and he was no longer there.

Even when she was married, the social contacts of C.N. (No. 36) were somewhat tenuous. Once she was widowed, they disappeared completely. She was keenly aware of her lack of social contacts, so much so, that she took this into account in her decisions regarding other matters too:

> When I came here to see the apartment, the owner introduced me to the neighbor, who said, "When you come to live here, you'll be with us, we won't leave you for a moment and you'll go out with us and with our crowd." So I moved in and she once invited me to go out—when they had tickets for a movie and her husband didn't want to go to that film, so she invited me. Well, she promised, but nothing came of all that. As far as social life goes, I'm sorry I took this apartment. I thought that they (the neighbors) would be good friends. But in the end I saw that it was all in their own interests—if they should want to go out, they would have a baby-sitter. So afterwards I stopped baby-sitting for them, because I saw they wanted me only for this.

C.N. was not particularly selective in her choice of contacts. She was ready to enter into any social contact which held out the promise of reciprocity in the relationship; nevertheless, as we learn from the passage quoted, she had considerable difficulty in finding partners for such a relationship. In her set of contacts with her neighbors, she felt marginal (a substitute for the husband who did not want to go to the movies) and exploited (a baby-sitter when needed). She did not succeed in penetrating a social group as an "equal among equals," as a "good friend." The need and desire to relate socially as an equal were expressed by S.E. (No. 17), who explained the difficulties in forming such relationships:

> For me, one of the basic things is that I don't want people to come to me out of pity, and from the very beginning I make sure that they come because they want my friendship. If someone comes to me because he recognizes my value, the value of the friendship that I can give and receive, then this can really be a true friendship . . . and from the social point of view there are a number of problems; there is the problem of the social vacuum . . . society accepts you but, somehow, with many reservations. It looks at you and really doesn't know what to do with you. It's the problem of a group that doesn't know how to relate to such a widow.

N.I. (No.23) also felt that she was something of a social misfit: ". . . you are uprooted from your own generation. I have already been through the period of being "single," and now I'm at the age of marriage—and not of old people who are alone again."

The only social contacts that ensured, almost automatically, the status of "equal among equals" were those formed with other war widows. Notwithstanding this, however, widows in the sample entered into such relationships with a great deal of hesitation and usually feeling that they had no other alternatives. Widows met one another in the Rehabilitation Department, at memorials and other ceremonies, or in various informal contexts, but they formed relatively few friendships or close friendships with one another. The attitudes of war widows in the sample to other war widows was a complex one and full of contradictions. On the one hand, they showed a great interest in what was happening in the lives of other widows, and they identified very strongly with their problems. On the other hand, a good many of the widows in the sample had reservations about any contact with other war widows. Those among the sample widows who desired close relationships with other war widows and sought them out were, for the most part, widows who saw both their personal identification and their social status as unequivocally dependent on the fact of their being war widows. Choosing other widows as friends meant electing to enter a group in which the widow had the status of "equal among equals," but the whole group was then itself an anomaly. Rejecting widows as friends, even potential friends, meant choosing an anomalous position in a social group which was itself not anomalous. Voluntary entry into a group which was out of the ordinary was usually done with some hesitation, as is evident from the words of I.B. (No. 3):

> I have a very good friend from (the seminary); her husband was also killed, not exactly in the war, but immediately after, and we formed a relationship. At first, I was very reserved when I met girls in my situation—it was difficult. I really didn't know how to relate to them . . . but slowly, slowly—and in the end we became friends. I don't believe we would have become friends if there had not been something deeper between us . . . what is strange about it is that, at the beginning, I was very reluctant, and in the end, this (being a widow) is what brought us together.

In the first stage of the research, that is to say three years after they became widows, there were only a few who maintained friendship or close friendship relationships with other war widows. Five years after they were widowed, some of the widows, mainly those whose social networks included a comparatively large number of friends and close friends, persisted in their rejection of social contacts with other widows. Others, feeling that they had virtually no alternative, did form new friendships and even close friendships with war widows. During the interviews it became very clear that the widows were reluctant to volunteer information about close contact with other war widows. The tendency was to belittle the importance of these relationships as though they would damage the interviewer's impression of the widow.

TECHNIQUES FOR ESTABLISHING SOCIAL CONTACTS

The various kinds of social contact described in this chapter (social events, groups, friendships, close friendships, acquaintance-ships) are shaped by the characteristics of those who are party to the relationship—their age and marital status, their social status and way of life, the community in which they live, and so on. At the same time, the kind of contact is in turn a major determinant of the various techniques employed for establishing the relationship and for maintaining its viability over time. Here, discussion will focus mainly on the significance of the factor of marital status in influencing techniques of social contact.

Widows in the sample, especially those of relatively young age, found themselves trapped in an anomalous and disadvantageous position, unable to conduct their social life as did either their married peers or their single friends. Techniques for establishing and maintaining social relationships available to these other categories could not be fully used by them, and the lack of normatively prescribed substitute techniques meant that, in time, the relationships tended to atrophy.

The style of the social life of married couples is dictated to a considerable extent by their family responsibilities. The amount of time they can allocate to social contacts and the nature and form of the contacts are circumscribed by factors like their children's study and leisure commitments, their schedule of meals, babysitting arrangements, and bedtimes. In order to meet all the demands upon them, married couples, especially those with small children, tend to plan social activities in advance, and spontaneous entertaining is generally precluded. With relationships accordingly formalized to a fairly high degree, visiting in private homes is usually arranged by prior invitation, while an evening out with friends will be planned to maximize the use of the babysitter, and will tend to include dining in a restaurant, as well as going to a theater or a nightclub. To a fair extent, these techniques for maintaining social relationships fitted in with the widow's schedules and coincided with her needs. She, too, had children requiring arrangements and an allotment of time similar to those of married couples. Social contacts between married couples usually took place on occasions and at hours when the widow was freed from her housework and the care of her children: social meetings planned in advance enabled her to make appropriate arrangements for the care of the children and facilitated her participation in them. However, her chances for full participation in the social life of her married friends were limited, as already discussed.

The style of social relationships among singles, on the other hand, differs completely from that of married couples. A considerable number of these social contacts take place in the kind of public setting that lends itself to informal meetings. Particularly in large cities, there are cafes or places of public entertainment where it is customary for single people to gather and strike up casual acquaintanceships without prior planning (Gordon 1976; Hunt 1966; Stein 1976). Here, at certain hours and at certain periods, people gather to exchange information about social activities such as place of parties and times of outings. Many make on-the-spot plans, arrange joint activities, or are invited to activities being arranged by others. In most cases, the circle of communication does not go beyond those people who are present. The planning here is usually short-term (for the same evening, or the end of the week). The times of such meetings are suited to the way of life of single people (late afternoon, after work, or early afternoon on Fridays when public places close for the Sabbath). It has already been pointed out that not all widows have access to social networks of single people. In the sample, it was mainly the widows living in big cities, and the comparatively young ones among them, that had contacts with networks of this kind. But even they could not fully participate in them since the timing and techniques involved in maintaining the contacts were in no way commensurate with their commitments to their home and children. S.E. (No. 17) described some of the difficulties in participating in singles' activities:

> In some way you fulfill the functions of a family. You're not an unmarried woman who can do what she pleases. You have responsibility, you have obligations, you carry a load on your back. And now, from the practical viewpoint, you are a family and you can't go out every evening. You have obligations—you have to get up at seven in the morning, take two children to kindergarten and then go to work. And in the afternoon, you have to play with them, and you have to put them to bed at night, and you have to go shopping, and you have to pay electric bills, and there are another hundred thousand things. You have obligations. You are not alone. You can't go back to the life of a young girl.

In individual, as opposed to group, arrangements, contacts between singles tend to be less formal, less structured, and less planned than between couples. This tendency is chiefly a function of the desire not to be committed to social activities in advance, so as to be free to exploit every possible last minute opportunity. "Going off for a cup of coffee" without arranging it beforehand, an invitation to the movies "in an hour's time," or the announcement of an outing being organized "for tomorrow morning and we don't know when we'll be back"— these are accepted forms in the patterns of relationships and techniques for establishing social contacts among singles (Gordon 1976, part 3). But the widows lacked the freedom of movement which most singles enjoy, and therefore their ability to accept last-minute invitations to social activities, or their opportunities to "run out for a cup of coffee" with their friends, were severely limited.

There is, however, one aspect of the widows' situation in which they had more to offer than other singles, namely, that the informal nature of the contacts made it fairly easy for them to entertain at home. In addition, since they ran regular, complete households (rare among singles), the chance that the visitor would be offered refreshments or a light meal, even without advance notice, added to the attraction of the visit. The unplanned visit was facilitated by the fact that widows, particularly those with small children, were to be found at home more than other singles. Furthermore, since the widow's freedom of movement was limited, such casual visitors could often avoid reciprocating the hospitality and, even if they went through the motions of inviting her at the last moment to a movie or an outing, they could anticipate that she would not be free to accept. Whether this kind of unbalanced relationship was preplanned or simply the outcome of lack of sensitivity and understanding of the built-in limitations of the widow's life, many widows perceived it as "being taken advantage of," and they tended not to encourage it. This situation epitomizes the hopelessness and impossibility for the widow of achieving the status of "an equal among equals."

The network of social relationships of each widow in the sample was unique to her and in many ways connected with her overall life situation, her social talents, and her personal attributes. The similarities or differences between the social networks in which the woman was involved before she became a widow and those which she had three years after varied from one widow to another. Of course, not every widow went through the same difficulties or the same experiences in attempting to form active, meaningful social connections for herself. For this reason, the different aspects and dimensions of the social life of U.G. (No. 51) which are presented below do not cover all the points discussed in this chapter. The purpose of presenting in full the available information concerning the social life of one widow is to give a clearer picture of the difficulties and dilemmas a widow faces in this area.

U.G. was neither among the most successful of the widows in her social life, nor was she among the least successful. Widowed at the age of 29, she had decided to start a new professional career, one which could be achieved only through full-time university study. The form her social life took resulted, on the one hand, from the relative freedom afforded her by her student life and, on the other hand, from the many constraints stemming from her position as a family head, woman alone and mother of small children.

Attenuation of social contacts from before widowhood; cessation of contacts with the group.

In the army (reserves), my husband was in a very special unit and they were a group that stuck together and we used to meet a lot before the war. There were outings and a close friendship. There was a lieutenant-colonel who was an unusually good-hearted fellow and he was like a "daddy" to all the others. And there was another one who was like a "daddy" and was also killed. After the two "daddies" were killed—I can't say that the contact was entirely broken, but the personal contact was broken. They (the unit) still remember birthdays and send the children presents. It's only terribly, terribly sad that the personal contact ended. If they had only picked up the phone once a year and let me know that they were coming, it would have been nice. So with all the friends, except one, I don't have contact any more. This man is very simple but unusually kind and for a while he kept up the contact with us. But today he's at sea somewhere, so with him too I've no contact. At the beginning, he used to come here whenever he was on shore and sometimes he even wrote us postcards. But, with time . . .

Friends from previous networks sever contacts.

Outside the army circle, our friends were quite a mixed group. I think the only one with a university education was my husband. Anyway, my husband was a very modest man, not at all a snob. And he also educated me very well, so that there's no lack (of friends) and, in this sense, I think I'm very lucky. Because I see what's happening and I talk to other widows about the social rejection. It's a phenomenon that exists. Other widows also complained that good friends stopped coming. Do you know that I had friends who told me that they have nothing to look for in this house now that my husband isn't here. There were those who said it to me straight out, and others who told it to a friend. One of them was asked, "Don't you come to U. any more?" and he replied, "There's nothing to do there. It simply isn't interesting any more." Society just rejects certain kinds of people.

Expectations of friendship, both in quality and quantity, are very modest.

I have many friends. What do I mean by "many"— even if there are only two or three couples that think about you when they go to the movies or on a picnic to the Sea of Galilee . . . that's enough—and in my situation today, that's even a lot. I take the children and go with them on trips. We go to the Sea of Galilee, we go to the seaside, and these are friends I always had.

Changes in style of social life; hostess role is reduced and limited to women only.

Today, I have completely stopped inviting people home, except girl friends who come for a cup of tea in the afternoon or in the evening—but never men.

Outings are reduced and have become dependent on others.

I often meet with these couples, although in the last two or three months I haven't been to a movie or a play. But I once went to a party, and once there was a tenth anniversary party, so I went out in the evening. And I have one couple that always asks me whether I'm interested in going to some performance. Now they've asked me if I'm interested in going to a certain play and have promised to buy me a ticket.

Continuation of contacts from before widowhood; unisexual close friendship.

I have one very close friend. My relationship with this friend was always very good—she's the kind of friend I'm not sure I could be. The friendship actually began with a mutual liking, since we took this apartment. At that time, only I worked and my husband was studying. And after I gave birth to our son, I got very attached to this friend. We weren't only good friends, but good neighbors.

New demands on friendship relationship develop.

The announcement (of the death of the husband) was brought to her. They came to my best friend and she said that it couldn't be, that she didn't believe them, and she fainted, and it was terrible. In any case, she told them that I was not at home and they said that they would come again in the afternoon. So she said, "Let her have her afternoon rest and then come to me". My friend took my daughter to her home and I took the boy with me to "sit shiv'a" at his grandmother's. The truth is that this friend wanted to protect me.

Husband of a close friend is called upon for help in specific areas.

They really tried to protect me and I felt it. You need one good friend—not more, only one. They (the friend and her husband) really helped me a lot. He came twice a week to put the children to bed, and she herself had three children at home. She always tried to reassure me that she doesn't do so much for me, but it's not true—she did a lot. They did what all the other friends didn't do—not one of them.

Formation of new social relationships and perceived constraints to the development of new social contacts.

In the university, the situation is peculiar. Either there are women older than I am—forty plus—with whom I became friendly, but this didn't really develop social contacts. Those old ones don't interest me. Not that they don't interest me, but . . . with one of them I've really formed a kind of friendship, so I can always pick up the phone and talk to her. I sometimes even go to her for a cup of coffee in the afternoon. My relationship with her is like with an older sister. And then, there are those little girls from the university—they're around eighteen (years old). Some are married and one is even in her first pregnancy. I think they enjoy my life experience, or something like that. Two of them are very religious.

I obviously don't go out with them, but sometimes they come to me or I go to them for a cup of coffee or a chat. It's not real social life, but it's a pleasant contact.

Partial contact with a group through a new relationship.

Here I have a wonderful neighbor, right next door to me. She's a good deal younger than I am, but it's interesting that with them I did form a social contact. She's part of a group and she always tells me ahead of time when they are coming to her and invites me as well. Or I just hear (that they are there) and I'm bored at home and I've had enough of studying, so I can knock at her door and go in. We are very free in our relationship, so I really do it. With them I found a common language, despite the fact that they are much younger than I am. But really to go out with them—I don't go. After all, they go to discotheques and so on, and that is already not for my age.

Failure to develop contacts with men.

If we are talking about social relationships—well, the idea is also to get married one day. You know, I tried in certain ways to form social contacts—mainly in order to meet someone. I thought that by meeting new people—but it was very hard. But I tried.

War widows are perceived as a deviant group and therefore rejected as potential friends.

What I do absolutely avoid is any contact with widows. I never go to those meetings with them. There was a period when they had organized tours for war widows and war orphans, and they always asked me, "Why don't you come?" I'm ready to go anywhere, but not there. I certainly wouldn't take the children—I want them to see normal life. On purpose, when I go on a trip, I go with couples. Then the man can take care of my kids and I can sit and rest and chat. If we go to the sea or the Sea of Galilee, there is always someone to keep an eye on them and to play ball with them. Who would play with them on a tour of widows?

VI

The Social Status of War Widows

This chapter will deal with the social status of war widows in Israel from the point of view of their place in Israeli society.[1] It will cut across, re-organize, and summarize much of the material covered in the previous chapters, but from a different viewpoint.

In modern societies, including that of Israel, achievement criteria are dominant factors in stratification: it is these criteria which, to a great extent, determine one's place in society. A person's achievements in areas relevant to the stratification system which obtains in society will determine the level of social rewards he will be given, as well as his place in the social hierarchy. But even in a society where achievement is the dominant factor in placing the individual in his social position, ascribed status also plays an important role.[2]

Ascribed-status criteria are of two kinds: a. Primary ascribed-status criteria (ethnic origin, sex, religion, nationality, and others) all have some weight in determining the possibilities and the opportunities for the individual to enter various areas of achievement. They also play a part in the way the individual is evaluated by society, and in the way rewards are accorded for achievements. b. Achievements themselves create ascribed-status criteria, in other words, certain achievements put the person who attains them into a particular social category. The very fact of belonging to such a social category or group brings with it status rewards which are in no way connected with the actual achievement itself. These status rewards are given to everyone who belongs to that group or category.

The achievement-stratification system appears to be an individualistic one—it demands achievement from every individual in society, and status is conferred on him in accordance with that achievement. This individualistic system of achievement-stratification does not apply equally in all cases. Two categories of individuals appear to be excluded, at least partially, from achievement competition and from the

145

process of status achievement—one category is youth and the other is women. Children and teenagers are not expected to enter those areas in which status can be achieved and rewards gained and, to a large extent, they are even prevented from doing so. Women's participation in achieving status is generally voluntary. They usually have a choice between creating their own achieved status or accepting that ascribed to them by virtue of being part of the family.[3] The exclusion of women and youth from participation in the system of status achievement (while not leaving them completely statusless) is possible only because the family is also a single-status unit.

In his discussion of American society, Parsons (1954) sees a man's achievement as the only source of status for the whole family, while the most meaningful status for woman is (in his view) that of successful marriage. Other scholars, however, do not accept Parson's opinion in its extreme form. Some hold that a wife contributes to the status of her family by virtue of her own achievements (Delphy 1976; Felson & Knoke 1974; Shamgar-Handelman 1972B), while others regard the positive connection between a man's occupational achievement and his married state as the only contribution of the wife to the status of the family (Blau & Duncan 1967). But all these scholars agree that marriage confers status on a woman comparable to the status which occupational achievement confers on a man. Since marriage is seen as an achievement for a woman (whether the sole or main achievement, or one among others), the fact that she is married constitutes, in and of itself, a positive component in the composition of her status. This is especially true in Israeli society where the rate of marriage is very high. In those groupings in which the majority is married, the minority group—the unmarried—does not receive certain social rewards that are accorded only to married people (Stein 1976).

In the light of the foregoing, the central question of this chapter is: what happens to the status of those comparatively young women who have lost their main status contributor, the husband? This question can be broken down into three sub-questions: a. What happens after widowhood to the status previously ascribed by the husband, and what is its place in the general composition of the widow's status? b. What kind of status is reserved in Israeli society for those who belong to the social category of "war widows?" c. What kind of status can a comparatively young woman, a mother of children, achieve through her own efforts in Israeli society, what areas of achievement are open to her, and what kind of social rewards can she gain by virtue of her own achievements?

Before their widowhood, the large majority of widows in the sample belonged to family units in which the occupation of the husband was the dominant component of status. The husband's occupation was the main source of economic rewards, of social prestige, of social connections, and of access to sources of information. It was also the source of additional benefits, such as entertainment, use of a car, trips abroad, and so forth. The participation of the women in creating family status was, in most cases, only minimal. Most were housewives and, as such, made it possible for their husbands to devote themselves fully to occupational roles. In some cases, the woman did play an active part in the occupational advancement of the husband— by participating in public appearances, by entertaining, and so forth (Burger 1970; Kanter 1977). Some few widows had worked and contributed to the economic resources of the family. Sometimes, however, the woman's occupation would downgrade the prestige of the family (for instance if she worked as a cleaning woman), and in this case, efforts were made not to disclose such information. Only in a very few cases had the woman been part of a family unit where both she and her husband simultaneously pursued careers which were more or less equal in terms of status and reward.[4]

One result of widowhood is that it not only brings about the breakdown of the status structure of the family unit as a whole, but that it also constitutes, simultaneously, a threat of further loss of status, both for the widow herself and for the family unit which she now heads. This threat of loss of status arises in three areas.

a. First, by definition, the widow loses the status of a married woman and joins the category of nonmarried women. This loss of status has significance in various ways: since marriage is a woman's sphere of achievement, the death of her husband means the loss of this. Differently stated, if marriage is seen as a woman's achievement, paralleling a man's occupational achievement, then becoming a widow may be seen as parallel to a man's loss of status when he loses his job because of the economic failure of his employer. The responsibility for such a loss of status is attributable neither to the woman in the former case, nor to the man in the latter. In both cases it results from external factors.

b. Since, in Israeli society, the rate of marriage is very high, women commonly live in a family framework of which the man is the head. The loss of the husband-father moves the widow and her family into a marginal or deviant social category. Being a nonmarried woman, in an age group where most women are married, is a basic status which affects all the roles and relationships of the widow (Epstein 1973; Lopata 1973A, 1973C).

c. A third kind of threat of loss of status lies in the loss of those social rewards accorded to the husband for the roles he performed in society and which, through him, were enjoyed by his whole family. The husbands had received different degrees, amounts, and combinations of types of reward (money, power, and prestige). After their death, the timing and pace at which the rewards taper off differ according to the reward in question. The point at which the salary of the late husband (an economic reward for his occupational achievement) stops being paid is quite clear. So, too, are the economic arrangements which exist for the family after his death. But in the nature of things, it is harder to assess the accumulation of power and prestige the family is left with, and it is not clear how and when they are lost. Thus, the loss of those social rewards which the family enjoyed by virtue of the husband and father occurs, not as a sudden event, but as a continuing process. The time span between the death of the husband and the total loss of all types of reward received through him by the family nevertheless provides an interim period which allows the widow some leeway to manipulate her status.

When the women became war widows, they also became the sole heads of their families. Accordingly, they took on the additional role of ensuring a new status for their family units. Widows were deeply aware of this obligation, and their aim was usually to prevent a loss of status for their families. The criteria as to what constituted such loss of status were not the same for all widows. In some cases, the main criterion was the composition of social rewards which the family unit had enjoyed before the loss of the husband. In others, the criteria were related to the status reference-group which the widow had prior to widowhood. In short, the aim of some widows was to maintain their prewidowhood rewards, while others tried to keep a status comparable to that of those family units within their reference-group.

The objective conditions, capacities, and resources at the disposal of the widow which enabled her to prevent a loss of status, as well as the level of status which was acceptable to her as a satisfactory minimum, were different for each widow. Every widow, in her specific situation, tried to manoeuvre in order to achieve the optimal combination of status rewards for herself and for her family unit.

To the extent that it derived from the personal status of the widow, a loss of family status could be prevented only in one way—by remarriage. Of all the widows interviewed in the course of this study, only one said she did not want to remarry. All the others saw remarriage as a desirable possibility, and attached a great deal of importance to the benefits of status which come with remarriage. I do not mean to suggest that women generally, or widows specifically, marry only to gain status. But an examination of those elements which were desirable in a partner for remarriage indicates that, in most cases, his status was expected to be at least equal to, if not higher than, that of the late husband (Shamgar-Handelman 1982). Although remarriage was considered a desirable solution to many problems in a widow's life, it was not an immediate one. In every case, there was a period in which this was either objectively impossible, or considered so. The awareness that this was not, and could not be, an immediate solution impelled the widow to try to crystallize a status alternative of her own.

Patterns of Status-Substitution Among War Widows

The widow's choice of her course of action in creating a substitute status depended on her objective characteristics and skills and on her particular aspirations. Her choice was also influenced by her desire to reattain certain rewards denied her upon widowhood. In addition, her course of action depended on the readiness of those who formed her social network to help her to attain her goals and meet her needs.

No information on the changes of status experienced immediately upon widowhood by the women in the sample could be included in this study since it was undertaken three years after the event. However, it seems reasonable to assume that the issue of status was of comparatively little importance to them in this period. Furthermore, in their newly-widowed state, they were generally so overwhelmed with grief, sorrow, and personal loss that the realization of changes in status was usually delayed. Nevertheless, whether the widow was conscious of it or not, the process of entering the status of a war widow began immediately after widowhood.

This study revealed three patterns of attempts to crystallize substitute status. It is, of course, possible that there are additional patterns which, for various reasons, did not appear in the sample. In any event, the fact that there are alternatives is added proof of the paucity of, or contradictions among, norms connected with the role composition of a war widow in Israeli society.

ADOPTING THE NEW STATUS OF WAR WIDOW

It was (and still is) difficult to determine the exact place of war widows in the status hierarchy of Israeli society. However, some general observations are possible:

a. The status of war widow was not at the bottom of the status ladder. Accordingly, a war widow could acquire three basic types of social reward—money, power, and prestige—even though their effect on her status may have been only transitory. Belonging to the category of war widow automatically brought with it the right to a monthly stipend according to fixed criteria based on size of family. Other types of economic reward existed potentially and were amenable to manipulation. Widows could exercise power, either on an organized basis through the Widows' Association, or in an individualistic way through attempts to influence the mass media, or to bring pressure on members of the Knesset, for example. Prestige was conferred through personal connections of significance, and through other channels, such as exposure through the mass media.

b. There were considerable fluctuations in the status level of a war widow, and in its place in the status hierarchy of Israeli society. A change in the value of this status affected the whole category of war widows. Thus, each war widow might gain or lose status according to fluctuations in the status of the whole category. These changes were closely related to the military situation prevailing in the country at any particular time. In periods of intensified concern for national security, the subject of war widows tends to be brought to the attention of the Knesset, the public, and the mass media, and the status of the whole category of war widows accordingly rises. This reflects, in turn, upon the social interaction of every individual war widow. It was during such a period, for example, that the activists in the Widows' Association began to use the tools at their disposal to gain ground for the whole category of war widows, to increase the benefits available to them, and to obtain other benefits previously unavailable. At such times, many widows were courted by the mass media, while each individual widow stood to gain more attention or prestige through her personal contacts. When the status of war widows failed to receive either ideological or situational encouragement for any protracted period, erosion of this status took place, and the expressions of status which the widow received through face-to-face interaction declined.

c. Belonging to the category of war widow did not provide an automatic guarantee either of its full status or of all its status rewards. Instead, it provided only the potential for gaining these, and very direct and active effort on the part of the widow herself was required in order to realize this potential. War widows in the sample who chose to crystallize this status maintained close contacts with one another, mainly through a group which served as a focus of communication in matters of mutual interest. In this way, their information concerning new rights, new regulations, and precedents was always up-to-date, and this helped them to defend their interests in their contacts with the Rehabilitation Centers of the Ministry of Defense. Before widowhood, the social activities of these particular widows had been rather limited. But the organized social activities for war widows now afforded them a way to acquire social contacts and some prominence, as well as a platform from which to present their opinions and make their influence felt. These women participated willingly and regularly in war widows' assemblies, in therapy groups organized especially for them, and in various recreational activities arranged for them, all of which demanded a considerable investment of time and effort on their part. However, the self-identification of a woman as a war widow went beyond the specific activities organized for this category, penetrating into all areas of her life. For example, those whose prestige derived mainly from this status often got work on the recommendation of the social worker. Sometimes they benefited from the special housing arrangements upon the recommendation of the Widows' Association. Others went abroad as representatives of the war widows at the expense of philanthropic hostesses. About half of the widows in the sample, for the most part those that did not enjoy very high family status before widowhood, chose to crystallize their substitute status around that of a war widow. For a certain duration, this substitute was satisfactory, and it answered their expectations of status. But those who continued in this status for a longer period found erosion setting in. The longer they maintained the substitute, the less was their ability to realize its potential status rewards.[5]

The frequency of war was an additional factor which influenced the status of war widows. The prestige of widows of a previous war declined greatly with the appearance of widows from a new war, and this limited the ability of veteran war widows to realize the potential of this status. The attitude of social workers to veteran widows has been mentioned before, in chapter II. In my opinion, this attitude is at least partially a result of the erosion in the status of the veteran widows. The following incident exemplifies the onset of status erosion of war widows in a framework where this was hardly to be expected. Both the social workers and the widows of the Six-Day War described to me the situation in the Rehabilitation Centers during the Yom Kippur War as one of overcrowding, confusion, and turmoil. To this extent, their reports coincided. But from this point on, the war widows' stories and those of the social workers differed. The social workers described what was virtually an "attack" by widows from previous wars upon the Centers, right at the beginning of the war. According to their account, the widows made a great number of unreasonable demands—all the more so in light of the crisis at the time. But the widows said that when they came to the Centers during the Yom Kippur War to arrange their routine affairs, they were pushed aside rudely by all the personnel, from porters to social workers, and this on the pretext that there were now more important widows to be dealt with.

In my interpretation of these two versions, the Six-Day War widows felt that the present war was catapulting into the headlines a new group of widows who would overshadow their importance in the Rehabilitation Centers. Thus, they presented themselves at the Centers hoping to prevent their relegation to widows of lesser status. However, by their action, they merely hastened this process. The workers of the Centers were unprepared for the outbreak of war and unready for the appearance of the Six-Day War widows. They reacted by postponing attention to them. This way they were transferred, ex post facto, to secondary importance in the priorities of the Centers. Such a transfer, in this context, constituted an erosion of status. In other words, the Six-Day War widows ceased to belong to the category of new widows (the most prestigious category) and became veteran widows (a less prestigious category).

At a certain stage in the time continuum, but unrelated to the advent of new wars, the status of a war widow was seen in a negative light and equated with that of a spinster (Bergguist 1972). Very often, the following description was applied to such a widow, both in writing and orally: "She is a widow from the War of Independence who is still not married." This suggests that remarriage became a status criterion for war widows as much as for other women in Israeli society. In a conversation about a certain war widow, the social worker said: "She was widowed in the War of Independence and never got married again, and till this day she thinks we owe her something." War widows who were widowed at a comparatively advanced age (in their forties), tended to drop the word "war" from the title of "war widow" after a fairly short time, and to present themselves simply as "widows." This seems to be an attempt not to be identified with those who lived as war widows for many years, and remained unmarried.

Because the war widow could not be easily identified as such through any external signs or symbols, the only way in which she could explain to other people, whether to an occasional acquaintance, a clerk in a government office, or any other casual interlocutor, that she was a war widow was by declaring, "I am a war widow." But to announce her status in this socially unconventional manner placed both the widow and her counterpart in an embarrassing position and the widow herself in a deviant catgory. B. Q. (No. 50) was sensitive in this regard: "All you want in a situation like this is to be on the same level as the woman who came here with her husband—everyone sees that he has a nose and he is limping. . . . Actually all you want is to put yourself on a level of equality and to begin from the same starting point." Thus, the necessity to declare herself made her feel that she was being relegated to a marginal position. Such an overt enunciation of her status made it impossible to do other than to continue the subject. One question which usually followed the declaration "I am a war widow" was, "From when?" Then the different reactions to the time elapsed since her widowhood were, for her, a measure of the extent of her own status erosion, just as they were a measure of the status erosion of the group to which she belonged. After a while, with growing frequency, another question followed her self-declaration: "You still haven't married again?" At this point, not to have remarried had become a negative component in the status of a war widow. As time passed, the status of the war widow underwent erosion, and she was forced to make a greater investment and effort in order to retain the same level of rewards.

The erosion in the status of a war widow impelled her to seek "status-strengthening" devices of various kinds. For example, some tried to overcome status erosion by increasing their consumption and usage of symbols which did not belong specifically to the status of war widow. Sometimes this particular device was a direct reaction to status deterioration in a specific social context. For example, after an incident where the social worker in the Rehabilitation Center did not give the war widow either the attention or the responsiveness which she expected, the widow started to appear at the Center overdressed and overly made-up. Another example is the war widow who thought that her children were affected by the erosion of their status as "orphans of a war hero" and tried to compensate them by buying them more toys and more expensive clothes and by inviting their friends to a very lavish children's party.

But such conspicuous status symbols were not always a direct reflection of those social areas in which status erosion was most strongly experienced. With the years, some widows accumulated status symbols of a more general nature: they moved into larger and better apartments, they changed their furniture, they bought especially big cars, and so on. These symbolized for them the higher standard of living for which they strove. It was made possible by the continual rise in the economic benefits which they received from the Ministry of Defense, benefits which were in excess of routine cost-of-living increases. The widows themselves explained their increased consumption as status-compensation for themselves and for their children: "He asked me for a bicycle. It's enough that he does not have a father. I bought him a bicycle so that he should not be ashamed in front of his friends" (B. B., No. 1). "When I was married, the furniture wasn't at all important. But today, if people come to my house, I don't want them to speak ill of me" (I. O., No. 39). These were typical explanations for acquisitions which, in many cases, could be classified as conspicuous consumption. While their children were still young, the widows could, in this way, cushion the erosion of their own status as war widows. But the major drop in status occurred when their children reached the age of eighteen and were no longer eligible for child support. As a result, the economic resources available to the widows greatly decreased.

Status-erosion could also be retarded by activating the war-widow status so that it became, in effect, a personal attribute which she could put to use as she did her talents or her skills. The widow who chose to adopt this course found that new spheres of action were now open to her. These spheres were unique to war widows but offered rewards similar to those accorded to professional or political activities in society at large. Some widows chose to activate the war widow status within the war widows' group, in which case her role could be expressive, administrative, representational, or political. But belonging to the category of war widow was a condition sine qua non for entering all or any of the roles. This set of roles was the product of organizational changes and of power struggles which arose from the demands of the widows themselves to become active participants in arranging their own affairs.

Alternatively, widows could choose to take on a representational role in one of the many public and political organizations (especially women's organizations) which tried to use war widows as their representatives, both within the country and abroad. The tendency to draw widows into such roles was most marked immediately after the war when their prestige was still at its peak. With time, these possibilities were reduced.

In the two areas of activity mentioned above, roles were defined either as "jobs," or as "voluntary jobs." The lines of demarcation between these two types of activity were not very clear. The best example of this was the role of the representative of the widows in Yad Lebanim. All members of the Yad Lebanim Center were volunteers. Its only full-salaried member, at the time of this study, was the representative of the war widows. The explanation offered was that this arrangement enabled a widow to take on such a role, whereas economically she could not afford to do so on a voluntary basis. In this case, a role which was defined as a voluntary job in fact yielded a salary comparable to that of a paid job.

In general, the attitude of widows to those who acted "as widows" in various frameworks was ambivalent. On the one hand, most war widows welcomed the opportunity of having their own representative participate in as many areas of public life as possible because, as they expressed it, "only a widow can understand the problems of another widow." On the other hand, it was thought to be somewhat indelicate to derive a benefit from being a widow. In all these instances, such widows were called in war-widow slang, "professional widows." If the benefits a widow got from a job were not very substantial, the title of "professional widow" was qualified by an expression of understanding and even of pity, as for instance: "If she starts now being a professional widow, she'll never escape from it"—that is to say, from the situation of widowhood. Often, jobs for "professional widows" carried comparatively high rewards, and then the title might have a derogatory connotation. They tended to command salaries which were high in relation to the professional competence or previous experience of the incumbent. All these types of activity undeniably offered rewards in terms of power (influence on policy, sometimes at the highest levels), and in terms of prestige (entering as equals into relationships with persons of high status). For war widows who took on such roles, these rewards were a kind of compensation for the process of status erosion.

PRESERVATION OF FORMER FAMILY STATUS

Some of the war widows found the status of a war widow unsatisfactory, even at its peak, and they never adopted it for themselves. In most cases, these were widows whose husbands' occupational achievements were rewarded not only, or even mainly, through monetary means, but also through prestigious social contacts and recognition. Their occupational achievements were accompanied also by a set of social benefits which accrued to membership in an elite social group.

Some of the widows made concentrated and focussed efforts in order to preserve the family status intact. To achieve their aim, they adhered consciously and meticulously to certain symbols, social contacts, and life styles: they made certain to keep alive the social memory of their previous family status in their circle of contacts. Those widows in the sample who chose this course clung very carefully to the set of mutual services which had existed between their family and other families before widowhood.

However, the partners to the previous social contacts were generally not very forthcoming about continuing them. Therefore, the initiative for maintaining these links had always to rest with the widow. The ideology of "warriors' friendship for life and for death" which prevails in the army legitimated the demands presented by the widow in the name of past friendship, and they were met, at least for a time, with a better response than they received from other social groups. The following is an example of this: B. B. (No. 1) was the widow of a high-ranking officer in the Permanent Army. She had chosen, whether consciously or not, to try to continue her previous social status, while totally rejecting that of a war widow. Immediately after the announcement of her husband's death, she told relatives, friends, and others who came to offer condolences that she absolutely refused to arrange her affairs through the Rehabilitation Center of the Ministry of Defense. The only official body whose intervention in her problems she was ready to accept was the army. Her late husband's friends, for the most part military people, took the responsibility for dealing with all her administrative affairs, and it was they who entered her name in the list of women eligible to receive financial benefits from the Ministry of Defense. (Details regarding this procedure are given in chapter II). A similar problem was presented by the army car which had been assigned for the family's use. B. B. refused to return the car, even though she was offered a very easy purchase arrangement on another one. In the end, she won out over all opposition and kept the car for quite a long time; moreover, it retained its army license plates, which was, in fact, her main reason for wanting it so much.

In her relationship with the army, and particularly with the regiment in which her husband had served, B. B. tried to continue to act as "the Commander's wife," a role which was largely expressive and charged with affect. For instance, very shortly after the war, she visited the soldiers serving in her husband's regiment. To them, she presented both her mourning and theirs as the product of a mutual loss, and she gave expression to social values which, in any other context and coming from any other person, would have been interpreted as sheer sentimentality. As the widow of one of the highest-ranking officers killed in the Six-Day War, B. B. was among those widows most sought after for newspaper interviews and public appearances, which she in turn perceived as part of her duty as a "commander's wife." In interviews, she emphasized those traits which characterize the hero-ine—the wife of a hero—and which express the most important values of the country and of the army. At the same time, she made it clear that she expected to continue to receive the same service that the army had given the family during her husband's lifetime. These expectations were met for a certain period of time: every few weeks, a soldier was sent to service the car; every Independence Day, the children were taken by the soldiers of the regiment to watch the parade; and, when necessary, the widow got services like transporting of furniture, use of army trucks, and so on.

It is important to stress here that the economic value of such services was quite without significance to this widow. The Ministry of Defense's monthly payment, an army pension, a life insurance policy, and the considerable estate left by her husband all afforded her a standard of living higher than she had enjoyed before widowhood. B.B. continued to act "the Commander's wife" for as long as she found others ready to respond positively to this role—in effect, as long as reporters wanted to interview her, and as long as officers in the army let her present, in public, their ideology and values. However, there is no place either in the structure of Israeli society in general, or in the structure of the army in particular, for a role of this nature: the role of "the wife of the late. . . ." The erosion of prestige of "the Commander's wife" began comparatively quickly, in spite of the widow's active desire to continue in the role. As the years passed, there was decreasing readiness to let her play this role and, by the same token, there was greater reluctance to acknowledge this role by continuing to supply her with the prestige symbols she so desired. In 1974, after the Yom Kippur War, and seven years after B.B. was widowed, she participated for the first time in an event organized by the Widows' Association. This participation was an admission that she was entering the group simply in the status of a war widow. For her this meant a great loss of status and the adoption, in its place, of a comparatively low one.

In the above case, the widow's attempt to preserve her family status mainly emphasized prestige and its symbols (the army license plates, refraining from going to the Rehabilitation Center, etc.) This emphasis was common among quite a number of widows of Permanent Army men. Similarly, it was typical for the widows of university staff members to try to retain their position within the group which was the source of their previous prestige. They tried to maintain this position through social contacts, through regular visits to the deceased husband's department, through contributions of money, and through work for social events connected with his group of colleagues (e.g., promotion parties and other celebrations). In all such cases, the widow was unable to continue as a member of the group for any length of time. Social contacts were broken, seemingly temporarily, for example because of a colleague's sabbatical leave, but they were never renewed. Moreover, personnel changes within the department altered the group's structure, and this made it very difficult for the widow to keep in touch. After a comparatively short time, contact continued, at best, only with the wives of her husband's colleagues. With their husbands, contact became limited to very specific matters, which could be interpreted as "asking for favors."

Attempts to preserve prewidowhood family status also took other forms. For instance, a widow might attempt to take over her husband's economic/occupational roles in the hope of assuring the continuation of social rewards which such roles had brought in the past. Attempts like these were made by some widows whose husbands had been self-employed, either independently or in partnership. In most cases, the remaining partner was opposed to continuing the partnership with the widow. Sooner or later, he made his feelings clear and the partnership was terminated, sometimes on a more, and sometimes on a less, equitable basis. Partnerships ended, in all cases, with the widow being obliged to withdraw. The story of B.C. (No. 7) describes such a situation:

We had friends who wanted to make a heroine of me. They said, "You can continue and you must continue" (partnership in a food enterprise in which her late husband had been a partner). So I really had a partner and it (the enterprise) began operating and I worked with him. But I saw that I couldn't be a business woman, and besides, my partner wasn't the kind of person I could get along with. He had the attitude—forgive me for the expression, it's his expression—that a woman is good for bed, but not for business. He wasn't even ashamed to tell someone that if I had agreed to go to bed with him, he would also have agreed (he would have been willing); but not to go into business with me. He didn't want to cooperate with me, so I saw it was no use going on.

Widows in moshavim were prominent among those who tried to continue their late husband's undertakings. Most of them tried, at least for a time, to carry on with the upkeep of the farm by themselves. The payments they got from the Ministry of Defense enabled them to hire the extra manpower necessary to work the farm. However, in spite of their efforts and of the enormous investment on their part, no widow succeeded for more than four years in running the farm, either as it had formerly been run, or on its former scale. From the descriptions given by widows in the moshavim, it appears that they retained the "rights" of the husband for a certain period, and the moshav tried to help them in those areas where activities were carried out collectively. But after a time, the widows dropped out of all the circles of informal mutual help and of informal social relationships. I would judge that, to a large extent, this was due to doubts about the widows' ability to contribute their share to these informal exchanges. It is customary in moshavim, for instance, for members to help one another in tasks of short or seasonal duration, like the repairing of buildings and the harvesting of crops. The widow was seen (by others, and in no small measure, by herself) as likely to be in need of such help, but seldom able to return it (the possibility of reciprocating this type of help with hired labor apparently did not occur to those concerned). The breakdown of the mutuality of informal help also harmed the position of the widow in areas of formal mutual help in the moshav. The widows found, in effect, that they were receiving only a very small proportion of the centralized cooperative services organized for all members by the moshav. It does not appear that those responsible for the distribution of services intended any harm to them, but the services they got came late, and the widows were, ex post facto, relegated to the end of the line as regards both quantity and quality of services.

Although a few widows in the moshavim managed to carry on with their farms for some years, the farms themselves became marginal, their development was stunted and, as a result, the credit of the widows in the moshav declined; the possibility of their obtaining loans began to diminish, farm development was impeded still further, and thus a vicious circle was set in motion. In this overall process, the position of the widow, as one who possessed equal rights with other farmers in the moshav, deteriorated. Taken at its best, her position became similar to that of a farmer who was not very successful. However, this failure was more likely to be forgiven, since in this case the farmer was a woman.

The possibility of preserving the former family status depended on the readiness of "meaningful others" to cooperate and/or to enter into a process of exchange with the widow through which she could get those status components she considered necessary. The quid pro quos which the widows were willing to offer in these exchanges were usually quite significant, yet they rarely succeeded in realizing them. There were two main reasons for this. The first was a tendency not to enter into such exchanges with widows, because the norms that governed them were, for the most part, neither very clear nor very well known. The second was that, even when there was a readiness to enter into exchanges with widows, what the widow offered in the exchange relationship deteriorated in value very quickly. Within a comparatively short period, the widow found herself in a situation where she could not "pay" what was required of her to maintain the exchange. For one reason or for another, the process of status-erosion began to accelerate.

SELF-ACHIEVED STATUS

Another way in which a war widow could create and crystallize status was to use her own resources in order to establish a self-achieved status consonant with the general criteria of success which were acceptable in Israeli society. As noted earlier, professional occupational status constitutes the main source of social rewards in every modern society, including Israel. Within the widows' grouping, the level of readiness and of skills necessary for entering into status-rewarding occupations was very diverse. There was also considerable variation in the accumulation of status with which the widows were left upon the death of their husbands (i.e., property, social contacts, and so on). The widow could enter into the process of crystallizing a self-achieved status in one of two ways: she could either accept (and to a great extent rely upon) the status accumulation she already had; or she could completely relinquish (and, in some cases, even reject) her pre-widowhood status accumulation, and start anew. In other words, she could try and go back to the position of a nonmarried woman, or she could try to achieve her own status as a widow.

Returning to the status of a non-married woman. If the widow decided to return to the place in society which was hers before marriage, she automatically gave up the status accumulated during her married life and, instead, entered the competitive social system in the same way as any unmarried woman. In most social contacts and role performances, the facts of her marriage and widowhood lost their significance and sometimes were not even known. Adopting this pattern was worthwhile for a widow only under certain circumstances: a. when she was still at an age when she could enter into, and assimilate within, a group of unmarried people without being conspicuous and without bearing the stigma of an "old maid;" b. when the status-accumulation of her prewidowhood family was comparatively insignificant, and as a result no great loss was felt in relinquishing it; c. when the widow could place her children in a social unit which carried a status no lower than their previous one. In this way, her going back to the situation of an unmarried woman did not involve her children in status-loss.

Among the widows in the sample, only a small minority (three) chose to return to their non-married status. It is possible that the criteria for selecting the sample might partly explain this small number. All the widows in the sample were mothers, so that there is reason to assume that their average age might be higher than that of widows without children. Of the three widows in the sample who adopted this pattern, all were very young (twenty years of age or less when widowed), had only one child, and were not yet economically well established. All three widows had been married to men from a social grouping similar to their own. All three placed their children entirely in the care of their parents, thus freeing themselves to take advantage of opportunities to work, study, and socialize. Widows of a similar age and also with one child, but who differed in other respects from these widows, looked for different solutions. Some young widows who had accumulated relatively high status while married tried to find solutions which did not oblige them to give up their existing status. Becoming a young nonmarried woman, without obligations to children, was practical from two points of view: on the one hand, it obviated to a great extent the loss of status which results directly from widowhood as such; and, on the other hand, it made possible the process of status-accretion in a way and in a form acceptable for all young women of a similar age in Israeli society. Two out of the three widows who adopted this pattern registered for further study. One went to a teacher's seminary, and the other continued her high school studies through evening classes. In these two cases, the widows were only one year older than the class average. This age difference was of no significance, and the widows participated as equals in the various social activities of the student group without appearing in any way deviant or unusual. The third widow lived in a small town. In her neighborhood, it was accepted for girls who were completing the last year of compulsory schooling to go into unskilled or semiskilled occupations until they married. The widow conformed completely to this pattern.

The option of returning to the status of a non-married woman is inherently limited by time. The marriage age in Israel is rather early in general. Even in those groups where it is acceptable to postpone marriage because of study or professional training, this delay is of short duration. Thus, widows who chose to return to their premarital status obtained the desired results only if they succeeded in a comparatively short time in overcoming the crisis of widowhood, in readjusting to the life of a nonmarried woman, in meeting and becoming attached to a man, and finally in remarrying. Otherwise, above a certain age (which differed from one social group to another) the widow faces the danger of being labelled an "old maid," in which case she might prefer the status of a "young widow" with a child. It is important to note that giving up the prewidowhood status constituted only a partial or temporary renunciation. The payments a woman received as a war widow continued, and since they were received by mail and no one needed to know that she received them, she was able to use this income to maintain her status as though she were unmarried. At the same time, even though her child was in her parents' care, she could take him back at any time. In view of these facts, when she passed an age consonant with the "unmarried" state, she could without any difficulty begin a new style of life better suited to her role as a "war widow."

Crystallization of self-achieved status as a widow. The majority of the war widows either could not, or did not want to, return to a pre-marital status. Those who chose to crystallize a self-achieved status embarked on this course as head of the family, aspiring to maintain an achieved status at least on the level of the pre-widowhood family status. There were various ways in which these widows chose to enter the competitive occupational arena:

a. A few widows had succeeded, despite the restrictions of marriage and child rearing, in establishing an independent career for themselves. The new situation and pressures of widowhood impelled them to invest even more time and energy in advancing their career.

b. Some of the widows had never seriously pursued an occupational or professional career, even though they had been fully or partially trained for it (Feldman 1973). Some of them felt now that their new status as head of the family charged them with an obligation to perform in the occupational sphere as well. They decided, therefore, to adopt as their main role what had been previously only a partial or secondary role. This change in emphasis was usually accompanied by other changes: a different attitude toward work achievement, a change in attitude toward professional advancement, a readiness to invest in occupational training, studies, etc. Some of the studies or occupational activities which were adopted by the widows involved them in an investment of both time and effort, and brought about significant changes in the everyday life-style of their families.

c. A considerable number of widows, who had worked and trained before widowhood in typically feminine spheres which did not command very high prestige (Epstein 1973), found these occupations unsatisfactory once they became the main source of status. Some widows abandoned their former occupations and began training for new ones, usually in spheres which commanded higher prestige, and often involving university training. Among those whose occupations before widowhood seemed to them to command insufficient prestige (especially school and kindergarten teachers), or negative prestige (mainly housemaids, charwomen, etc.), there were a few widows who preferred to abandon such occupations altogether and to content themselves with the rewards they received by virtue of their "war widow" status. It was common for women whose family status before widowhood had been relatively high to leave typically feminine occupations. On the other hand, widows who had had a low status before widowhood made a great effort to acquire such occupations because, in comparison with the status of their previous low-prestige jobs, feminine occupations offered a higher status.

d. Some widows tried to crystallize a self-achieved status in spite of the fact that they had neither preparation nor resources for this. Most of them had little formal education, and they lacked professional or occupational training. Their previous work experience, if any, was very limited, was always of the lowest level, and had been undertaken in order to solve serious economic problems in their single lives. Their recognition of the consequences of this lack of educational and occupational experience, and the advice and guidance of the social workers in the Rehabilitation Centers, induced most of these widows to try and acquire at least minimal skills in office services such as typing, IBM card punching, and the like. Not all of the widows who tried, succeeded in acquiring such skills. But some did and, in the process, they also acquired such routines as getting to work on time, being properly dressed, and learning to fit themselves into, and become part of, a mixed social group which was different from that to which they were accustomed. This was quite an achievement and a source of status for them. Their low place in the group did not disturb them; it appeared to them as the "natural" place for a woman, and especially a woman without a husband. In most cases, these widows did not see their position as a real compensation for the married status they had lost. But they also did not conceive of it as a failure since they accepted as fact that there was no way in which a woman could compensate for that status which was lost with her husband.

In a very few cases, widows who made this attempt succeeded in achieving independently a comparatively high status, which was more of a real compensation for the status-loss which had resulted from widowhood. The following are two typical examples of such instances. I.H. (No. 13) emigrated from Morocco to Israel when she was fourteen years old. In Israel, because of the special conditions which prevailed in the 1950s, the family suffered a serious status-loss. All the children in the family were forced by circumstances to leave school and take on paid work in order to help support the household. I.H. married at the young age of sixteen. According to her, one of the reasons for this early marriage was her desire to escape from the difficult economic situation in the family. With marriage, she stopped working outside her own household. After she became a widow, in spite of the necessity to work in order to supplement the family income, and against the advice of the social worker in the Rehabilitation Center, I.H. decided to complete both her elementary and her secondary formal education. Her aim was to enter one of the institutes of higher learning in the country. The alternatives she set for herself were either to study engineering at the Haifa Technion, journalism at the Hebrew University or, if she were unable to realize these aspirations, to go to a teachers' seminary. In the first year of widowhood, she successfully completed elementary school and was accepted as a student at an evening high school. While the research was in progress, she finished the first two years of high school and succeeded in passing the first stage of the matriculation examination. She then entered the eleventh grade of high school. In explaining the supreme efforts she had made, I.H. emphasized many of the social status advantages accruing to a formal education.

Although B.C. (No. 9) had lived in Israel for seven years when she was widowed, her poor Hebrew did not enable her even to do her own shopping. In all those years she had never left the house by herself, not even to spend an afternoon with women friends in her neighborhood. She had lived in a small town but, after being widowed, moved to one of the major cities in order to be closer to two of her married sisters. Shortly thereafter, it became clear to her that her sisters would not be able to protect her as her husband had done. According to her description of events, the knowledge that only she herself would be able to regain at least part of what she had lost with his death both frightened her and compelled her forcefully to try to crystallize an independent status. B.C. studied Hebrew intensively for a year. She was then able to read and write, while her command of spoken Hebrew became sufficient for most communication. After completing this language course, she took and completed a course in cosmetics, passing both the practical and theoretical tests. With the help of the Ministry of Defense, she purchased all the necessary equipment and opened a beauty salon in her own apartment. The income from this business allowed her a considerable rise in her standard of living; she moved to a larger apartment in a better neighborhood, bought a car, and so forth. In one of my informal visits to her home, I expressed admiration for her achievement. Her reply was: "Well, at last we live the way we used to." There is no doubt that her standard of living at this point was much higher than anything she had known before widowhood. It would appear that, by this stage of her self-attained achievement, she felt that she had succeeded in reaching a level which was a real compensation for the status she had lost with her husband. After the Yom Kippur War, payments by the Ministry of Defense to war widows increased considerably, and all widows, including those of the Six-Day War, benefited. This gave B.C. the freedom to stop working as a cosmetician, and instead she took a part-time job punching IBM cards in the research department of a major bank. Her explanation for this move was: "Now that I get enough money from the Ministry of Defense and have already bought everything we need, I want a better social position. Now I want to go to a concert and meet friends from work there." In sociological terms she renounced economic rewards, of which she had plenty, in order to gain more prestigious social benefits that were, for her, relatively rare.

Most of the widows who tried to activate their own resources, and to compete for positions in the open job market, attained levels of occupational achievement consonant with their education and professional training. These levels were comparatively high, much higher than those they had attained before widowhood, and the formal rewards they received were in keeping with their achievement. In fact, that status which was built on the widow's self-attained achievement was the only type, among all those described above, which was not eroded directly by time. Moreover, in most cases such status tended in absolute terms to gain ground with time. Nonetheless, it must be kept in mind that a desirable status for a widow was usually calibrated according to prewidowhood status. Measured by this yardstick, even such independently achieved status did not usually satisfy the aspirations of the widow, nor did it prevent a decline in status for herself and her family. If this did not apply in all cases, according to absolute criteria, it did apply in almost all the cases, according to relative criteria. In Israeli society in general, it is common for a husband to have higher skills than his wife, and the widows in this sample were no exception. Given this basic premise, it was very difficult for a widow to reach the same occupational level as her late husband. Only those women who had begun to develop their own careers before widowhood had succeeded, three years later and with considerable investment of effort, in doing so. Even in those cases, however, they were not able to create a status for themselves and for their families which was similar to that of their prewidowhood lives. For this there were two reasons:

a. In Israel, like in many other societies, the social rewards for a man performing a role are different from those accorded to a woman in the same role (Aloni 1976; Ozerman 1976; Padan-Eisenstark 1974; Tamari 1974). In most cases, this difference does not lie in the formal rewards that accompany the role, but in the symbolic "padding" of benefits and prestige which are accorded to a man but not to a woman (Astin 1969; Barad 1966; White 1970). Since the status of the family is an ascribed one, the importance of such symbols is very great. Thus, the wife of a man who fulfills a certain role enjoys, through the benefits and prestige symbols of her husband, a higher status than does a woman who herself fulfills the same role.

b. When her status was measured by her position among friends of her late husband and herself, the widow inevitably found that it had lagged, even where she had succeeded in reaching an occupational level identical with that which her husband had achieved. This status-lag resulted from the fact that, while she was trying to catch up with his occupational status, the occupational achievements of their friends continued to advance and so remained ahead of hers. Thus, she could not retain that place which her husband would have had within the group at this later point. Only when her occupational sphere was completely different from that of her husband could she create for herself a separate friendship- and/or a different reference-group. In such cases, her status-lag was no longer, or was only partially, relevant to her present status.

At the outset, I argued that there were two main sources of erosion in the status of the war widow: one was the loss of that status which was ascribed to her by virtue of her husband's achievement, and the other was that loss which occurred in her transfer from the category of "married woman" to that of "unmarried woman" or, using Parson's terminology, the loss of that most meaningful achievement of a woman. It was almost impossible for a widow to compensate fully for the loss of the first type of status through her own resources. At the same time, the more she was able to compensate for this type of status, the more she reduced her chances of attaining the other type of status—that is, through remarriage, since the higher the self-achieved status of the widow, the greater were her expectations about the status of a candidate for marriage. Even if she were ready to deviate from this norm, which usually was not the case (Shamgar-Handelman 1982), and to reduce the qualifications she expected of marriage candidates, the men themselves held to the same norm, and therefore were looking for spouses whose status was lower than their own. Thus, the higher the achieved status of the widow, the less desirable she was as a candidate for marriage to a man whose achieved status was lower than hers. Widows were quite aware of this attitude, and they acted accordingly. It was not at all uncommon for a widow to be faced with the choice either of advancing professionally, or of increasing her chances of remarriage.[6] In some instances, widows in the sample consciously limited their professional advancement in order to increase their marriage possibilities; in other instances, widows decided to advance their careers, although they realized that in so doing they were limiting or obviating their chance of remarrying.

The widow could escape from this "status catch" by joining groups in which the norms of marriage, of discrimination against women, and so forth, either were not as strong as in Israeli society in general, or were different. One possibility was to throw in her lot with the bohemian community. Among bohemians, to be unconventional or "different" is a social advantage of sorts, and one which they often try hard to achieve. Unusual marriages, in terms of age and status (e.g., marriage between a very successful actress and a stagehand), are not subjected to sanctions as they would be outside this circle, and there is far less emphasis on couples than there is in "established society." Friendship between the individuals of one couple and those of another is freely acknowledged and approached with a relaxed attitude. The achievements of both men and women are rewarded more or less equally in those occupations usually prevalent in this grouping (i.e., plastic arts, music, theater, and other similar areas of activity). The widow who developed her own career through such activities could receive adequate rewards for her achievements, including prestige, fame, and invitations to prestigious functions. Her loss of status due to the fact that she was not married was comparatively slight in this grouping, and being without a spouse would not prevent her from enjoying fairly wide social contacts within the group. Moreover, since there are comparatively few norms for mate selection among bohemians, her occupational achievements would compromise her chance of remarrying less than they would in Israeli society at large. Among the widows studied, a few tried to join such groups, but only two, who had developed their artistic hobby into careers, succeeded in participating fully in the bohemian community.

The bohemian community was not the only one that afforded the widows comparatively satisfying rewards; other marginal and deviant groups, such as the golden youth and beatniks, offered similar advantages. However, only a very small minority of the widows entered such groups, or even attempted to do so. For the most part, they continued to function in the same types of settings in which they had lived before widowhood, even if not always in the same specific group.

The Manipulation of Status Alternatives

The status alternatives described above created for the widow an area of freedom within which to maneuvre. The extent to which she used the different alternatives to achieve status, and the degree of efficiency with which she manipulated their use, depended on her personal attributes, talents, skills, and resources, as well as on her ability to understand her situation, and on her willingness to pay the price for those benefits she got from the various types of status. It should not be overlooked that different types of status were, to some degree, mutually exclusive. The simultaneous use of more than one status was possible only where the settings and contexts in which the statuses were activated were separated one from the other. In the same way, neither were all combinations of status simultaneously possible. When a widow used several types of status simultaneously, she did so through "situational selection:" thus, she chose to present herself in a given situation in that image which, according to her assessment of that situation, would give her the maximum benefit (Goffman 1959; Schutz & Luckmann 1973; Warriner 1970). The story of Z.Z. demonstrates how different statuses could be maneuvred simultaneously.

Z.Z. (No. 26) completed her academic studies before marriage. For the sake of her husband's career, the family moved to a small town. At that time, the couple had two small children and it was not too difficult for Z.Z. to give up her own occupational advancement in favor of his. However, when she became widowed, there was no doubt in her mind as to the direction she would choose. Her former place of work in the city offered her quite an important position, with good prospects of future advancement. She decided to return there and to put all her efforts into her own career. Firm in this resolve, Z.Z. approached the Rehabilitation Center worker in the city and asked for her help in solving the problem of temporary housing. Such housing would enable her to give her new job a trial period before deciding on a permanent move to the city. However, the social worker tried to persuade her not to make this move and, when she could not influence her, rejected her request for aid with temporary rental payments in the city (this type of help was given almost automatically in most cases). The social worker explained that the purpose of this move was wholly career-motivated and that this did not justify help from the Ministry of

Defense. Z.Z. rejected this decision and made another appeal for assistance, this time invoking the help of the social worker in the town where she was still living. This worker gave her recommendation and the application was accepted.

The tone of the relationship between Z.Z. and the Rehabilitation Center social worker had been set at their first meeting. At this point, Z.Z. decided that their approaches to matters of "common concern" were so divergent that there was no way of bridging the gap between them. Accordingly, she limited her contacts with the Rehabilitation Center to wholly administrative and technical matters. As a result, and quite aware of what she was doing, she gave up a considerable part of the supplementary benefits to which she was entitled as a war widow. For example, because of her lack of contact with the Rehabilitation Center workers, only after a year did she discover that war widows were eligible for a kindergarten allowance. But, because of this long delay, she had become ineligible for such payments, and she could not receive them retroactively. She incurred similar losses in connection with her right to a reduction in car insurance. In spite of these losses, however, she refused to perform as "war widow" in these contexts. Still, she was prepared to accept both the role and the status of "war widow" in other contexts. For example, Z.Z. participated for a long time in a therapy group for war widows. She tried to select and to control those statuses which she presented in different social contexts. Thus, while she was willing to be a "war widow" within the therapy group, she refused for many years to have her personal status changed in her identity card to that of "widow", until she discovered that without this change she could not get a passport.[7] She also recalled that when on one occasion she needed the services of a government office which did not deal specifically with war widows, she deliberately played the role of a "war widow" who could not find her way about the administrative maze. The kindhearted clerks reacted to this by attending to her business quickly and efficiently so as to make matters easier for her. It is interesting to note that although, according to the values of Israeli society, a sympathetic attitude towards a war widow, especially on the part of public servants, is expected, Z.Z. felt that she hoodwinked these clerks and got from them a more helpful response than was actually due her.

The above is a typical example of the simultaneous use of status alternatives where different statuses were activated in different contexts to reach different aims. Although the widow usually saw one particular status as dominant, she did not necessarily abandon the other types of status. In this case, Z.Z. conceived her place in society as a combination of her professional and her economic achievements, her political affiliation, her life-style, and so forth. But, at the same time, she accepted her war widow status as relevant to certain social contexts. Defining a situation, determining her aims, and evaluating her power within this situation—these were the factors that guided her in selecting the specific status she would present in a particular context.

The story of Z.Z. exemplifies the simultaneous use of status alternatives. Another way of manipulating available status alternatives was the transfer from one type of status, which was used in most areas of a widow's life, to another type of status which, temporarily, became the dominant one. This use of statuses was periodical rather than simultaneous.

Shifting from one status to another was one of the ways of dealing with different social contexts. A widow could shift status in order to test out or familiarize herself with new situations. Such shifts enabled her to gauge the benefits and the drawbacks of various status alternatives and thus to decide which she preferred. Another reason for shifting status resulted from changes in the widow's situation. For example, a widow who returned to her premarital status at the outset of her widowhood would abandon that status if she had not remarried within a few years but had, nonetheless, reached an age where she could no longer realize all the potential benefits of her nonmarried status. On the other hand, as time passed, she may have learned a trade or a profession and started upon an independent career, so that she then found that there were benefits to be gained in the status of a woman who, as head of a family, had her own self-achieved career.

The most common transfer of status found among the widows in the sample was from a type of status which tended to erosion (like the status of "war widow," or the previous family status) to a self-achieved status. This represented a clear attempt on the widow's part to escape the process of erosion which lay ahead. Since the pace of status erosion is unpredictable, it was hard to say when such a shift in status would occur for any one particular widow. In addition, some widows might have continued to hold on to this type of status in spite of the process of erosion. In any event, the adoption or renunciation of one or another type of status did dictate certain forms of behavior on the part of the widow and made it necessary for her to give up certain rewards in favor of others.

Widows differed in their awareness level of possible alternatives and, therefore, in their capacity to assess the realization of these alternatives. At times, widows found themselves in particular social positions without knowing how they got there or how to disengage from them. On the other hand, in a number of cases, widows used their alternatives in a planned and conscious way and well understood which benefits and drawbacks to expect. The following stories of widows, and quotations from interviews with them, are intended to demonstrate both the way in which status alternatives were manipulated by them and their high level of awareness of the alternatives available to them.

N.A. (No. 54), at the time of our interview, was what the widows called "a professional widow," involved with various social activities, some of which were directed toward helping other war widows. In spite of, or perhaps because of, this involvement, she began to question whether this status suited her. In an account of how she handled problems connected with the status of a "professional war widow," N.A. recalled an argument with one of her friends of very long standing:

> It didn't seem right to her (the friend), the new way of life I had—a lot of travelling and going out with new friends and becoming quite detached from my old social contacts. Once we had an argument, and she hinted that I made the whole thing (widowhood) into a tool to be used. And, at that time, she was right. I think it was a very important remark. Perhaps this is a very serious danger. Somehow, war widows have a certain standing—position—in Israel—I don't know how to say it. I have new friends, and the way they invite—well, it's terrible to say this, but the way they invite me is the same way they would invite a scientist or a doctor. They don't invite me because of myself; they invite me so that they can say, "I had a war widow at my party." At the beginning, it quite shocked me and then I thought to myself, "the hell with that!" I enjoy it, they're nice people, they're people who one day might be important to me, so why not? I'll come the way everyone else comes. Like the journalist, who isn't insulted at being invited as a journalist; so why should I give it a thought? This week I was invited by very nice people, who also invited R.B. He had interviewed me once and I understood what the hostess was after. She thought it would be a bit piquant—the interviewer with . . . oh, never mind. He is a very pleasant person and nothing of the sort happened: nothing was said about the interview. I remember sitting there in a very charming living room with really fantastic things, and I thought to myself, "to hell—she invites the journalist, the judge, the doctor, and me—then that means she's inviting the best."

N.A. accepted her widowhood virtually as a professional status, akin to that of a doctor, journalist, or judge.

As in any other role, however, the widow had obligations as well as social rewards, and in some situations N.A. found those obligations beyond her strength. Her involvement in public activities as a war widow began almost immediately after the war. Around that time (according to her), she suggested forming a group within one of the women's organizations to help war widows whose names and addresses were provided by the Ministry of Defense. The members of the group began to visit the widows at home and to help them with initial arrangements. Out of this activity, therapy groups developed under the guidance of psychologists who were members of the women's organization. These groups aimed at giving psychological aid and support to the widows. In this situation, N.A. had a dual role: with respect to the therapy group, she represented the organization; but with respect to the organization, she was a war widow, a member of the therapy group and, as such, she represented the group. She came under much pressure because of this dual role, and it proved too much for her:

> Sometimes, when I didn't come (to therapy) they asked, "Why didn't you come? What's the matter, doesn't it suit you any more?" It's unpleasant for me, all the public striptease (but her status obligated her in this context). I got to the point where I just asked questions simply to participate. I sucked questions out of my thumb, so as not to sit there and not do anything. It was very unpleasant. The circumstances were too difficult and too serious for me to play the role (of "professional widow") among my friends.

Unable to meet the demands of the therapy group, N.A. left it. At the same time, she shifted the focus of her activities in the women's organization to a solely representative role. This change of emphasis was made entirely according to N.A.'s dictates, and the organization gave her a free hand to choose her area of activity. To my mind, this demonstrates the importance attached to the high prestige and repute of the role of "war widow" within the organization, particularly at that time. N.A. took on various tasks, for example, as head of the cultural committee (a position she filled only in a perfunctory way), and was accorded many of the rewards connected with such roles, usually reserved for veteran members of the organization. For example, she represented the organization at a women's conference in Europe and undertook a lecture tour of selected European Jewish communities. A year after the interview quoted, she married and cut all formal connection with the organization. Even her informal contacts with most of those she had come to know during the period of her public activities became fewer and more distant until they were dissolved completely, to the point where not one of her former friends in the organization could help me find her after her remarriage. It would appear from the foregoing that for N.A. the women's organization had served as a convenient framework within which to activate her status as a "war widow." As soon as she left this status category, however, the organization ceased to be a source of benefit for her. Conversely, once she had lost the status of war widow, the organization could no longer use her to represent the war widows' grouping.

The story of N.A. demonstrates the high level of awareness, at least of some war widows, about the status alternatives open to them.

An additional example of such maneuvering is seen in the calculations of B.B. (No. 1) when she faced problems similar to those of N.A.

Before widowhood, B.B. was the wife of a high officer in the regular army. The separation of their respective areas of activity was described in the following way: "With us, everything was shared with the Army. This means that we (the family) got very little. He loved the home, but when I said to him once, 'give us not fifty percent, give us ten percent,' he replied, 'You are here, and you take care of everything and I don't have to worry. But there, I have a thousand boys I have to take care of.' " During my research, B.B. still continued to try to maintain her prewidowhood status. However, after three years of widowhood, she became sensitive to social pressure to relinquish this attempt and began to create a new status for herself, more in keeping with her situation. As she described it:

When my husband was alive, no one ever asked me why I don't work. As though once he had said it (that I don't have to work), that was the end of it. But now, not only friends, close friends, but everyone, even total strangers, ask me, "Why don't you work? It would be much better for you, you'd be among people. Don't remain at home—you will degenerate!" I really can't move ten steps away from the house without someone asking me about it. I can't explain to everyone that I am not frustrated by the fact that I am raising my children. But, just in order to stop the whole thing, I have decided to look for work—only part-time, not full-time and not every day, because I want one day for myself.

As a result of social pressure, B.B. began to examine the possibilities open to her:

I was offered a lot of jobs. The interesting ones are full-time, really careers. At the university, for instance, as an assistant to the Academic Secretary. There was another job, as secretary to the Dean. That is a full-time job, plus afternoon meetings. It's clerical work, which is interesting. You need an academic education, and you have a lot of contact with students and professors. But they're full-time jobs and I can't take them.

Another possibility, of which B.B. was aware, but which she rejected, was to develop an independent career. From what she said, it was not clear whether this rejection was due to her unwillingness to break away from her past status, or because she thought that any self-achieved status she could create would not be a true compensation for the status which she had made such effort to maintain. The career path was not the only possibility open to B.B. however:

A year ago, I got an offer to go as a delegate to the Working Women's Organization to represent the city I was living in. I never was in the Organization, so I asked, "Why suddenly me—you have a lot of working women here?" So she said, "You're young and charming, and from an Oriental background." I got endless suggestions of this kind. Today, a war widow is a "brand name."

During this research, B.B. was still quite satisfied with her success in maintaining her prewidowhood family status. At the same time she was fully aware of other possibilities open to her and of the differences between them. Thus, a career was a big investment (a full-time job involving afternoon meetings, and giving up, to a great extent, the role of child-raiser), but it had obvious advantages (interest, contacts with students and members of staff). On the other hand, because being a "professional widow" was a temporary phenomenon (fashionable, a "brand name"), she thought it perhaps "worth getting into." A few years after she was interviewed for this research, B.B. was still managing to maintain her pre-widowhood status, albeit at a steep and ever increasing price. As already mentioned, my last meeting with her took place at a point where she had to compromise and to accept the status of war widow in place of that which she had tried to maintain.

The last example, that of S.E. (No. 17), exemplifies the complexity of status manipulation as experienced by the widows in this study. While she was married, S.E. was a teacher and her husband was at the outset of his academic career at the university. Considering the young age of this couple and the fact that they already had two small children, their achievements (together and individually) were comparatively high. Since most of this young family's resources were invested in the husband's professional career, when he died all the family resources were lost as well. S.E. had to start from the beginning to crystallize status for herself and for the family she headed. The following quotation from the interview with her explains how she did it:

Statement defining high status of a war widow as reflecting society's central values.	My symbol is that I gave my husband for the State and I'm proud of it, because this is my homeland. The label "war widow" brings obligations. My status as a war widow obligated me—it obligates me in the eyes of my children, and in the eyes of the public.
Refusal to exchange the high status for obviously meager return.	I had an incident in the kindergarten today. Once a year we pay IL 55 for dancing lessons and other activities. So I gave them a check dated the first of the coming month, as this month I am very short of money and have a lot of expenses. The kindergarten

teacher said to me, "I thought that from you I wouldn't ask for the money, so make the check out for only IL. 30." I said, "No, I pay like everyone else." I don't ask favors of anyone. I don't define myself (in this context) as a widow. I'm a woman and not a widow with a sign.

Willingness to exchange the status of a war widow for a position of political influence and prominence.

Before the cease-fire there were negotiations and Gahal (a party in the government coalition at the time) was about to leave the Government. I felt I couldn't bear it any more. I said to myself. 'S., it would be immoral for you not to do something now.' So what did I do? I wrote a letter to the Prime Minister. To this day, I have not received an answer. I had asked her (Golda Meir) to think it over (returning Sinai), so that the time should not come when my daughter would be writing her a letter also as a war widow. After this, I went to A.L. of the Land of Israel Movement[8] and said to him: "Look, I feel I can't stand aside any more. I want to do something." He was delighted. I explained to him who I was, what I am. I told him that I, more than others, can create an image which cannot be ignored, and that if I find another five widows like myself, we could make a lot of noise—noise which would have more effect than asking a thousand people to demonstrate (against the return of Sinai). I said that I know that in this country the status of the war widow is valued and revered and I feel that I shouldn't use it in unimportant matters; but here our very lives depend on it and I believe that if I don't use my special position (as a widow) this would be a mistake.

Exchange negotiation breaks down because widow's evaluation of war-widow status not reciprocated, and return offered deemed insulting.

So this man offered me a position as a secretary and asked me if I knew how to type. I couldn't sit there any more. I was disgusted. (S.E. subsequently moved to another city.)

Leaving "feminine" career track yielding only low status in order to pursue new career track with potentially higher status rewards.

I said to myself that I want to leave teaching (at that time S.E. had a university teaching diploma that enabled her to teach in high school). I said that I don't want to go back to teaching because I feel I shouldn't be in this limited setting of a school. I feel that I can deal with high administration—that's what I like and I want to try it.

Attempts to use war widow status to facilitate entry to self-achieved high status track; first attempt through Rehabilitation Center meets with failure and frustration.

(S.E. tried to hold the Ministry of Defense to its promise to take care of all the problems of war widows, and approached the Rehabilitation Center with a request for help in finding work suited to her own evaluation of her aspiration and talents.)

They offered me all kinds of small secretarial jobs. That's the problem. A widow wants to rehabilitate herself and here she finds a wall—a social worker who is herself a little thing who sits there and gets her salary, can solve problems only up to a certain level, and from there on she is incapable. When I arrived there, they had nothing to offer me. They had nothing to say to me. I had no one to approach. Who at the Rehabilitation Center will help me (in employment matters)? They're not capable of doing anything. If the widow is a housemaid, she (the social worker) can place her with one of her friends; or if she's a little secretary, she can place her with the Histadrut (General Federation of Labor) or the Mo'etzet Hapo'alot (Working Women's Council).

Second (independent) attempt meets with success despite, rather than because of, war-widow status.

(By chance, S.E. learned of an opening in the field of public relations.)

There was an application committee. Some ten candidates came to be interviewed. I was one of them. One of the things on which the committee attacked me the most was the question of how I, a widow with two children, would manage. This was a blow below the belt. Because you know my situation. A woman who goes to work knows that she has to find someone to stay at home with the children, so don't exaggerate your investigation.

Self-achieved status: New career yields rewards commensurate with its "market value"—power, money and prestige— satisfying status aspirations.

(S.E. was hired for the job, and described it as follows):

I direct a department for special public relations at the institution. I deal with scientists and scientific delegations, presidents of universities, deans, and Nobel Prize winners. I am the liaison officer in the institution. When I got the job, I had no secretary, no desk; but today I have a whole department—two secretaries, an accountant, a complete set-up. I'm not going to leave this work, and the people there know it. They know that this is my life now. They know I created it. I have status in the institution, and today if S.E. calls, it is not the secretary who answers her, but the head of the department himself. He comes and listens carefully to what I have to say, because I have created a name for myself and a position, and they all know me.

Conflict between career status and personal status; after three years of widowhood, remarriage seen as desirable and attainable, though not pressing issue.

(First Interview)
I am a woman. I'm very much a woman, and I'm not ugly. I am an attractive woman. My appearance is a bit like a "glamour girl." I'm young—I'm twenty-seven—and I'll certainly be able to remarry. Of course, I want to rehabilitate myself in this way as well.

After five years of widowhood, conscious attempts to increase chances of remarriage and attempts to create potential for new social contacts.

(Second interview)
Last year I got tired of work, of the job, of everything. I thought I must change things a bit, my surroundings as well, the social contacts. It's very hard, as you know. That's not new. There's a surplus of women and it's the same old story. We talked a lot in the first interview about the surplus of women. This is a problem that everyone wants to solve for herself. I thought that perhaps the best thing for me is to get away from it all. I thought maybe a trip. But that's not so simple. So I thought, perhaps through the Ministry of Foreign Affairs.

Sacrificing career and potential advancement for benefits of social/ geographical relocation; using war widow status, where its value is perceived highest in the marriage market; remarriage perceived as central issue—fighting for life.

The post of Administrative Secretary in Embassy "X" is not a rise in level for me. It is not up to the types of job I have already held. But from the interest point of view, and being in the center of things, it's not so bad. My thought was obviously not only the job itself. The job is the key, because I can't manage without it; but the idea was to make contacts in the Jewish community in "X." For them, I wouldn't be a "local," I wouldn't be the average woman—not that I'm the average woman here. But here there is a problem, a whole generation of men gone—men who might have been acceptable candidates for marriage. And you are left alone, alone, alone, alone. And you try to break through . . . I thought that (going away) may be the solution. And so, in spite of the fact that the status aspect is not enough for me, from the point of view of the interest and the place, I thought it might be good. He (her superior) understood my motives in going away. At first he tried to stop me. He said that there is a jungle out there, that I shouldn't go, that he is terribly worried about me, that he is afraid I won't be happy, and so on. I told him that I have no other solution, that I'm fighting for my life. I'll be abroad for two years and I'll get something out of it, all kinds of things, a new experience. I don't see going to find a husband as the only aim, but the idea is that—maybe. Here I'm not getting anywhere and I can't go on any more. So—maybe.

Nonetheless, candidate for remarriage has to have matching status.

I can't marry just anybody. He has to be able to stand up to me.

Failure of plans result in new situation demanding extreme solutions: renouncing all previous achievements; starting a new career track.

(For various reasons, S.E.'s plan to go abroad did not materialize) In (the institution where she had previously worked) they offered me a few things. But you understand that what they now offered was even more difficult, with more responsibilities. It was no longer somewhere in the middle. Everything I was offered was something enormous, that demands the whole of you. So I decided to go and study. I registered, but I don't know if I have been accepted. This year there are problems—there are a thousand candidates for eight places. I took the examination and I hope I was accepted.

Epilogue

Between the years 1972 and 1976, the Widows' Organization gained a lot of ground. The newly-elected director used the power of the organization to achieve both actual benefits and public recognition. Her position within Yad Lebanim was strong—she was highly appreciated and well-liked, so much so in fact that she was able to make sure that no serious decision would be made without taking into account its relevance to the widows. In spite of the strong support and recognition by both widows and officials that she was a most able representative of the widows, she had to resign her job once she remarried. Neither she nor her colleagues and supporters could overcome the prevalent assumption that once a widow remarried, her past life was no longer relevant. She forfeited her right to speak for the widows and became a stranger among them.

After the 1973 Yom Kippur War, the assumption that the State owed the widows only minimum subsistence was publicly questioned for the first time. The initiators of this public debate were the parents of war widows who formed an ad hoc small organization to bring the whole issue to the attention of the mass media. At the heart of the matter lay an objection in principle to the minimum subsistence criterion. They claimed that although in fact the State supported the widows on a higher level than minimum subsistence, it was shameful to use this criterion, basically derived from welfare policy, in the context of war widows' rights. Their achievements were few, and the organization itself folded after a short time. Nonetheless, for the first time, parents of the widows, as opposed to parents of the dead soldiers, appeared as a concerned group with something to say in this context. It is important to note that my material shows a very high level of involvement by the widows' parents in the lives and problem-solving process of the widows. The parental investment of money, time and consideration in the lives of their daughters and grandchil-

179

dren was very high. This investment went virtually unrecognized by the public, by the authorities, and often even by the widows themselves. As a result, the parents of the widows had no recourse to help, support or guidance from any official body. The reader might recall the few situations described where parents were refused cooperation from social workers on the grounds that they had no official standing. This attempt by the widows' parents to gain some recognized status as involved parties to the widows' affairs met with total failure.

The bereaved parents, on the other hand, did succeed in gaining an officially recognized status, in this instance vis-à-vis their grandchildren. A long and very painful debate eventually engendered a law according to which paternal grandparents of children who lost their fathers in war have the right to be heard in court hearings concerning the adoption of their grandchildren by the mother's new husband. It is worth noting that this is the only case in Israel in which any considerations other than the welfare of the child are introduced into adoption proceedings.

During the years that have passed since the formal conclusion of the study, I have had the opportunity to meet again with many of the women that appear in this book. Most of them are by now middle-aged, and some are already elderly. Each in her different way has her own tale to tell. Many (almost half) of them have remarried, some while they still had a chance to create a new full family by having children with a new husband; for others, even those that wanted it very much, it was too late. Most of their children, even those born after their father's death, have by now left home or will shortly join the army.

Some of the women have kept me informed about the major events of their lives. S.E. (No. 17), for example, finished law school and embarked upon another new career. She later married a colleague and moved to another city. K.M. (No. 33) is still working as a librarian. Both of her children are doing their army service. Not long ago I met M.S. (No. 60) on the street with her new husband, pushing a baby carriage. She introduced me to her husband and proudly showed me her grandson. This baby, like many grandchildren of fallen soldiers, was named after his grandfather. C.M. (No. 27) reached retirement age long ago, but she still keeps her part-time secretarial job, hoping not to be forced into full retirement in the near future. T.N. (No. 35) is by now a full professor in an institute of higher learning. N.A. (No. 54) remarried and retreated into quiet family life. S.B. (No. 47) has also remarried, and has achieved fame as a volunteer in a charity organization.

Those of the women that have remarried no longer have rights in the Rehabilitation Department, and consequently the rights of their children have eroded as well. Those who have not remarried experienced a serious reduction in their standard of living once their children came of age, and are now forced to rely on their own financial resources. Their connections with the Rehabilitation bureaus are minimal. The only widows that still have intensive contacts with the Rehabilitation workers are the three unfortunate ones that lost sons in war—one in the Yom Kippur War (1973) and two others in the 1982 Lebanon war—now under their new designation as "bereaved parents."

New generations of widows have entered the system since the study took place. Many of the social workers have left and new ones have taken their place. New Ministry of Defense Rehabilitation Centers have opened. Some administrative changes in their organization and in the delivery of services have been introduced. These changes are considered by the Ministry of Defense Rehabilitation Department to be "radical changes." Whether they have really altered the essence of the relationship between the Ministry of Defense and the war widows is questionable. The last time I visited one of the centers, I witnessed a young girl, the daughter of a dead soldier, inquiring about her entitlement to a Ministry of Defense university tuition grant. This is one of the rights due to her by law as the daughter of a fallen soldier. The welfare officer (a clerk) assured her that she was indeed entitled to this grant, but it could only be awarded after she had met with the social worker. I could not but conclude that compliance with "treatment" was still necessary in order to realize financial rights. The point of view of the widows was expressed clearly by B.Q. (No. 50), whom I still meet at infrequent intervals on the street. She "assures" me that the only thing that has changed in the Rehabilitation Center is ". . .that the social workers are younger and less-experienced and I'm older and have much less patience for them."

During the war in Lebanon, the following report on a Knesset proceeding appeared in the Jerusalem Post under the heading, "Debate on war widows' pensions:"

> Should war widows who remarry continue to receive their monthly pensions? The present law says no, but Moshe Shahal (MK, Alignment) disagrees. Because of that provision in the law, he says, many widows prefer not to marry, living with men they would otherwise wed.
>
> Shahal yesterday presented a private member's bill that would remove the financial obstacle to holy wedlock.
>
> Defense Minister, Moshe Arens, replying for the government, said that it was perhaps "understandable, human and somewhat regrettable" that some war widows act as Shahal had described. But their behavior is basically the same as that of workers who reject job offers because they prefer to draw unemployment insurance, he said.

There is no reason to pay pensions to war widows who remarry, Arens said. Nevertheless, he agreed that the bill be referred to the Labour and Social Affairs Committee, and the Knesset did so.

Michael Bar-Zohar (Alignment), in a motion for the agenda, proposed that war widows' pensions be linked to the average wage, to prevent their further erosion.

Arens replied that while there is no limit to the country's debt to these widows, there is a limit to the resources it can allocate for the purpose. He noted that the pension of a woman with two children is greater than the take-home pay of a breadwinner with two children, who earns the average wage in the economy.

The motion was referred to the Foreign Affairs and Defense Committee (*Jerusalem Post*, Thursday, November 10, 1983, p. 3.).

Reading this article gave me a sad feeling of dèjá vu.

Appendix I

Research Methods and Sources of Information

$\mathbf{A}$s was mentioned before (chapter I), there is very little systematic sociological knowledge either on war widows in general, or on war widows in Israeli society in particular. This fact, together with my concern not to bind the study to untested theoretical assumptions, sent me into an unstructured hunt for information concerning war widows. In the course of the field work, relevant sources of information were revealed, and one source led to another. At the same time, analytical questions led to the search for answers in yet other directions. In order to understand the multi-faceted aspects of the widow's situation, I felt it necessary to study those with whom the widow came into contact as well, and this attempt further extended the sources of information that I used. The accumulated material was derived from two types of sources: documentary and other written information, and personal information.

I. The documentary information.
   A. The files of the Rehabilitation Department of the Ministry of Defense furnished both concentrated data on the whole group of war widows and some personal information on individual widows in the study. This material provided the basic demographic and socio-economic data for this study, as well as practical tools such as the list of names and addresses that was the basis for sampling and that enabled me to reach the widows to be studied.
   B. The records of all Knesset (Parliament) debates that concerned war widows from the early years of the State up to the end of 1975 were collected. This material served as a basis for establishing the formal position of a war widow in the State of Israel.
   C. All the articles, stories, news items, and letters to the editor concerning war widows that appeared in the three most widely-read daily newspapers in Israel from the outbreak of the Six-Day War

until the end of 1975 were collected. That material served a parallel purpose to the one above—that of establishing the social position of war widows in Israeli society.

II. Personal information

A. Many people, usually from the helping professions, were involved in administering the special services designated for war widows. The main "gate keepers" of these services were the social workers employed by the Ministry of Defense, and in this capacity they were brought into frequent contact with the war widows. The services themselves were delivered variously by psychologists, psychiatrists, counsellors, army welfare officers, and lay volunteers. All the social workers assigned to work with war widows, and representatives of all other helping professions, were interviewed systematically. Twenty-one people were involved altogether in these interviews.

B. Often during an interview with a widow, she would say: ". . .you should talk to my lawyer/friend/parent/parent-in-law about . . .." I frequently did. The information gathered from those people was not collected systematically; they often refused to be tape-recorded or quoted, and in most cases the conversation with them took the form of an informal exchange of opinions or ideas. The material was always recorded as soon as possible after the conversation had taken place. References to it appear throughout the body of the work, generally to illustrate a point. Nonetheless, the main value of this data lay in the deep insights and help it afforded in understanding the situation of the war widows.

C. The main source of personal information about the situation of war widows was, of course, the war widows themselves.

The War Widows

Of the 315 wives and mothers who were widowed during the Six-Day War, eighty-one did not qualify to participate in the first stage sample of this study because they were kibbutz members.[1] One-third (78) of the 234 women that constituted the population of this study were sampled for interview, and of them, seventy-one actually participated. These seventy-one widows represented 30 percent of all the eligible study population, or 91 percent of the sample. The sampling method was based on two main assumptions. The first was that the social environment of the widow would most likely be relevant to the understanding of her situation. In order to include the maximum variation of social environments in Israel, 25 percent of the 234 widows in the population were randomly sampled across the country. As a result, this part of the sample included widows living in the four main cities of Israel, as well as those living in smaller old and new towns, and in agricultural settlements, except for those living on a kibbutz.

The second assumption was that war widows might have the tendency to stick together and to create their own social networks and mutual support systems. In order to test this assumption, all the widows who lived in one of the major cities in Israel were included in the sample. The 25 percent sample across country, plus the whole population in one of the major cities, constituted a third of all the widows in the eligible population. All seventy-one widows were interviewed for the first time during 1970. The twenty widows, that composed the total Six-Day War population of widows of one of the major cities, were systematically interviewed for the second time during 1972. From 1970 to 1975, I was in continuous contact with the War Widows Association. I attended many of its meetings and kept in close contact with its leaders. Personal relationships developed between myself and some of the widows in the sample, and we maintained contact for some years after the systematic field work for this study ended. My presence at many of the meetings and ceremonies organized for war widows, together with the long hours I spent in the waiting rooms of the offices of the Department of Rehabilitation, brought me into contact with widows of other wars as well as with widows of the Six-Day War who were not included in the sample.

After some time, and especially after the final report to the Ministry of Defense was submitted, voluntary and unprompted information started to come my way. The informants were war widows from all the wars, their parents or parents-in-law, their friends, and sometimes people from the helping professions who included army personnel whose job was to deal with war widows' problems. Occasionally, a woman's voice on the telephone would say: "My name is . . . I'm not sure whether you still remember me, but you interviewed me some time ago. I have something to tell you that I'm sure will be interesting for your study." Sometimes, an unknown voice would say: "You don't know me but I've heard that you are writing a book on war widows and I wanted you to know that. . ." In many cases, either by phone or in writing, I received requests for advice or information that I could conceivably have given. However, given the confidentiality of information I had collected, and my own lack of training to counsel on personal problems, I always refused. The answer was almost always, ". . . so at least listen to my story. Maybe you'll decide to include it in your book." Such volunteered information was recorded and is incorporated in the body of this book.

The Interviews

The interviewing technique used in every case was that of the partially structured, open-ended interview. All interviews, whether with the widows themselves, with the social workers, or with other members of the helping professions, started with one general question: What does it mean to be a war widow in Israeli society of the 1970s. The interviewee was directed, when it was necessary, to address himself or herself to various specific aspects of widowhood: for example, the economics of widowhood, household management, the relationships between the widows and the Rehabilitation Department of the Ministry of Defense, child rearing, and the relationships within social and kinship networks. The length of the interviews with the widows ranged between two hours for a short interview and fifteen hours (in three sessions) for the longest one.

The second round of interviews with people from the helping professions was conducted specifically in order to obtain information about the widows in the sample. In these interviews, the main question was: "Please tell me whatever you know and think about Ms. X." Here again, the interviewee was directed to touch upon the same general areas that were specified above for each widow who was assigned to his or her care. All of the interviews, with widows and others, were carried out after a telephone conversation that specified the aim and the subject of the interview. The interviews were tape recorded and later were transcribed verbatim. Incidental conversations with widows and others in various settings were not recorded, but were written down later as accurately as possible.

Changes in Widows' Household Composition*

	Before Widowhood	Between beginning of widowhood and beginning of this study	Type of household by end of study
B.B. (1)	Joint household with husband's mother	1. Decrease—removal of husband's mother	Nuclear family household
T.B. (2)	Nuclear family household for childless couple	1. Joint household with friends 2. Dissolution of joint household 3. Joint household with widow's sister and her family 4. Increase—birth of a child 5. Decrease—exit of widow's sister and family	Nuclear family household
I.B. (3)	Kibbutz household	1. Joint household with widow's parents in parents' house 2. Semi-joint household with widow's parents, widow's daughter remained with widow's parents	Semi-joint household
N.B. (4)	Nuclear family household	1. Joint household with widow's sister and sister-in-law, located in widow's house 2. Decrease—exit of sister-in-law	Joint household
I.C. (5)	Nuclear family household	1. Decrease—removal of son to educational institution 2. Decrease—first daughter inducted into army 3. Decrease—second daughter inducted into army	Nuclear family household

*Households which underwent no change are not included in this presentation.

	Before Widowhood	Between beginning of widowhood and beginning of this study	Type of household by end of study
B.C. (7)	Nuclear family household	1. Decrease—older daughter inducted into army 2. Decrease—marriage of older daughter 3. Decrease—second daughter inducted into army	Single person household
A.C. (8)	Childless couple living in permanent army personnel housing on army base	1. Kibbutz household for single person 2. Increase—birth of a child 3. Nuclear family household in city	Nuclear family household
M.H. (10)	Nuclear family household for childless couple	1. Joint household with widow's parents 2. Increase—birth of a child	Joint household
B.H. (12)	Nuclear family household	1. Joint household with widow's sister 2. Increase—birth of a child 3. Increase—addition of two of widow's sisters to the household 4. Decrease—exit all of widow's sisters from household	Nuclear family household
T.H. (13)	Nuclear family household	1. Joint household with widow's parents, located in parents' home 2. Semi-joint household with widow's parents	Semi-joint household
W.H. (15)	Joint household with widow's father-in-law	1. Decrease—removal of father-in-law from household 2. Joint household with widow's mother 3. Decrease—exit of widow's mother from household 4. Increase—widow's sister-in-law joins household	Joint household
T.E. (18)	Nuclear family household	1. Joint household with husband's parents, in parents' house 2. Dissolution of joint household	Nuclear family household
K.I. (19)	Nuclear family household for childless couple	1. Increase—birth of a child	Nuclear family household

	Before Widowhood	*Between beginning of widowhood and beginning of this study*	*Type of household by end of study*
I.X. (20)	Nuclear family household	1. Decrease—removal of child to widow's parents' care	Single person household
B.I. (22)	Nuclear family household	1. Joint household with parents-in-law and late husband's unmarried siblings, located in household of parents-in-law 2. Increase—birth of widow's child 3. Joint household with widow's parents and her unmarried siblings, located in parents' house 4. Joint household with widow's parents, located in widow's house	Joint household
N.I. (24)	Nuclear family household	1. Joint household with widow's parents in their house 2. Dissolution of joint household—exit of widow from parents' house, her daughter remains in widow's parents' care	Single person household
C.M. (27)	Joint household with widow's grandmother	1. Decrease—removal of grandmother from joint household	Nuclear family household
I.M. (28)	Nuclear family household	1. Increase—birth of a child	Nuclear family household
A.M. (29)	Nuclear family household for childless couple	1. Joint household with parents-in-law in their house 2. Increase—birth of a child 3. Dissolution of joint household	Nuclear family household
L.M. (30)	Nuclear family household	1. Joint household with widow's sister and her family, located in widow's house 2. Decrease—death of a child 3. Decrease—exit of widow's sister and her family	Nuclear family household
I.M. (31)	Nuclear family household	1. Joint household with widow's mother, located in widow's house	Joint household

	Before Widowhood	Between beginning of widowhood and beginning of this study	Type of household by end of study
E.M. (32)	Joint household with husband's parents in moshav	1. Decrease—death of husband's father 2. Decrease—exit of husband's mother	Nuclear family household
T.N. (35)	Nuclear family household	1. Semi-joint household with widow's parents	Semi-joint household
C.N. (36)	Nuclear family household	1. Joint household with widow's mother, sister and sister's children, located in widow's mother's house 2. Increase—birth of widow's child 3. Joint household with widow's mother, located in widow's house	Joint household
N.N. (38)	Nuclear family household in moshav	1. Nuclear family household in the city 2. Increase—birth of a child	Nuclear family household
I.O. (39)	Nuclear family household	1. Decrease—exit of mature son	Nuclear family household
M.N. (40)	Joint household with husband's parents	1. Joint household with widow's parents located in their house 2. Increase—birth of a child 3. Dissolution of joint household—exit of widow and children 4. Joint household with widow's parents in widow's house 5. Decrease—exit of parents 6. Joint household with widow's sister, located in widow's house	Joint household
B.O. (41)	Nuclear family household	1. Joint household with widow's mother, located in widow's house 2. Decrease—exit of mother 3. Semi-joint household with widow's mother	Semi-joint household
S.T. (43)	Nuclear family household	1. Joint household with husband's parents, located in their house 2. Dissolution of joint household—exit of widow and daughter	Nuclear family household

	Before Widowhood	Between beginning of widowhood and beginning of this study	Type of household by end of study
S.T. (44)	Nuclear family household	1. Decrease—exit of mature son	Nuclear family household
I.B. (45)	Nuclear family household	1. Joint household with widow's sister located in widow's house 2. Decrease—exit of sister	Nuclear family household
K.B. (46)	Nuclear family household	1. Total dissolution of household, placement of children with relatives and boarding school, widow lives in hospital dormitory 2. Reassembly of household 3. Increase—joint household with widow's sister	Joint household
B.T. (49)	Nuclear family household	1. Joint household with mother-in-law, located in widow's house 2. Dissolution of household—widow moves to another city	Nuclear family household
B.Q. (50)	Nuclear family household	1. Increase—birth of a child	Nuclear family household
O.M. (52)	Nuclear family household	1. Joint household with widow's mother, located in widow's house 2. Increase—birth of a child 3. Dissolution of joint household—widow moves to another city, mother returns to her own home	Nuclear family household
N.A. (54)	Semi-joint household with widow's father	1. Decrease—father exits from semi-joint household to remarry	Nuclear family household
K.L. (55)	Nuclear family household in moshav	1. Semi-joint household with husband's brother's family 2. Increase—brother-in-law's thirteen-year-old daughter moves into widow's house	Semi-joint household
N.S. (61)	Nuclear family household	1. Decrease—death of a child	Nuclear family household
N.T. (63)	Nuclear family household	1. Joint household with widow's mother located in widow's house 2. Increase—birth of a child	Joint household

	Before Widowhood	Between beginning of widowhood and beginning of this study	Type of household by end of study
Z.T. (68)	Joint moshav household with husband's parents	1. Decrease—exit of husband's parents from household 2. Decrease—removal of child to special education institution	Nuclear family household
C.B. (71)	Nuclear family household	1. Joint household with widow's mother, located in widow's house 2. Decrease—mother returns to her own home	Nuclear family household

Profiles of War Widows

B.B. (No. 1): The mother of two children, B. was thirty-seven years old when she was widowed, after thirteen years of marriage. Her husband was a permanent army officer, one of the highest-ranking officers killed in the Six-Day War. Both husband and wife were upwardly mobile. Although a teacher by profession, B. had not taught for several years. Her occupational experience included many different secretarial jobs, and she had also worked as a youth leader in various frameworks.

T.B. (No. 2): T. was widowed at age twenty-six after four years of marriage. Her only child, a son, was born after his father was killed. T. herself was an orphan from early childhood. She immigrated to Israel from Austria at the age of nineteen, and worked variously as a typist in an office or in a free-lance capacity at home. Her husband, born in Tunisia, held a medium-level administrative post in an airline company.

I.B. (No. 3): Born in Israel to a European family, I. was married at age eighteen to a man who immigrated to Israel from Morocco with Youth Aliya. Both of them were members of a kibbutz at the time. After being widowed at the age of twenty-one, she left the kibbutz with her only child, a daughter, and entered a teachers' seminary. She never returned to the kibbutz.

N.B. (No. 4): N. was married at nineteen to a man she had known since her childhood in their home town in Morocco. Both came from large working-class families. During their three years of marriage they met with very little success in overcoming their severe economic problems. Their only child was three years old when her father was killed.

I.C. (No. 5): At the age of fourteen, I. married a man twelve years older than herself. She and her husband had both emigrated from Iraq to Israel at an early age, having acquired only elementary school education. When the husband, a building constructor, was alive, I. was a full-time housewife, taking care of their four children. Accordingly, when she was widowed at age thirty-three, she had very little experience in any activities outside the home and no occupational experience whatsoever.

N.C. (No. 6): N. was thirty years old when widowed after four years of marriage. She and her husband, both Israeli-born and with university education in the same field, worked in the same profession. Their only child, a son, was one year old when his father was killed. After she was widowed, N. abandoned her plans to continue her education to Ph.D. level. She remarried five years after being widowed.

B.C. (No. 7): Forty-seven years old when widowed, B. was the oldest widow in the sample. In 1939, when Poland was invaded by the Germans, her youth movement leader offered to marry her so that she would be included in the entry permit he had received to a South American country. She accepted this offer, but by the time all the official arrangements had been made, they could no longer leave Poland and each was sent to a concentration camp. After the war, B.'s husband, a survivor of Auschwitz, spent months looking for her in the various camps for displaced persons, and he found her at last somewhere in Germany. In 1947 they came together to Israel as illegal immigrants. Neither of them had had the opportunity to acquire a full high school education and, in their first years in Israel, supported themselves with various unskilled types of work. With time, her husband succeeded in building up a business marketing agricultural products, and the last thing he did before going to the war was to connect his new cooling plant to the electricity system. When he was killed, his older daughter was already a student living away from home and his younger daughter was in her last year of high school.

A.C. (No. 8): A. was twenty-seven years old when widowed after three years of marriage. Her husband was a kibbutz member who served in the permanent army throughout their married life. Their only child, a son, was born two months after his father was killed. A. stayed on in the kibbutz until her son was a year old; she then moved to the city, where she trained and subsequently worked as a kindergarten teacher.

B.C. (No. 9): B. had been married for seven years when she was widowed at the age of twenty-nine. Her husband was a draftsman and, like her, of Moroccan origin. They married immediately after immigrating to Israel. Together with three children, they led a very close family life within a North African immigrant community, so that when B. was widowed, her knowledge of Hebrew was insufficient to cope with even the most basic day-to-day demands. She had serious difficulties in handling the necessary contacts with bureaucratic institutions, such as banks, the electricity company, the municipality, etc. Immediately after being widowed, she took a Hebrew language course and, upon completing it, she began taking a correspondence course in cosmetics. At the beginning of the study, she was working as a cosmetician at home. Subsequently, she took a clerical job in an office.

M.H. (No. 10): M. was twenty-four years old when widowed after four years of marriage. She and her husband were both born in North Africa and immigrated to Israel as children. M.'s husband had ten years of schooling, and began working as an unskilled laborer in his early teens. The news of the birth of his second daughter reached the father when he was already in army service, a few days before the outbreak of the Six-Day War. From the time that she became a widow, M. devoted herself to the house and her two daughters and refused any offers of work.

S.H. (No. 11): Widowed at the age of twenty-eight, S. had been married for four years and had one son. She was born in Iraq and her husband was Israeli-born, of Persian origin. He was a skilled worker in a factory and S., not having completed high school, worked as a kindergarten teacher's aide. After she was widowed, she left this job and took part-time clerical work.

B.H. (No. 12): B. was widowed at the age of twenty after three years of marriage. Both she and her husband had only an elementary school education. The husband, a skilled diamond cutter, supported the family well, and B. did not feel the need to go out to work after she was married. Her only child, a daughter, was born a few days before the outbreak of the Six-Day War, after the father had already been called up. Her attempts to find a job after she was widowed were not successful.

I.H. (No. 13): Widowed at the age of twenty-four, I. had been married for seven years and had two children. Both she and her husband immigrated to Israel as children from Tunisia. Her husband had partial high school education and was a semi-skilled construction worker. I. came to Israel at the age of twelve and, although she entered school immediately, had to begin working before she was able to finish elementary school. After she was widowed, she made exceptional attempts to further her education. At the time of the study, she had already succeeded in completing her elementary education and was continuing at high school level. She planned to enter the university and to study journalism.

S.H. (No. 14): S. was twenty-four years old when she was widowed. She had been married for five years and had one child. Both she and her husband were Israeli-born, of European origin. Her husband left school at the age of fourteen, went into the building trade, and eventually became a building contractor. S. herself had completed high school and was a full-time housewife until she was widowed. After becoming a widow, she took on her first job working as a bank clerk.

W.H. (No. 15): W. was married for eight years and had three children before she was widowed at the age of thirty. Both she and her husband were born in Turkey. The husband immigrated to Israel with his family as a child. W. and her older brother were sent from Turkey to a boarding school in Israel when she was twelve years old. Her husband was a semiskilled worker. She herself had two years of high school education and during her marriage was a full-time housewife.

C.H. (No. 16): C. was married for seven years and had two children before she was widowed at the age of thirty. Her husband was a permanent army officer. She was an elementary school teacher by profession.

S.E. (No. 17): S. was widowed at the age of twenty-five after five years of marriage. She was Israeli born, of European origin. Her husband was born in Italy to parents who fled from Germany when World War II broke out. Before the Six-Day War, S. was an elementary school teacher and her husband was a Ph.D. student. Their two daughters were born within a year of each other. After she became a widow, she completed her BA and MA degrees while at the same time holding a top executive position. By the time the study was drawing to an end, she had left that position and was accepted at law school. It is known that she finished her studies and passed the Bar examinations.

T.E. (No. 18): T. immigrated to Israel at the age of eight and entered elementary school. She left school after sixth grade and at the age of fourteen began working as a charwoman. She married at twenty-three. Her Moroccan-born husband also had only an elementary school education. When she met him, he was an unskilled worker on a boat. When they married, he left the sea and went into partnership in a small removal business. T. was widowed at the age of twenty-six and had one child, a son. After becoming a widow, she began working as a cashier in the student cafeteria of a university.

K.I. (No. 19): K. and her husband, both Israeli-born and of European origin, had known each other from high school days. She was widowed at the age of twenty-three after nine months of marriage. When she was widowed, she was in the second month of pregnancy, a fact which her husband learned only a few days before he was called up. Before she became a widow, K. was a school teacher, a profession she decided not to continue after she was widowed. On the basis of her previous Bachelor's degree, she was accepted at a school for librarians and, at the time of the study, was working as a librarian in a government office.

I.X. (No. 20): Israeli-born, I. was married at the age of seventeen to a man born in Poland, nine years her senior. Their only child, a son, was born in the first year of their marriage. The husband, a self-employed contractor, did not want his wife to work. Two years after they married, the husband was killed and I. tried to finish her high school studies which she had abandoned in the middle because of her marriage. At the time of the study, she was living by herself, while her son was living with her parents. She was the only widow with whom communication was problematic. Some time later, she was admitted to a mental hospital where she remained for a prolonged period.

O.X. (No. 21): O. and her husband were born in the same small town in Rumania. They both immigrated with their families as teenagers and were able to acquire a few years of high school education in Israel. She was eighteen and her husband twenty-four years old when they married. They had three children of their own and also raised the daughter of O.'s deceased sister. O. was twenty-eight years old when she was widowed, at which point she took her first job as a low-level clerk in an office.

B.I. (No. 22): Both B. and her husband were born in North Africa and immigrated to Israel as children. Her husband studied in high school, but did not complete his education. B. herself had almost no formal education. She started working as a cleaner at the age of eighteen until her marriage a year later. Her husband was a motor mechanic who earned a fairly good living. She was married for one year and eight months. Their second child, a son, was born after the father was killed.

N.I. (No. 23): N. and her husband were both born in Libya. Her husband was a permanent army officer. The couple was married for thirteen years and had three children. She trained as an infant nurse, worked regularly after finishing her studies, and continued to do so after she was widowed at the age of thirty-three.

N.I. (No. 24): N. was Israeli-born of Yemenite origin. Her husband immigrated from Yemen to Israel at the age of ten. They married when she was seventeen and he twenty-five. He was then working as a house painter. They were married for three years and had one child, a daughter, before he was killed. In spite of her low level of formal education (she completed one year of high school), she succeeded in establishing herself after she was widowed as a practical occupational therapist in an old people's home.

K.J. (No. 25): K.'s husband immigrated with his mother from Europe after his father died in a concentration camp during World War II. He was educated at an agricultural high school. K., moshav-born, met her husband during his agricultural training at her moshav. He then completed his engineering degree at university and returned to the moshav, where they married and he became a farmer. They were married for two years and had one daughter when K., aged twenty-five became a widow. At the time of the study, she was contemplating moving to the city and taking a full-time job as an instructor in therapeutic gymnastics.

Z.Z. (No. 26): Z. was widowed at the age of thirty-three after eight years of marriage. Both she and her husband were Israeli-born of European origin, and both had MA degrees. The husband's job required that the family move to a small town. After she became a widow, Z. left this town and moved with her two sons back to the city where she was offered a job in her own profession. At the time of the study, Z. had been promoted in her job and was doing well in her professional career.

C.M. (No. 27): Both C. and her husband were born in Rumania. Caught as children in World War II, neither of them had a chance to complete their formal education. They married when C. was nineteen and her husband twenty-three. A few years after their marriage, the husband decided to complete his basic education and go on to obtain professional qualifications. The whole family, the parents and their three daughters, invested tremendous resources and effort to this end. The husband studied every night and could contribute very little to the family life, and a considerable sum of money out of their already scarce financial resources was invested in his studies. The entire family treated his excellent educational achievements as their common achievement. The husband was killed a few months before he was to receive his engineering diploma.

I.M. (No. 28): I. was widowed at the age of twenty-eight after six years of marriage to a permanent army officer. Their second child was born after his father was killed. Until her husband's death, I. lived in officers' quarters in an army base and had a life style typical of that community. However, her way of life changed totally after she became a widow. She moved to the city and began studying art seriously on a full time basis. By the time of the study, she was already an integrated member of a bohemian community, a full time artist, and recognized by the art establishment in Israel.

A.M. (No. 29): A. was born in Poland and came to Israel at the age of twelve. At twenty-six, she married a second-generation Israeli of Spanish origin. Each was an only child in their respective families. The husband was on the faculty of a university, and A. had a BA degree in Social Science. A year after their marriage they went on a sabbatical and returned a few months before the outbreak of war. She was three months pregnant when her husband was killed. Both before and after the birth of the child, she held part-time jobs which she quite frequently changed. At the same time, she slowly completed her MA degree. She was well supported by the combination of Ministry of Defense payments and the university pension arrangement, and treated her jobs as the best way of passing time. She was never either very committed to, or interested in, any of the jobs she held. As the mother of the only grandchild of her parents and of the parents of her late husband, she found herself in a very complicated, restrictive, and obligating set of relationships.

L.M. (No. 30): Both L. and her husband were Israeli-born of Middle-Eastern origin. Neither had completed elementary school. The husband was a member of a bus cooperative and supported his family very well. L. was widowed at the age of thirty-two after seven years of marriage. Their only son, the youngest of three children, suffered from a malignant disease from which he died two years after his father was killed. At the time of the study, she was just starting to reorganize her little family, after losing two of its members. She did not work, but she was well supported by the combination of Ministry of Defense payments and the cooperative's pension arrangements.

I.M. (No. 31): I. was born in Morocco and made a second marriage at the age of twenty-seven to a man of Italian origin. From her first marriage she had a daughter who was always raised in children's institutions, and from the second marriage she had two sons. Neither she nor her husband completed elementary school and neither ever held a permanent, steady job. She was working as a charwoman, paid by the hour, before she became a widow, and continued to do so afterwards. She was widowed at the age of thirty-nine, having been married to her second husband for twelve years.

E.M. (No. 32): E. and her husband were born in the same moshav, went to the same school, and both left school a year before the end. They married after both had completed army service, came back to their home moshav, and joined the husband's aging parents on their farm. E. was widowed at the age of thirty-three, after thirteen years of marriage. Two years after her husband was killed, his father died and his mother was placed in an old people's home. E. stayed on the farm with her three daughters. At this point, she started reducing the farm's functions to a minimum, disposed of all the livestock, and worked only those parts of the farm which were cultivated cooperatively by the whole moshav. She took a part-time job in the laboratory of the local school as an untrained laboratory technician. Although she very much wanted to leave the moshav, she did not do anything actively to carry out her plans.

K.M. (No. 33): K. and her husband were both Israeli-born, of European origin. The husband held a high executive position in a bank, and K. was a school teacher. They had three children, two daughters and a son, and had been married for seventeen years when she was widowed at the age of thirty-six. After becoming a widow, she continued her studies with the aim of becoming a junior high school teacher.

U.M. (No. 34): U.'s husband was a permanent army officer, born and raised on a kibbutz. After a short attempt to live on his kibbutz, they left and went to live in the city. Her insistence on leaving the kibbutz created a deep estrangement between her and her husband's family. She was widowed at the age of thirty-four after thirteen years of marriage and was left with two children. After becoming a widow, she continued her job as a teacher and educational adviser in an elementary school; however, she devoted most of her time and energy to painting, which she hoped would eventually become her main occupation.

T.N. (No. 35): Both T. and her husband were faculty members in an institution of higher learning where he held a post one grade higher than that of his wife. They were married for fifteen years and had a daughter and two sons. T. was widowed at the age of thirty-seven. After becoming a widow she continued successfully in her academic career.

C.N. (No. 36): C. was born in Turkey and immigrated to Israel as a child. After completing seven years of schooling, she started working in an unskilled capacity. At seventeen she married a man born in Morocco, who had immigrated to Israel at the age of eighteen. The husband had a full high school education, was a skilled factory worker, and supplemented his income as a movie operator in youth clubs. C. was widowed at the age of twenty, after three years of marriage, and gave birth to their second child, a daughter, after her husband was killed. At the time of the study, she was a waitress and cleaning woman in a milk-bar.

H.N. (No. 37): H. was born in Egypt. In 1956, following the Sinai Campaign, her family, like most Egyptian Jews, had to leave Egypt. They settled in France where she finished high school and worked as a secretary. She immigrated to Israel at the age of twenty in order to marry her cousin, whom she had met on a previous visit to Israel. Their only son was born a few weeks before the outbreak of the Six-Day War. H. was widowed at twenty-two, after only one year of marriage. After she became a widow, she devoted all her time to her child and did not look for a job, even though her financial situation was not very secure. She had quite substantial technical and emotional support from the extended family to which both she and her husband belonged.

N.N. (No. 38): At the age of nineteen, N. married a member of a religious moshav. They lived together on the moshav for thirteen years. Although she had completed a kindergarten seminary, she never worked in this profession. Immediately after becoming a widow, she left the moshav with her two daughters and her son and moved in to live with her parents in the city. Two months later, she gave birth to her fourth child, a daughter. At the time of the study she was living in a flat of her own and was taking a secretarial course with a view to getting a job to supplement her income.

I.O. (No. 39): I. and her husband were born in the same city in Poland and knew each other as children. From the beginning of World War II, they were both members of the underground, fled together to Hungary, and came to Israel together in 1948 as illegal immigrants. She was widowed at the age of forty-three, after twenty years of marriage. Her husband was a member of a bus cooperative and his pension, together with her salary as a bookkeeper, enabled her and her two children to live quite comfortably. At the time of the study, the older son was already at university and the younger son was in the last year of high school, planning to start his two-year period of army service.

M.N. (No. 40): M. was Israeli-born of Yemenite origin. At the age of eighteen, she married a man born in Afghanistan. Both she and her husband had only an elementary school education. He was a semi-skilled worker and she an unskilled worker. M. was widowed at twenty-three after four years of marriage. When she became a widow, she had a son and a daughter, and a second son was born after his father was killed. At the time of the study, she was working as a charwoman.

B.O. (No. 41): B. was born in Bulgaria and her husband in Rumania. Both immigrated to Israel as children. They married when she was twenty-one years old and had just finished her training at a teachers' seminary, while her husband, then aged twenty-four, had received his Bachelor's degree and was continuing his studies. B. had a full-time teaching job at an elementary school, and her husband worked part-time as a teaching assistant at a university. At the time of his death, he had expected to get his Ph.D. within the year. B. was twenty-six when she was widowed. She and her husband had been married for five years and had a son and a daughter.

S.T. (No. 42): S. and her husband studied together at law school. They married while still students and, on completing their studies, each took a first job as a legal adviser. S.'s husband was the only son of elderly parents and felt obliged to live next door to them. They had been married for six years and had one son when, at the age of thirty, she was widowed.

S.T. (No. 43): S. and her husband were born in Iraq and both immigrated to Israel in their early teens. Both had only elementary school education. The husband was a chauffeur and, before their marriage, she was an aide in a kindergarten. They had one daughter and had been married for six years when S. was widowed at the age of twenty-four.

S.T. (No. 44): S. and her husband were both born in the Balkans and came to Israel as teenagers. Both had only elementary school education, and the husband worked as a shoemaker. They had three children and had been married for thirteen years when she became a widow at the age of thirty-one. Then she went out to work for the first time, finding a job as a kindergarten aide.

I.B. (No. 45): I. immigrated to Israel from Yemen at the age of seven; her husband was sixteen when he immigrated from Aden. Both had a partial high school education. The husband was a skilled worker and I. had an irregular job in a post office. She was widowed at the age of twenty-six, after seven years of marriage, and had two sons. A year after becoming a widow, she moved from the small town where they lived to the city.

K.B. (No. 46): K. and her husband immigrated to Israel from Morocco as teenagers and met in the small town where they lived. They married when both were twenty-two years old. Her husband was a porter in an agricultural products concern. She was widowed at the age of thirty-six, after fourteen years of marriage, and had four children. Immediately after she became a widow, she entered a practical nursing course which she completed a year later. She moved from the small town to the city and, at the time of the study, was working as a practical nurse in a psychiatric hospital.

S.B. (No. 47): S. and her husband were both Israeli-born of European origin. He was a medical student and supported his family by doing numerous summer jobs. S., who had no education beyond high school, held a half-time job as a secretary in a research institute. She was widowed at the age of twenty-nine, after five years of marriage, and had one son. She continued working in the same job and later married her husband's best friend.

A.B. (No. 48): A. and her husband were Israeli-born, of Yemenite origin. Both had only an elementary school education. Her husband worked in his family's transport company and provided well for his wife and two children. During the war, A. gave birth to a stillborn child. She was widowed at the age of twenty-eight after seven years of marriage. She never held a job, either before or during her marriage, and refused job offers after she became a widow, in spite of the fact that she experienced a very serious reduction in her standard of living. She expected her husband's family to contribute financially to her support, which they refused to do.

B.T. (No. 49): B. and her husband were born in Morocco. B. immigrated to Israel when she was seventeen and was married at nineteen. She had a partial high school education, and her husband had only a few years of formal schooling in Morocco. He immigrated to Israel at the age of twenty-one and was immediately recruited into the army. After his two years of compulsory service, he remained in the army on a permanent basis, with the rank of sergeant. They had been married for four years and had two children when the husband was killed. A year later, she moved from the small town, where the couple had lived next door to the husband's parents, and went to the city where her own family lived. Although she had never held a job while married, at the time of the study she was working part-time in a refreshment kiosk owned by her brother.

B.Q. (No. 50): Both B. and her husband were born in Israel of European origin. They had known each other from childhood and were married when both were about twenty years old. After their marriage, they continued their education at university level. B.'s husband was a regimental commander in the permanent army at the time of his death. She was thirty-five when she was widowed and had two sons and a daughter. A few months later, she gave birth to their fourth child.

U.G. (No. 51): U. and her husband were both Israeli-born of European origin. U.'s husband was a self-employed engineer and, during her marriage, she herself worked as a bank clerk. She was widowed at the age of twenty-nine, after eight years of marriage, and had two children. After becoming a widow, she embarked upon a university education and was engaged in this at the time of the study.

T.G. (No. 52): T. was Israeli-born of Balkan origin, as was her husband. She was twenty-four when she was widowed and by that time the mother of two and expecting a third child. As neither T. nor her husband came from rich families, they decided to start their life together in a small, developing town which gave the husband a good opportunity for occupational mobility. Immediately after becoming a widow, with the help of friends, T. moved to the big city in which she was born and where her parents still lived. Three years later she regretted this move and was talking with nostalgia about life in the small and friendly town. T. never completed her high school education, and although she was employed before her marriage, perceived herself as unemployable. She had a very pessimistic view of her future which she saw as solely bound up with raising her three children.

C.Q. (No. 53): C. was Israeli-born, of Yemenite origin. Her husband, also Israeli-born, was of European origin and was an engineering technician by profession. C. had only partial high school education. She was twenty-three when she was widowed after eighteen months of marriage, and had one daughter. After she was widowed, she tried to complete her high school studies, but her efforts met with only partial success. During the time of the study, she had a part-time job in the Telephone Department and, although very dissatisfied, was unable to find a more suitable position.

N.A. (No. 54): N. was born in Yugoslavia and immigrated to Israel at the age of ten. Her Israeli-born husband had been her boyfriend from the age of fourteen. They were in the same class in school, finished high school together, served together in the army, and married when both were twenty-four years old. N.'s husband was a computer programmer in a big company. She had completed a teachers' training course, but worked as a teacher for only a few years. After that, she devoted her time to voluntary activities and was still involved in these at the time of the study. She was widowed at the age of thirty-three, after nine years of marriage, and had two sons.

K.L. (No. 55): During the German occupation of Poland, K.'s parents fled to Belgium where she was born. When Belgium was overrun, her parents could not keep her any longer and gave her to a Christian family to raise. By a lucky chance, they were able to inform a relative about this arrangement. The parents were killed by the Nazis. After the war, this relative told the story to the child's uncle living in the U.S.A. He brought K. to the States and she was raised in his childless home. Her relationship with her uncle, which at best might be described as "correct," deteriorated as time went on and, at the age of nineteen, she immigrated to Israel where she married. Her husband had come to Israel with his parents as a teenager. The family settled on a moshav, where K.'s husband and his two sisters were each given a farm when they married. When at the age of twenty-six she was widowed, she had two children, and a third child was born after the father was killed. After much deliberation, she decided to remain on the moshav. This decision made her very dependent on her late husband's family—his parents and two married sisters. They, for their part, did all they could to help her keep the agricultural farm going as a viable entity and treated her and her children as an integral part of the family.

O.L. (No. 56): Both O. and her husband were born in Yemen and immigrated to Israel as children with their families, who settled on a moshav. Both finished elementary school in the moshav and, when they got married, received their own farm. O.'s parents subsequently left the moshav and settled in a nearby town. She was widowed at the age of twenty-one, after three years of marriage, and had a son and a daughter. Her farm on the moshav was tended mainly by her brother-in-law with the help of some other relatives, both her own and her husband's. It seemed that the relatives on both sides agreed to free her from any obligation to work the farm. At the time of the study, she was using this freedom to take a course for instructors in folk dancing.

T.L. (No. 57): T. was born on a kibbutz. Her husband's parents, along with thousands of other refugees from Europe, tried to enter Israel illegally with their child in 1946. The boat was caught by the British authorities and the whole shipload of new immigrants was transferred to a camp in Cyprus. In 1947, after the Declaration of Independence of the State of Israel, the family finally settled in Israel. T. was an elementary school teacher and her husband was a lieutenant-colonel in the permanent army. The family moved around the country according to the demands of the husband's occupation, but their permanent home was in a housing development for army veterans, to which T. returned with her two children when, at the age of thirty-one, she became a widow. Ten years of marriage with an army officer left her with many contacts among army personnel, which she made serious efforts to continue.

S.L. (No. 58): S. and her husband were both born in Yemen, and both had partial high school education. The husband was a diamond cutter. She had no occupational training and only a very short experience working as an unskilled worker. She became a widow at the age of twenty-seven after nine years of marriage. Thereafter, she continued much the same way of life as before—she remained a housewife, took care of her three children, kept up minimal contacts with relatives and, even three years after becoming a widow, had no plans to alter or to broaden her life.

S.L. (No. 59): Both S. and her husband were born in Rumania and came to Israel as teenagers. The husband was an automobile mechanic and, a few years before he was killed, he joined forces with his brother in buying a lorry, on the basis of which they started a transport company. S. had almost no formal education and, since her marriage at the age of eighteen, had devoted all her time to housework and to their only son. At thirty-six years old she was widowed and, at that point, went out to work as a supermarket cashier. She proved to be very successful in managing her financial affairs and succeeded in winning a complicated legal battle against her brother-in-law for her share in the transport company. At the same time, she considerably raised the standard of living for herself and her son by very cleverly manipulating her rights with the Ministry of Defense.

N.S. (No. 60): N. and her husband were both born in Poland and came to Israel as children with their families. She was twenty-one years old when they married and had just finished nursing school. Her husband was two years older than she and, by the time they married, he had completed his army service and joined his father in the building industry as a foreman. N. had one daughter when her husband was killed six years later. She moved to another town and, consequently, to another job. She cut off her contacts with her husband's parents almost completely. She also made no effort to retain the social contacts of her married life. As a result, these were lost. A year later she left the nursing profession and made a serious attempt to enter the world of the mass media. During the follow-up study, five years after she became a widow, she and the man she was living with were planning to marry, and her daughter was already proudly introducing him as her father.

N.S. (No. 61): N. and her husband, both Israeli-born, were married for fourteen years and had two children when the husband was killed. She was then thirty-three years old. Two years after she was widowed, the older son died of a malignant disease. At the time of their marriage, N. and her husband were members of a kibbutz, but left it a few years later when her husband joined her father in his business. She was a high school teacher and continued in her job after she was widowed. Her family (parents, a married sister, and a brother) got together to provide her with maximum support and help after her double loss. During the follow-up study, she and her daughter were abroad, where N. was finishing her university education. It is known that she remarried upon her return to Israel two years later.

O.T. (No. 62): Of European origin, O. was born on a kibbutz. At age twenty-two she married an Israeli-born man of Yemenite origin and left the kibbutz. Her husband was a member of a bus cooperative and she was a housewife. Their son was born in the first year of their marriage. She was twenty-five years old when, after three years of marriage, she was widowed. Then, for the first time in her life, she had to cope with all the unfamiliar and complex bureaucratic and technical aspects of city life. This demanded considerable effort on her part. At the time of the study, O. was about to start working in a clerical job. She already felt more confident in her ability to control her own life.

N.T. (No. 63): N. and her husband were both Moroccan-born. Members of a Zionist youth movement, they immigrated to Israel with a pioneer group planning to settle in a kibbutz. After a few years on the kibbutz, they left and moved to the city. She worked as a nurse in a hospital, a profession she had acquired while still in Morocco, and her husband worked as a technician in a factory. N. was widowed at the age of twenty-nine, after six years of marriage, and had a daughter. Her son was born after the father was killed. Her parents moved in with her. But, despite their help, it was difficult for her to continue her work in the hospital after the birth of her son. Her efforts to find a suitable alternative job were unsuccessful. At the time of the study, she was still dissatisfied with the part-time job she had and was considering finding some suitable, more satisfying work—the only way she saw of rebuilding her life.

B.T. (No. 64): B. was born in Morocco and came to Israel at the age of eighteen. Almost immediately upon her arrival, she met the man who later became her husband. He was of European origin and nine years older than she, and this match met with great opposition from her family. Soon after the marriage, her parents cut their contact with the couple almost completely. B. had only six years of schooling and during her married life was a housewife. The husband, an agricultural instructor, provided well for his family. He left her with two daughters when she was widowed at the age of twenty-two after four years of marriage. Even after she became a widow, her relationship with her family was not restored and, as her husband had no family in Israel, the feeling of isolation was one of the most difficult problems with which B. had to cope.

M.T. (No. 65): M. was born on a moshav and, at the age of eighteen, during her army service, met the man who subsequently became her husband. They joined her parents in living and working on the family farm. They were married for seventeen years and had three daughters. When M. was widowed at the age of thirty-five, she decided for the first time in her life to take a job outside the family farm, which continued to be run by her father. She proved herself to be a natural organizer and, at the time of the study, was in charge of housekeeping services in some ninety regional medical clinics. The occupational and financial independence she gained compensated for the awkwardness she felt about living in her parents' household and reverting in it to her role as a daughter.

N.T. (No. 66): N. was born in a cooperative moshav. Her Belgian-born husband joined the moshav when they were married. She had one daughter when she was widowed at the age of twenty-seven. After she became a widow, she started and completed a course for dental assistants. At the time of the study she was working in the moshav dental clinic. Her family, including her parents and a married sister who lived in the same moshav, participated very actively in the routines and arrangements of N.'s household and in this way allowed her a good deal of freedom for her own needs and interests.

I.T. (No. 67): I. was married at the age of twenty-four, had one son, and was widowed when she was thirty. She was a teacher of home economics in an elementary school, and her husband was a gymnastics teacher. After becoming a widow, she started university studies with the aim of being a high school teacher. At the same time, she continued her job at the elementary school.

Z.T. (No. 68): Z.'s husband was born in Germany and came to Israel as a child with his parents, who joined a moshav. After they married, she and her husband joined his family farm and lived there together for about twelve years. After becoming a widow, she decided that she could no longer take care of her father-in-law who, by that time, was an old and sick widower. The old man was placed in a home for the aged. At approximately the same time, the elder of Z.'s two sons showed learning difficulties and was placed as a boarder in a special education school. The burden of keeping the farm going was too great for her and her younger son, then still in elementary school, and she decided to take a job in the nearby town. At the time of the study, it was recognized that her farm was not functioning and Z. was considering selling it and moving to the town.

Z.T. (No. 69): Z., Israeli-born, was married for seven years and had two children when she was widowed at the age of thirty. Her husband, who had immigrated from Poland to Israel when he was thirteen years old, was a university lecturer. Because of his very low medical profile, he was released from military service. On the first day of the Six-Day War he volunteered to serve as a civilian in an army camp and was killed the following day, a few hundred meters from his house. Before she became a widow, Z. was an elementary school teacher but felt she could not go back to teaching after her husband was killed. She took a course for librarians and, upon completion, found a job as librarian in an institute of higher education.

T.T. (No. 70): Both T. and her husband were born in Rumania and immigrated to Israel in the early '50s. Her parents had been killed in the Holocaust, and she herself had spent several years in concentration camps and in camps for displaced persons in Europe. The Second World War interrupted the education of both T. and her husband, and neither was able to finish high school. At the time of their marriage, her husband was serving in the Border Police and she was working as a kindergarten aide. After the birth of the second of their three children, she stopped working and her husband left the Border Police and was accepted as a technician in military industry. T. had been married for twelve years when she was widowed at the age of thirty-five.

C.B. (No. 71): C. and her husband moved from Argentina to Israel with one child in the early sixties after three years of marriage. In the neighborhood in which they settled there were many other new immigrants from Argentina. The second child, who was born not long after the family came to Israel, kept C. attached to the home and the neighborhood where she felt very comfortable and made little effort to adjust to the new society in Israel. She was widowed at the age of thirty-one after ten years of marriage. Without her husband, she discovered that she was almost incapable of managing her life. Her mother, who came from Argentina to help her, lived with her for six months, and at the end of this time took her and her children back to Argentina with her. A few months later, C. returned to Israel and tried to start her new life as head of her family. She took a part-time job and made a serious effort to improve her Hebrew. At the time of the study she had lost her job, her Hebrew was very poor, she considered her efforts to function as head of her family a failure, and she had decided to go "back to mother" in Argentina.

NOTES

Prologue

1. The initiator of this study was Naomi Golan (now professor of social work at Haifa University). From the outset her partner was Ruth Grushka, M.S.W. For personal reasons, Professor Golan had to leave Israel for a prolonged period. I accepted the offer to take over this study. During the first stage of the research Ruth Grushka was a full partner, and we shared equally the work as well as the responsibility. Ms. Grushka left the project before the final report to the sponsor was prepared.

Chapter I

1. An exception to this is the chapter on widows in Waller's (1951) book.
2. Shiv'a—the seven-day mourning period obligatory in the Jewish religion after the death of a close relative.

Chapter II

1. Hereafter referred to as the "Families of Soldiers . . ." law.
2. In this context, "privilege" is defined as "benefits, rights, exemption from obligations, or immunity granted either by law or custom to a selected social group, persons who fulfill certain functions, or a social strata" (Gould & Kolb 1964).
3. In this respect the situation of the widow differs from that of the other groups covered by the "Families of Soldiers" law. While all the other groups retain their entitlement even in the event that they form relations of a nature similar to those they had with the fallen, the widow's entitlement, in similar cases, expires. For example, "bereaved parents" retain their legal status even when an additional child is born to them; the status of a fallen soldier's children remains unchanged even when they are adopted by a man who is not their biological father, such as their mother's second husband.

It appears that the law reflects values generally held by society as a whole. In terms of values, the emotional ties between husband and wife and what their relationship stands for are one and the same. The existence of ties of this nature, and a relationship of this type within one dyadic system, constitute a sort of admission that they have expired in any other. These values generally provide the backing for monogamous ties. As mentioned earlier, psychologists also consider a widow's ability to form meaningful emotional ties with another man as proof that her emotional ties with her dead husband have been severed.

Many war widows adhere to these values. Their reluctance to remarry is often explained by the fact that their emotional ties with their husband are still intact. This attitude was expressed publicly during a meeting of the Widows Organization in 1974: a member of the organization was recounting her difficulties in finding suitable candidates for remarriage, and her problems in forming relationships with men. As she spoke, the audience was nodding in affirmation. She concluded her narrative: "About half a year ago, I married a man who understands the situation. He even accompanied me when I went to place flowers on my late husband's grave. . . ." Her words were interrupted by angry calls from the audience; "Get off the stand," "Get out of here," "You don't belong here anymore, you are not a widow." She was forcibly removed from the podium, and order was not restored until she was outside the meeting hall.

4. Through the mediation and good offices of Yad Lebanim, many specific arrangements were made for the benefit of bereaved parents not routinely included in the "indigent" group. For instance, bereaved parents who needed assistance on a one-time basis, or those requiring admission to a home for the aged or some form of special care, received these services "extra-legally," often through the efforts of Yad Lebanim, which pleaded their case before the Rehabilitation Department.

5. The impression created from the interviews with the social workers of the Rehabilitation Department was that the main communication channel ran vertically, only from the top downwards. Very little pressure and information was conveyed from the bottom up. A typical example of this was the answer given by one of the rehabilitation workers when I asked her how the widows managed to support themselves on the meager budget provided by pension payments at the time: "I don't know and I don't want to know, because if I did know, I'd have to do something about it."

6. The earlier figure (IL 240) quoted by S.E. was the sum given to widows with two children prior to the Six-Day War, and the figure given to S.E.'s friends that came to inquire a few days after the war. This sum was adjusted to the cost-of-living index a couple of weeks after the war and was set at IL 365 per month.

7. These three papers were chosen because their combined readership represents the vast majority of the daily newspaper readership in Israel (Kahana & Kana'an, 1973).

8. In the years following the Six-Day War, either as the result of past experience or due to changes of policy, the Minister of Defense (and/or the Rehabilitation Department) gave up its "fight" to participate in and supervise all the "help" offered to war widows. Thus it saved itself, in certain cases, a great deal of trouble and criticism. For example, in 1974, the Jewish community in London invited twenty war widows for a two-week holiday in the city at its expense. The Ministry of Defense refrained from handling this matter, but neither did it attempt to have the invitation called off. The matter was handed over to the Widows' Organization, and somehow twenty widows were selected to take the trip. This matter created a great deal of controversy among the widows: accusations of favoritism were hurled at the organization's activists, and plans for a "rebellion" were brewing among various groups of widows. For several weeks, the organization's activists were kept busy trying to appease the "rebel widows."

9. The reference in the original version of the law to its framework of implementation is summed up in the following two subsections: "4. a) The Ministry of Defense shall appoint a Pensions Officer or Pensions Officers for the purpose of this law. b) Notice of the appointment of the Pensions Officer and his address shall be published in 'Reshumot' (Book of Laws)." (Book of Laws, 1950, p. 163.)

10. The affairs of the disabled were also handled by the Pensions Officer and remained under the jurisdiction of the Rehabilitation Department as services were expanded. Within the Department itself, a distinction was drawn, particularly by the field staff, between the "Disabled" and the "Families of Soldiers." Here, reference to the Rehabilitation Department applies to its section dealing with war widows only.

11. In the course of this study, I met quite a number of war widows who lost their husbands during the 1948 War of Independence or later, and who had never visited the Rehabilitation Bureau. Several of them were not even fully aware of the existence of such a bureau until the Six-Day War.

12. A detailed discussion of this issue appears in a report on the subject submitted to the Ministry of Defense (Shamgar-Handelman 1972A).

13. Among the first changes introduced into the Rehabilitation Bureaus after the Six-Day War was the change in the plaques on the doors of the social workers' offices, from "social worker" to "rehabilitation worker." This change was made under pressure from the widows who refused to be "social cases."

14. Reportage and descriptions of this type are the best available substitute for "case histories," as there was no orderly, systematic, written material on the widows in the personal files of the Rehabilitation Department.
15. In connection with such processes of labeling, see Becker (1963), Goffman (1961), Scheff (1966), and Schur (1973).
16. In this regard, the view of the social workers, of the widows, and apparently of society at large, tended to concur. The "breaking-up of a home" by a woman was not to be condoned. A widow whose ties with a married man caused him to leave his family was considered immoral. In general, the man involved was not censured to the same extent as the woman. This matter is discussed in greater detail in chapter V.
17. Defense Ministry personnel, questioned anonymously about the case, admitted that it was by no means clear-cut.
18. The State Comptroller's Report of 1969 (Vol. 19, p. 562) called attention to the fact that war widows under the care of the Rehabilitation Department did not receive all of the benefits to which they were entitled. In his report a year later (1970, Vol. 20, p. 674) the State Comptroller regretted to state that, despite some administrative attempts to improve the situation, no actual improvement could be found.
19. The importance of these mechanisms is discussed extensively in Goffman (1959). An interesting discussion of their significance in the system of relationships with social workers can be found in Cohen (1976).

Chapter III

1. Data published by the United States Bureau of Census (Bureau of Census Vols. 92, 93, 96, 98, 104) show that, at least for the last ten years, the typical female-headed household of all types (divorced, widowed, unwed mothers) was composed of a mother and one (over 50 percent) or two (over thirty-five percent) children. That is to say, one-parent households generally are small, a fact that casts doubt on the validity of the argument of overload on the single parent. Data of the same nature was found by Roter & Keren-Ya'ar (1974) concerning one-parent families in Israel.
2. Appendix II presents the households that underwent changes in composition from the beginning of widowhood until the end of this study.
3. In this work, a joint household was defined as meeting, at least partially, the following criteria: a. the household included more members than just the widow and her children; b. the residential unit was shared by all members of the household, and served them all, at least in part; c. the household functioned as a single service and consumption unit for all its members; d. the household maintained, at least to some extent, a "common budget," and all the members who had some means contributed to the funds; e. within the household unit there was division of labor, and division of the power and authority which derived from the structure of the unit and the interaction between its members (Bar-Yosef 1973).
   When a household met most of the above criteria, but with the major modification that not all the members of the household unit shared the same sleeping quarters, it was defined as a semi-joint household. Generally, a semi-joint household comprised two closely situated units, one functioning as a service center for all household members, the other mainly providing sleeping accommodation (Bar-Yosef & Shamgar-Handelman 1972).
4. This is an agricultural settlement where the homestead, including the household, is privately managed, but many of the major agricultural functions are carried out collectively.
5. In this work, a household was defined as "reduced" when, in addition to the loss sustained through the death of the husband-father, one or more other members of the household were intentionally removed from it. Those removed from the household could belong to one of two categories: a. household members who did not belong to the nuclear family; b. children who belonged to the nuclear family. In either case the widow retained the position she assumed on her husband's death as head of the household.
6. A household was defined as having undergone a life-cycle change when changes in its composition resulted from birth, children leaving home, marriage of one of its members, or death (Glick 1947, 1955; Lansing & Kish 1957).

Chapter IV

1. Other aspects of social life are dealt with in Chapter V.
2. The central ceremony of Passover is the Seder, in which the history of the Exodus from Egypt is retold and symbolically reenacted. The ceremony is conducted by the male head of the family, but children play an active role too (Fredman 1981). A festive meal is an integral part of the Seder.

Chapter V

1. Among the few studies dealing with married women are: Adams (1974), Booth (1972), Williams (1958), Lynd & Lynd (1929).
2. Some exceptions are found in the works of Adams and Butler (1967), Babchuk (1965), Babchuk and Bates (1963), Bott (1957).
3. U.M. (No. 34), for example, was highly aware of the restrictions imposed upon her: "If it was up to me, I would have gone back to work the day after the funeral, but I was simply afraid of public opinion." In addition, she told the interviewer about a vacation organized by the army for its members and their families in which she participated approximately a month after she was widowed. In response to the question whether she participated on her own initiative or whether she was invited by the organizers, she answered: "Obviously, I asked, and was not offered. Who would offer me something like this?"
4. It should be pointed out that the designations applied to these five types are not necessarily those used by all informants, but many of them did use this terminology.
5. According to Jewish religion and tradition, a boy reaches maturity at the age of thirteen. From this time on, he is responsible for his actions before man and God. This occasion is celebrated by both religious and non-religious families, usually according to the traditional form. It should be stressed that this religious norm does not correspond with the legal situation in Israel where, according to the civil law, a person reaches maturity at the age of eighteen.
6. The widows' descriptions of close friends are very similar to the one which appears in Lopata's book (1979, Chapt. 6). The only difference between the two is that Lopata claims that this type of friendship does not, and cannot, exist in American society today while, according to my information, it can and does exist in Israeli society.
7. Lopata's findings concerning the source of widows' female friends (op cit) contradict those of Babchuk and Bates (1963). The findings of this study are consistent with those of Babchuk and Bates. Lopata's sample was much older, on average, than either the sample of this study or the sample studied by Babchuk and Bates. This suggests that sources of friendship may change with stages in the life cycle, and that dormant friendships from the early stages can be renewed in the later stages but may be totally inoperative in the middle stages of the life cycle.
8. This phenomenon may be explained on the one hand by the tendency of friendship relationships to be established among people who have certain important characteristics in common and, on the other hand, by the important role of the family in Israeli society (Peres & Katz 1981).
9. Simmel (1964) deals with the disruption in the balance of a relationship when it changes from dyad to triad. Here the discussion deals with this kind of disruption when the relationship contracts and changes from a quartet to a triad, using the numerical characteristics of the different groups as described by Simmel.
10. The image of the unmarried or formerly married woman as a danger to the married life of her friends gets "scientific" backing from different disciplines. Cochrane (1936) claims that widows are very attractive to men sexually, as a sexual relationship with them symbolizes the victory of male oedipal fantasies. Lepp (1968), a priest and psychiatrist by profession, on the basis of his professional case histories and of saints' stories from Catholic mythology, warns against too close a relationship between a married couple and an unmarried woman. Weiss (1975) "recommends" that relationships after divorce should continue only with friends of the same sex. He bases his recommendation on the awareness that a friendship

relationship that is not unisexual might "deteriorate" into an "affair." None of these scholars raise the question—and certainly they do not answer it—to what degree is a friendship relationship between a married man and a single woman more dangerous to the marital relationship than a friendship relationship between a married man and a married woman who is not his wife.

11. It should be assumed that this story has another side unknown to us. But, even according to the widow's description, it is clear that everyone involved (the widow, the husband, the "betrayed" wife, the neighbors, and the friends) all agreed that "a widow is not allowed to destroy a marriage." The only question in doubt is whether the widow really did so. In the case described, she was not even given the benefit of the doubt.

12. Friendships, as described and characterized by the widows in the sample, partly overlapped into the categories of both "casual friendship" and "expedient friendship", as defined in Cohen's (1961) paper.

Chapter VI

1. In spite of the varied definitions of the term "status," most people working in relevant areas accept status as being the place of a person in the social system within which he lives and functions (for instance, Linton 1945; Parsons 1951). The place of a person within the social system determines the kinds and the levels of social rewards—economic, power, and prestige rewards—allotted to him (Davis & Moore 1945).

2. In Israel, as in other modern societies, profession-occupation is the dominant area that determines a person's status in his society (Eisenstadt 1962, 1971). The importance of ascribed status components is discussed in general in Lenski (1966) and their particular meaning in Israeli society in Lissak (1969). Of special relevance to the subject of this book is the meaning of gender as a status criterion. A comprehensive survey of the literature on this subject can be found in Hochschild's (1973) article.

3. The degree of freedom given a woman to choose between using ascribed or achieved status differs from one society to another and from one historical period to another. It is questionable whether the obstacles to getting self-achieved status faced by American women in the seventies, as described by Musgrave & Wheeler-Bennet (1972), still exist today, or whether the situation would be more similar to that of Russian women, as described by Mace & Mace (1964), where choosing ascribed status was not considered fully legitimate.

4. Here I refer to families in which the occupational structure, the pattern of division of labor, the style of life, and the inner power relationships between the couple are similar to those described by Rapoport & Rapoport (1971) or Holmstrom (1972).

5. It is difficult to determine the exact pace of erosion in the war widows' status since this did not depend entirely upon the factor of time.

6. Women's tendency to refrain from "too much" success is discussed intensively by Horner (1972). Other scholars argue that this phenomenon increases or decreases according to the social conditions in which the women function. But all agree that under certain circumstances refraining from success is a common tendency among women (for instance, Levine & Crumrine 1975).

7. Every Israeli citizen is required by law to carry his identity card on his person at all times. A similar phenomenon is reported by Barrett (1977).

8. This is a social-political movement which arose after the Six-Day War, the main plank of which was objection to returning any territory conquered during the war.

Appendix I

1. The decision to exclude widows living in kibbutzim, as well as widows from the non-Jewish population was made by the Israeli Ministry of Defense. The understanding was that the unique conditions of these groups called for a study designed specifically for their situation. For reasons irrelevant to this book, the study of sub-groups among the war widows was never carried out.

REFERENCES

Abrahams, R. B. "Mutual Help for the Widowed." *Social Work* 17 (1972): 54-61.

Acker, J. "Women and Social Stratification: A Case of Intellectual Sexism." *American Journal of Sociology* 78 (1973): 936-945.

Adams, M. "The Single Woman in Today's Society—A Reappraisal." *Intimacy, Family and Society*. Edited by A. Skolnick and J. H. Skolnick. Boston: Little, Brown, 1974.

Adams, B. N., & J. E. Butler. "Occupational Status and Husband-Wife Social Participation." *Social Forces* 45 (1967): 501-507.

Aitken-Swan, J. *Widows in Australia—A Survey*. Sydney: Council of Social Services of New South Wales and the Australian Council of Social Services, 1962.

Aloni, S. *Nashim k'benei-adam* (Women as People). Jerusalem: Mabat Press, 1976.

Amir, D. *"Ba'alei Miktzoa K'mitnadvim—Alternativa Lepitaron Machsor B'koach-Adam B'shirutim B'zman Chirum oh Milchamah."* [Professionals as Volunteers—an Alternative Solution to Manpower Shortage in Services in States of Emergency or War]. Research report. Tel Aviv University: School of Social Work, 1976.

Angell, R. C. *The Family Encounters the Depression*. New York: Charles Scribner's, 1936.

Astin, H. *The Woman Doctorate in America*. New York: Russell Sage Foundation, 1969.

Averill, J. R. "Grief, its Nature and Significance." *Psychological Bulletin* 70 (1968): 721-748.

Babchuck, N. "Primary Friends and Kin: A Study of the Associations of Middle Class Couples." *Social Forces* 43 (1965): 483-493.

Babchuck, N., & A. P. Bates. "Primary Relations of Middle Class Couples." *American Sociological Review* 28 (1963): 377-384.

Barad, M. "Ha-isha B'tafkidei Nihul B'Yisrael" *(Women in Positions of Management in Israel)*. *Ha-isha B'chevra Ha-modernit (Women in Modern Society)*. Edited by Y. Golan, M. Rosner, & S. Shofti. Tel Aviv: The Workers Press, Kibbutz Ha' artzi Ha-shomer Ha-tzair, 1966.

Barrett, C. J. "Women in Widowhood." *Signs* 2 (1977): 856-868.

Barton, A. H. *Communities in Disaster*. New York: Doubleday Anchor, 1970.

Bar-Yosef, R. W. "Household Management: An Organizational Model Applied to Comparative Family Research." *Human Relations* 26 (1973): 581-598.

———. & D. Padan-Eisenstark. "Role System Under Stress: Sex Roles in War." *Social Problems* 25 (1977): 135-145.

———. & E. O. Schild. "Pressures and Defenses in Bureaucratic Roles." *Bureaucracy and the Public*. Edited by E. Katz & B. Danet. New York: Basic Books, 1973.

———. & L. Shamgar-Handelman. *Some Problems of Definition of the Modern Family*. Paper presented to the 7th International Seminar on Family Research, Moscow, 1972.

Becker, H. *Outsiders*. New York: The Free Press, 1963.

Belcher, J. C. "The One-Parent Household: A Consequence of the Isolated Nuclear Family?" *Journal of Marriage and the Family* 7 (1967): 534-540.

Berardo, F. M. "Widowhood Status in the United States: Perspective on a Neglected Aspect of the Family Life Cycle." *The Family Coordinator* 17 (1968): 191-203.

211

Bergquist, L. "How Come a Nice Girl Like You Isn't Married?" *Toward a Sociology of Women.* Edited by C. Safilios-Rothschild. Lexington, Mass.: Xerox Publishing, 1972.

Blau, P., & O. D. Duncan. *The American Occupational Structure.* New York: John Wiley, 1967.

Boissevain, J. *Friends of Friends.* Oxford: Basil Blackwell, 1974.

Booth, A. "Sex and Social Participation." *American Sociological Review* 37 (1972): 183-192.

Bossard, J. H. S. "War and the Family." *American Sociological Review* 6 (1941): 330-344.

———. *Parent and Child.* Philadelphia: University of Pennsylvania Press, 1953.

Bott, E. *Family and Social Network.* London: Tavistock, 1957.

Bowlby, J. "Processes of Mourning." *International Journal of Psychoanalysis* 62 (1961): 317-340.

Brain, R. *Friends and Lovers.* New York: Basic Books, 1976.

Brewster, H. H. "Grief: A Disrupted Human Relationship." *Human Organization* 9 (1950): 19-20.

Bunch, J. "Recent Bereavement in Relation to Suicide." *Journal of Psychosomatic Research* 16 (1972): 361-366.

Bureau of the Census. *Statistical Abstract of the U.S.A.* vols. 92, 93, 96, 98, 104. Washington, D.C.: United States Department of Commerce.

Burger, V. H. *The Executive's Wife.* London: Collier Books, 1970.

Caine, L. *Widow: the Personal Crisis of a Widow in America.* New York: William Morrow, 1974.

Caplan, G. A. "Patterns of Parental Response to the Crisis of Premature Birth." *Psychiatry* 23 (1960): 365-374.

Caplan, G., E. A. Mason, & D. M. Kaplan. "Four Studies of Crisis in Parents of Prematures." *Community Mental Health Journal* 1 (1965): 149-161.

Cochrane, A. L. "A Little Widow is a Dangerous Thing." *International Journal of Psychoanalysis* 17 (1936): 494-509.

Cohen, R. *Machleket Sa'ad Ironit (A City Welfare Department)* Master's dissertation, University of Tel-Aviv, 1976.

Cohen, Y. A. "Patterns of Friendship." *Social Structure and Personality.* Edited by Y. A. Cohen. New York: Holt, Rinehart & Winston, 1961.

Davidson, C. S. *When You're a Widow.* London: Concordia, 1968.

Davis, K., & W. E. Moore. "Some Principles of Stratification." *American Sociological Review* 2 (1945): 242-249.

Delphy, C. "Continuities and Discontinuities in Marriage and Divorce." *Sexual Divisions and Society: Process and Change.* Edited by D. Barker, L. Allen & S. Allen. London: Tavistock, 1976.

Deutsch, H. "Absence of Grief." *Psychoanalytic Quarterly* 6 (1937): 12-22.

Durkheim, E. *The Elementary Forms of the Religious Life.* 1915. New York: Collier Books, 1961.

Duvall, E. M. *Family Development.* Philadelphia: Lippincott, 1962.

Dyer, E. V. "Parenthood as Crisis: a Re-Study." *Journal of Marriage and Family Living* 25 (1963): 196-201.

Dyk, R. B., & A. M. Sutherland. "Adaptation of the Spouse and Other Family Members to Colostomy Patients. *Cancer* 9 (1956): 123-138.

Eisenstadt, S. N. *Ha-chevra Ha-Yisraelit—Reka, Hitpatchut U'ba'ayot (Israeli Society—Background, Development and Problems).* Jerusalem: Magnes Press, 1962.

Eisenstadt, S. N. *Social Differentiation and Stratification.* Glenview, Illinois: Scott Foresman, 1971.

Eliot, T. B. "The Adjusted Behavior of Bereaved Families: A New Field of Research." *Social Forces* 8 (1930A): 543-549.

———. "Bereavement as a Problem for Family Research and Technique." *The Family* 11 (1930B): 114-115.

———. "The bereaved family." *Annals of the American Academy of Political and Social Science* 160 (1932): 184-190.

———. "Bereavement: Inevitable but not Insurmountable." *Family, Marriage and Parenthood.* Edited by H. Becker and R. Hill. Boston: Heath, 1955.

———. "Adjusting to the Death of a Loved One. *Marriage and the Family in the Modern World.* Edited by R. S. Cavan. New York: Thomas Crowell, 1969.

Engel, G. L. "Is Grief a Disease?" *Psychosomatic Medicine* 23 (1961): 18-22.
Epstein, C. F. *Woman's Place*. Berkeley: University of California Press, 1973.
Farber, B. "Family Organization and Crisis." In *Readings on the Family and Society*. Edited by W. Goode. Englewood Cliffs: Prentice-Hall 1964.
Feldman, S. D. "Impediment or Stimulus? Marital Status and Graduate Education." *American Journal of Sociology* 78 (1973): 982-994.
Felson, M., & D. Knoke. "Social Status of the Married Woman." *Journal of Marriage and the Family* 36 (1974): 517-521.
Fredman. R. G. *The Passover Seder: Afikoman in Exile*. Philadelphia: University of Pennsylvania Press, 1981.
Freud, S. "Mourning and Melancholia." Vol. 4 of *Collected Papers*. 1917. New York: Basic Books, 1959.
Freudenthal, K. "Problems of the One-Parent Family." *Social Work* 4 (1959): 44-49.
Fromm-Reichmann, F. "Loneliness." *Interpersonal Dynamics* (2nd. ed.). Edited by W. G. Bennis, E. H. Schein, D. E. Berlew, & F. I. Steele. Homewood, Ill.: The Dorsey Press, 1968.
Glasser, P., & E. Navarre. "Structural Problems of the One-Parent Family." *Social Issues* 21 (1965): 98-105.
Glick, I. O., R. Weiss & O. M. Parkes. The First Year of Bereavement. New York: John Wiley, 1974.
Glick, P. C. "The Family Cycle." *American Sociological Review* 12 (1947): 164-174.
———. "The Life Cycle of the Family." *Marriage and Family Living* 17 (1955): 3-9.
Goffman, E. *Asylums*. New York: Doubleday Anchor, 1961.
———. *The Presentation of Self in Everyday Life*. New York: Doubleday Anchor, 1959.
Goode, W. J. *Women in Divorce*. New York: The Free Press, 1956.
Gordon, S. *Lonely in America*. New York: Simon & Schuster, 1976.
Goren, D. *Sodiut, Bitachon V'chofesh Ha-itonut (Secrecy, Freedom of the Press and National Security)*. Jerusalem: Magnes Press, 1975.
Gorer, G. *Death, Grief and Mourning*. New York: Doubleday, 1965.
Gould, J., & W. L. Kolb (eds.). *A Dictionary of the Social Sciences*. London: Tavistock, 1964.
Greengain, R. F. "A Symbolic Action During Bereavement." *Journal of Abnormal and Social Psychology* 37 (1942): 403-405.
Handelman, D. "Bureaucratic Transactions: The Development of Official-Client Relationships in Israel." *Transaction and Meaning*. Edited by B. Kapferer. Philadelphia: ISHI, 1976.
———. "Bureaucratic Affiliation: The Moral Component in Welfare Cases." *A Composite Portrait of Israel*. Edited by E. Marx. London: Academic Press, 1980.
Hart, N. *When Marriage Ends*. London: Tavistock, 1976.
Herzog, E., & C. E. Sudia. "Fatherless Homes: A Review of Research." *Children* 15 (1968): 177-182.
Hill, R. *Families Under Stress*. New York: Harper & Brothers, 1949.
———. "Social Stresses on the Family." *Sourcebook in Marriage and the Family* (2nd ed.) Edited by M. B. Sussman. Boston: Houghton Mifflin, 1963.
Hobbs, D. F. "Parenthood Crisis: A Third Study." *Journal of Marriage and the Family* 27 (1965): 367-372.
Hobbs, D. F., Jr. "Transition to Parenthood: A Replication and an Extension." *Journal of Marriage and the Family* 30 (1968): 413-417.
Hochschild, A. R. "A Review of Sex Role Research." *American Journal of Sociology* 78 (1973): 1011-1029.
Holstrom, L. L. *The Two-Career Family*. Cambridge, Mass.: Schenkman, 1972.
Horner, M. S. "Toward an Understanding of Achievement: Related Conflicts in Women." *Journal of Social Issues* 28 (1972): 157-175.
Hunt, M. *The World of the Formerly Married*. New York: McGraw Hill, 1966.
Kahana, R. & S. Kana'an. *Hitnahagut Ha-itonut B'matzavei Metach Bitchoni V'hashpa'ata al Temichat Ha-tzibur B'memshal. (Press Behavior Under Defense Stress Situations and its Effect on Public Support of the Administration)*. Jerusalem: Levi Eshkol Institute for Economic and Policy Research in Israel, Hebrew University of Jerusalem, 1973.
Kanter, R. M. *Men and Women of the Corporation*. New York: Basic Books, 1977.
Katz, E., & S. N. Eisenstadt. "Some Sociological Observations on the Response of Israeli

Organizations to New Immigrants." *Bureaucracy and the Public*. Edited by E. Katz & B. Danet. New York: Basic Books, 1973.

Kimmerling, B. "Tfisat Ha-status shel Ha-tafkidim Ha-bitchoni'im B'Yisrael. (Perception of Status of Security Positions in Israel)." *Medinah u'Mimshal* A (1971): 141-148.

Kna'ani D. ed. *Intziclopedia Le-mada'ei Ha-chevra (Encyclopaedia of the Social Sciences)*. Merhavia: The Workers Press, Kibbutz Ha'artzi Ha-shomer Ha-tzair, 1962.

Koos, E. L. *Families in Trouble*. New York: Kings Crown, 1946.

———. Class Differences in Family Reactions to Crisis. *Journal of Marriage and Family Living* 12 (1950): 77-79.

Kubler-Ross, E. *On Death and Dying*. London: Collier-Macmillan, 1969.

Lansing, J. B., & L. Kish. "Family Life Cycle as an Independent Variable." *American Sociological Review* 22 (1957): 512-519.

Lazarsfeld, P. F., & R. Merton. "Friendship as a Social Process." *Freedom and Control in a Modern Society*. Edited by T. Abel & C. Page. New York: Van Nostrand, 1954.

Lehrman, S. R. "Reactions to Untimely Death." *Psychiatric Quarterly* 30 (1956): 564-578.

LeMasters, E. E. "Parenthood as Crisis." *Marriage and Family Living* 19 (1957): 352-356.

Lenski, G. *Power and Privilege*. New York: McGraw-Hill, 1966.

Lepp, I. *The Ways of Friendship*. New York: Macmillan, 1968.

Levine, A., & J. Crumrine. "Women and the Fear of Success: a Problem of Replication." *American Journal of Sociology* 80 (1975): 964-974.

Lindemann, E. "Symptomatology and Management of Acute Grief." *American Journal of Psychiatry* 101 (1944): 141-148.

Linton, R. *The Cultural Background of Personality*. New York: Appleton-Century, 1945.

Lissak, M. *Social Mobility in Israeli Society*. Jerusalem: Israel Universities Press, 1969.

Litwak, E., & I. Szelenyi. "Primary Group Structures and Their Function: Kin, Neighbors and Friends." *American Sociological Review* 34 (1969): 465-481.

Lopata, H. Z. "Loneliness: Forms and Components." *Social Problems* 17 (1969): 248-261.

———. "The Social Involvement of American Widows." *American Behavioral Scientist* 40 (1970): 41-57.

———. *Widowhood in an American City*. Cambridge, Mass.: Schenkman, 1973A.

———. "Social Relations of Black and White Widowed Women in a Northern Metropolis." *Changing Women in Changing Society*. Edited by J. Huber. Chicago: University of Chicago Press, 1973B.

———. "Self-Identity in Marriage and Widowhood." *Sociological Quarterly* 14 (1973C): 407-418.

———. *Women as Widows—Support Systems*. New York: Elsevier, 1979.

Lynd, R., & H. M. Lynd. *Middletown*. New York: Harcourt, Brace, 1929.

McCall, G. J., ed. *Social Relationships*. Chicago: Aldine, 1970.

———. & J. L. Simmons. *Identities and Interactions*. Glencoe: The Free Press, 1966.

Mace, D., and V. Mace. *The Soviet Family*. Garden City, New York: Doubleday, 1964.

Maddison, M., & W. L. Walker. "Factors Affecting the Outcome of Conjugal Bereavement." *British Journal of Psychiatry* 113 (1967): 1057-1067.

Marris, P. *Widows and Their Families*. London: Routledge & Kegan Paul, 1958.

———. *Loss and Change*. London: Routledge & Kegan Paul, 1974.

Marsden, D. *Mothers Alone: Poverty and the Fatherless Family*. Rev. ed. Harmondsworth: Penguin Books, 1973.

Miller, A. A. "Reaction of Friends to Divorce." *Divorce and After*. Edited by P. Bohannan. New York: Doubleday, 1970.

Mitchell, J. C. ed. *Social Networks in Urban Situations*. Manchester: Manchester University Press, 1969.

Mitchell, N. D. "The Significance of the Loss of the Father Through Death." *American Journal of Orthopsychiatry* 34 (1964): 279-280.

Morris, P. *Prisoners and Their Families*. New York: Hart, 1965.

Musgrave, B., & J. Wheeler-Bennett. *Women at Work: Combining Family with a Career*. London: Peter Owen, 1972.

Nye, R. E. "Child Adjustment in Broken and in Unhappy Unbroken Homes." *Journal of Marriage and Family Living* 19 (1957): 356-361.

Ozerman, A. "Lo Ha-kol Matok B'mamlechet Elit" (Not All is Sweet in the Elite [chocolate] Kingdom). *Dvar Ha-poelet*, 2 (1976): 609-611.

Padan-Eisenstark, D. "Shivion V'shamranut Meshamshim B'irbuviah (The Interplay of Egalitarianism and Conservatism)." *Dvar Ha-poelet.* Special edition to mark International Woman's Year. (1974): 406-412.

Paine, R. "In Search of Friendship: An Exploratory Analysis in Middle-Class Culture. *Man* 4 (1969): 505-524.

Palgi, P. *Death, Mourning and Bereavement in Israel Arising Out of the War Situation.* Jerusalem: Jerusalem Academic Press, 1973.

Parad, H. J., & G. Caplan. "A Framework for Studying Families in Crisis." *Social Work* 5 (1960): 3-15.

Parkes, C. M. *Bereavement: Studies of Grief in Adult Life.* New York: International Universities Press, 1972.

Parsons, T. *The Social System.* Glencoe: The Free Press, 1951.

———. "Age and Sex in the Social Structure of the United States." *Essays in Sociological Theory.* Glencoe: The Free Press, 1954.

———. & R. F. Bales. *Family Socialization and Interaction Process.* Glencoe: The Free Press, 1955.

Peres, Y. & R. Katz. "Family and Familism in Israel." *Megamot* 26 (1980): 37-55.

———. "Stability and Centrality: The Nuclear Family in Modern Israel." *Social Forces* 59 (1981): 678-707.

Pollock G. H. "Mourning and Adaptation." *International Journal of Psychoanalysis* 42 (1961): 341-361.

Rapoport, R., & R. Rapoport. *Dual-Career Families.* Harmondsworth: Penguin Books, 1971.

Rees, E. D. "The Hallucination of Widowhood." *British Medical Journal* 4 (1971): 37-41.

Rosenblatt, P., P. Walsh, & D. A. Jackson. *Breaking Ties with a Deceased Spouse.* Paper presented at the IXth International Congress of Anthropological and Ethnological Sciences, Chicago, 1973.

Roter, R., & C. Keren-Ya'ar. *Mishpachot Chad-horiyot B'Yisrael (One-Parent Families in Israel).* Jerusalem: National Insurance Institute, 1974.

Ryan, William. *Blaming the Victim.* New York: Pantheon Books, 1971.

Safilios-Rothschild, C. *Toward a Sociology of Women.* Lexington, Mass.: Xerox Publishing, 1972.

Scheff, T. *Being Mentally Ill.* Chicago: Aldine, 1966.

Schur, E. *Labeling Deviant Behavior.* Englewood Cliffs: Prentice-Hall, 1973.

Schutz, A., & T. Luckmann. *The Structures of the Life-World.* Evanston, Ill.: Northwestern University Press, 1973.

Scott, J. F. "Brief Comment on Situational and Social Structure Implications for the Loss of a Loved One." *The Loss of Loved Ones.* Edited by D. M. Moriarty. Springfield, Ill.: Charles Thomas, 1967.

Seligman, E. R. A. ed. *Encyclopedia of Social Sciences.* New York: Macmillan, 1931.

Shamgar-Handelman, L. *Almanot Milchemet Sheshet Ha-yamim (The Six-Day War Widows).* Final Report. Jerusalem: Ministry of Defense, Rehabilitation Department, 1972A.

———. *Ha-kesher Ben Shiyuch Ma'amadi Atzmi V'avodat Nashim B'ochlosit Ovdei Medinah V'iriyot B'Yisrael (Self-Ascribed Status and Working Wives Among a Government-Employed Male Population in Israel).* M. A. dissertation, The Hebrew University of Jerusalem, 1972B.

———. "Ma'arechet Sherutit Le-mishpachot Chad-horiyot: Shirutei Misrad Ha-bitachon Le-almanot Milchamah Veyeladeyhen. (A Service System for One-Parent Families: Ministry of Defense Services for War Widows and Their Children)." *Bitachon Sotziali* 8 (1975): 106-113. (English summary.)

———. "The Concept of Remarriage Among Israeli War Widows." *Journal of Comparative Family Studies* 13 (1982): 359-372.

Shelsky, H. *Wandlungen in der Deutschen Familien in der Gegenwart (Current Changes in the German Family).* Stuttgart: Enke-Verlag, 1954.

Shuval, J. *Immigrants on the Threshold.* New York: Atherton Press, 1963.

Sills, D. L. ed. *International Encyclopedia of the Social Sciences.* New York: Free Press, 1968.

Silverman, P. "The Widow-to-Widow Program." *Mental Hygiene* 53 (1963) 333-337.

Simmel, G. *The Sociology of Georg Simmel.* Edited and translated by K. H. Wolff. New York: The Free Press, 1964.

Spiro, J. D. *A Time to Mourn: Judaism and the Psychology of Bereavement.* Philadelphia: Bloch, 1967.

Stack, C. B. *All Our Kin.* New York: Harper & Row, 1974.

State of Israel—Official Publications. *Divrei Ha-Knesset (Knesset Record)* Vols. 4, 49.

———. *Reshumot: Sefer Ha-chukim (The Book of Laws).* 1952.

———. *Shnaton Statisti Le-Yisrael (Statistical Abstract of Israel).* 1970, 1975.

———. *Doch Mevaker Ha-medinah (State Comptroller's Report).* Vols. 19, 20. 1969, 1970.

Stein, J. P. *Single.* Englewood Cliffs: Prentice-Hall, 1976.

Stein, Z., & M. Susser. "Widowhood and Mental Illness." *British Journal of Preventive Social Medicine* 23 (1969): 106-110.

Suttles, G. D. "Friendship as a Social Institution." *Social Relationships.* Edited by G. J. McCall. Chicago: Aldine, 1970.

Tamari, R. "Nashim Ovdot Adayin lo B'tzameret (Female Employees Still Don't Reach the Top)." *Dvar Ha-poelet.* Special edition to mark International Woman's Year. (1974): 427-434.

Thomas, M. "Children with Absent Fathers." *Journal of Marriage and the Family* 30 (1968): 89-96.

Townsend, P. *The Family Life of Old People.* London: Routledge & Kegan Paul, 1957.

Volkart, E. H., with S. T. Michael. "Bereavement and Mental Health." *Death and Identity.* Edited by R. Fulton. New York: John Wiley, 1965.

Waller, W. *The Family* rev. ed. New York: Dryden, 1951.

Warriner, C. K. *The Emergence of Society.* Homewood, Ill.: Dorsey Press, 1970.

Weiss, R. S. "Helping Relationships: Relationships of Clients with Physicians, Social Workers, Priests and Others." *Social Problems* 20 (1973): 319-328.

———. *Marital Separation.* New York: Basic Books, 1975.

White, H. C. *Chains of Opportunity.* Cambridge, Mass.: Harvard University Press, 1970.

Whyte, W. H. *The Organization Man.* New York: Simon & Schuster, 1956.

Williams, J. H. "Close Friendship Relations of Housewives Residing in an Urban Community." *Social Forces* 36 (1958): 358-362.

Wylie, H. L. "A Pattern of Mother-Son Relationship Involving the Absence of the Father." *American Journal of Orthopsychiatry* 29 (1959): 644-649.

Wynn, M. *Fatherless Families.* London: Michael Joseph, 1964.

Zelditch, M. "Role Differentiation in the Nuclear Family: A Comparative Study." *Family Socialization and Interaction Process.* Edited by T. Parsons & R. F. Bales. Glencoe: The Free Press, 1955.

INDEX

Other Books of Interest from *Bergin & Garvey*

Women & Change in Latin America
New Directions in Sex and Class
JUNE NASH, HELEN I. SAFA, & CONTRIBUTORS
"When women's issues are made paramount then we must question development goals that emphasize production for profit rather than concern for quality of life."
— FROM THE INTRODUCTION
384 Pages   Illustrations

In Her Prime
A New View of Middle-Aged Women
JUDITH BROWN, VIRGINIA KERNS, & CONTRIBUTORS
"These ethnographies are fascinating, heartening, and provocative."
— WOMEN'S REVIEW OF BOOKS
240 Pages   Illustration

Nicaragua — *The People Speak*
ALVIN LEVIE
Introduction by Richard Streb
"Outstanding . . . For everyone questioning Nicaraguan self-determination."
— Ed Asner, ACTOR
224 Pages   Illustrations

The Politics of Education
Culture, Power & Liberation
PAULO FRIERE
"Here speaks a teacher who lives life, a revolutionary with hope."
— CHANGE
240 Pages   Illustrations

Applied Anthropology
An Introduction
JOHN VAN WILLIGEN
320 Pages   Illustrations

Now in Paper!
Spiritualist Healers in Mexico
KAJA FINKLER
Foreword by Arthur Kleinman
272 Pages

Crisis in the Philippines
The Making of a Revolution
E. SAN JUAN
288 Pages   Illustrations

Recalling the Good Fight
An Autobiography of the Spanish Civil War
JOHN TISA
265 Pages   Illustrations

Beyond Revolution
A New Theory of Social Movements
DANIEL FOSS & RALPH LARKIN
Introduction by Stanley Aronowitz
256 Pages

The Struggle for Rural Mexico
GUSTAVO ESTEVA
320 Pages

Sex & Class in Latin America
JUNE NASH, HELEN SAFA & CONTRIBUTORS
352 Pages   Illustrations

Women and Colonization
MONA ETIENNE, ELEANOR LEACOCK & CONTRIBUTORS
352 Pages   Illustrations

Political Anthropology
An Introduction
TED LEWELLEN
Foreword by Victor Turner
160 Pages   Illustrations

The Nicaraguan Revolution in Health
From Somoza to the Sandinistas
JOHN DONAHUE
188 Pages   Illustrations

Women & Nutrition in Third World Countries
SAHNI HAMILTON & CONTRIBUTORS
160 Pages

Now in Paper!
Transnationals & the Third World
The Struggle for Culture
ARMAND MATTELART
192 Pages

Escape From Auschwitz
ERICH KULKA
Foreword by Herman Wouk
224 Pages   Photographs

Jewish Experience In The Art Of The 20th Century
AVRAM KAMPF
240 Pages   193 Illustrations   16 Color Plates

Victims & Neighbors
A Small Town in Nazi Germany Remembered
FRANCES HENRY
Foreword by Willy Brandt
216 Pages   Illustrations

Ended Beginnings
Healing Childbearing Losses
CLAUDIA PANUTHOS & CATHERINE ROMEO
240 Pages   Illustrations

BERGIN & GARVEY PUBLISHERS INC.
670 Amherst Road,
South Hadley, Mass. 01075
(413) 467-3113